NKRUMAH AND
THE GHANA REVOLUTION
| | | | |

NKRUMAH AND
THE GHANA REVOLUTION

| | | | |

C. L. R. JAMES

Introduction by Leslie James

DUKE UNIVERSITY PRESS   DURHAM AND LONDON   2022

© 2022 Estate of C. L. R. James
All rights reserved
Printed in the United States of America on acid-free paper ∞
Project editor: Lisa Lawley
Typeset in Arno Pro and Gills Sans Std by
Copperline Book Services

Library of Congress Cataloging-in-Publication Data
Names: James, C. L. R. (Cyril Lionel Robert), 1901–1989, author. |
James, Leslie, [date] editor.
Title: Nkrumah and the Ghana revolution / C. L. R. James,
Leslie James.
Other titles: C.L.R. James Archives (Series)
Description: Durham : Duke University Press, 2022. | Series: The
C. L. R. James Archives | Includes bibliographical references and
index.
Identifiers: LCCN 2021034984 (print)
LCCN 2021034985 (ebook)
ISBN 9781478005452 (hardcover)
ISBN 9781478006220 (paperback)
ISBN 9781478007128 (ebook)
Subjects: LCSH: Nkrumah, Kwame, 1909–1972. | Nationalism—
Africa. | Ghana—Politics and government—To 1957. | BISAC:
HISTORY / Africa / West | POLITICAL SCIENCE / Colonialism &
Post-Colonialism
Classification: LCC DT512 .J35 2022 (print) | LCC DT512 (ebook) |
DDC 966.705/1—dc23/eng/20211027
LC record available at https://lccn.loc.gov/2021034984
LC ebook record available at https://lccn.loc.gov/2021034985

Cover photograph: Government officials carry Prime
Minister Kwame Nkrumah following Ghana's independence
from Great Britain, April 14, 1957. Courtesy of Bettmann/
Getty Images.

CONTENTS

The 1977 edition of *Nkrumah and the Ghana Revolution* is reprinted here in its original form with only minor insertions or deletions to clarify typos or supply dropped words.

All spellings and capitalization, along with most punctuation, remain as they appeared in the first edition despite any changes in common usage since 1977. For example, "Marxism" has been retained as "marxism."

Readers may also note the spelling of "Nkrumaism." The second commonly used spelling retains the "h" in Nkrumah's name. Although both spellings have existed since the 1960s, the spelling "Nkrumaism," used by C. L. R. James, was most common at the time (including in the Ghanaian press) while "Nkrumahism" has become more common in recent years.

ACKNOWLEDGMENTS

The introduction to this volume would not have been possible without the consistent wisdom and support of Robert Hill. His careful eye on drafts was always firm and strong. Most of all, I thank him for inviting me in as a collaborator, and for his warmth and hospitality in our meetings in Jamaica. The two anonymous reviewers also significantly improved the first draft of the introduction.

I want to thank Margaret Busby for meeting with me and sharing her experience of working with C. L. R. James on the original publication. And I want to thank Christian Høgsbjerg and John Williams for their insights into the appendices.

Finally, I want to thank the wonderful archivists at The University of the West Indies at St. Augustine, Trinidad and Tobago, as well as at Howard University's Moorland Spingarn Research Center. My multiple trips to both archives over the past decade proves the invaluable and brilliant support they consistently provide.

INTRODUCTION | Ghana and the Worlds of C. L. R. James

LESLIE JAMES

By the time C. L. R. James published *Nkrumah and the Ghana Revolution* in 1977, it seemed as if James's book had been eclipsed. Originally drafted in 1958, by 1977 the transformative social and political revolution of Kwame Nkrumah and the Convention People's Party (CPP) that James analyzed was well and truly over. A coup in 1966 deposed Kwame Nkrumah and overturned the government of the CPP. James himself publicly broke with Nkrumah in 1964 after Nkrumah deposed a sitting chief justice in order to impose his will on the courts. Yet James's book was never intended as a simple commentary or celebration of the transition of one state from colonial to sovereign status; it was an explanation of Africa's contribution to revolutionary theory. Determined to see his work gain life as a public document, James added a series of letters and speeches created after 1960 and published his analysis in two parts nearly two decades after he first sat down to write it. Today its context, its meanings, and indeed its very content hold such an array of possibilities for readers because it is not, and never has been, one work.

First, *Nkrumah and the Ghana Revolution* is a work that displays James's intellectual practice. It demonstrates his utter conviction in his arguments and gift for determined polemic, alongside a purposeful commitment to adjusting analysis and strategy to current conditions. Consider James's introduction to the book in 1977: by this time not only had James broken with Nkrumah but Nkrumah had survived numerous assassination attempts (the closest were in 1962 and 1964), along with the coup that deposed him, forcing him to live in exile until his death in 1972 in Conakry, Guinea. Despite all these changes, James remained firm in his analysis: "Events since 1958 give me no reason to modify and bring up to date what I wrote in 1958" (6). We see the same confidence in the preface to the 1963 revised second edition of James's masterpiece, *The Black Jacobins*, which we know he was working on at the same time as he wrote the manuscript on Ghana (see appendix 1). "This book was written in 1938," he writes. "Today, I have little to add to or subtract from the fundamental ideas which governed its conception."[1] In the basic ideas and arguments of both texts, James was sure. Yet he leaves an opening. In 1963 James added an appendix to the *Black Jacobins* titled "From Toussaint L'Ouverture to Fidel Castro," which he wrote for "West Indians, a people of the *middle* of our disturbed century, concerned with the *discovery* of themselves."[2] In 1977 James explained *Nkrumah and the Ghana Revolution* as a record of "a *sequence of political responses* to an extreme political situation, the African situation, as it has developed" (18). Together, both texts are not an end point. Rather, they are situated in the midst of history and among a people in development; they are made as a tool for learning and growing.

Why was James so sure of what he wrote in 1958? The short answer is that he was not merely commenting on a sequence of events—he was adding new implements to revolutionary theory. James drafted part I of the book in the midst of coauthoring a book on the 1956 Hungarian Revolution, *Facing Reality*. Indeed, as the letters in appendix 1 of this edition show, James set *Facing Reality* aside to prioritize his manuscript on Ghana. He completed the first draft just as he returned to his native Trinidad, where he became directly involved in Caribbean politics for the first time since he had departed for England in 1932. Crucial elements of part II of the book were written during his time in the Caribbean; others were written as James engaged with the rise of Black Power in the Caribbean, the United States, and Canada, as well as with a new set of African socialist leaders, particularly Julius Nyerere in Tanzania. This book was forged, then, both in and by the actions of peoples in Africa, the Caribbean, North America, and Europe. What James was interested in, broadly, was theorizing how collective action took shape in specific classes and contexts and analyzing what particular historical moment and set of factors converged to move people toward internal creative action.[3] *Nkrumah and the Ghana Revolution* was James's version of what he argued he saw in Caribbean people as a whole in the 1960s: "Passion not spent but turned inward."[4]

What was James's experience in the time between writing and publishing this piece? And what have we learnt in the decades since it was published in 1977? I want to attempt to answer these two questions before returning to how *Nkrumah and the Ghana Revolution* extended several key themes in James's lifelong enquiry into the nature and practice of social and political revolution, and why this work remains relevant to us today.

When James attended Ghana's independence ceremony in March 1957, where he says he first got the idea to write his book on Nkrumah and the CPP, he was no Caribbean outlier in Ghana, nor was he a rare African diaspora intellectual and activist to ally himself with Nkrumah's project. African diaspora commitment to Ghana was real and material. We know that many African Americans worked, traveled, and lived in Ghana in the years after independence.[5] Indeed, African American presence in Ghana far exceeded the famous intellectuals like W. E. B. Du Bois and St. Clair Drake, artists and writers like Maya Angelou, and labor leaders like Vicki Garvin and George McCray.[6] Ghana sought the aid of both Jamaican chief minister Norman Manley and Trinidadian chief minister Eric Williams to send legal experts to help the new state.[7] Nkrumah also recruited two Caribbean-born, UK-based men to advise the new Ghanaian government in 1957: the illustrious Saint Lucian William Arthur Lewis became Ghana's first economic advisor, and the Trinidad-born George Padmore became Nkrumah's Advisor on African Affairs.

Padmore was a crucial anticolonial organizer who served as a connecting point for many colonial travelers who arrived in London from Africa, South and Southeast Asia, and the Caribbean during the 1930s, 1940s, and 1950s. Padmore, a lifelong Marxist, turned his nom de guerre (he was born Malcolm Nurse) into a well-known name through his work for the Communist International in the early 1930s, when he also edited the globally circulated *Negro Worker*. This period of his life also facilitated the theoretical knowledge and organizational networks that he harnessed after he broke with the Communist Party and moved, by 1935, to London. James and Padmore, in fact, had known each other since their boyhood together in Trinidad. Once each of them separately made their way to London, they collaborated closely through an organization and paper they helped to found: the International African Service Bureau and *International African Opinion*. At the end of 1938 James left for the United States, and for the next decade and a half the two men worked from different poles. However, they remained in contact, and it was James who introduced Kwame Nkrumah to Padmore via a letter in 1945.

James first met Nkrumah in 1943 through his close political comrade, Raya Dunayevskaya, when she took James to Lincoln, Pennsylvania, where Nkrumah was a student.[8] Throughout the rest of World War II the two men met to discuss political strategy, as James tutored Nkrumah in the skill of underground political work. And although James introduced Nkrumah to Padmore by stating, famously, that Nkrumah was "not very bright," James later claimed that Padmore knew exactly what he meant by the statement: "The man is a born revolutionary, devoted completely," but his intellect needed a deeper education in Marxist theory.[9] Nkrumah's contact with Padmore throughout the late 1940s and 1950s was frequent and detailed. Although Nkrumah returned to the Gold Coast in late 1947, they maintained regular correspondence, a connection aided by Nkrumah's secretary after 1952, Trinidadian Joyce Gittens.[10] In 1954, Padmore also produced a book on developments in Ghana, *The Gold Coast Revolution*.

James remained in touch with Nkrumah in a more limited capacity after 1945. Grace Lee (Boggs), James's political comrade, whom Nkrumah also befriended while he studied in the United States, facilitated their communication.[11] Indeed, Lee Boggs traveled from Detroit to London in 1957 to assist him in the preparation of the Ghana manuscript.[12] Lee Boggs, James, and Dunayevskaya collaborated closely in their writing and political organizing throughout the 1940s and 1950s, shaping their political ideas into a distinctive group on the US left known as the Johnson-Forest Tendency. But while James's contact with Nkrumah was somewhat limited, his return to England in 1953 afforded a closer connection again with Padmore. And when Ghana celebrated its independence in March 1957, both James and Padmore traveled from London to Accra as invited guests. James stayed in Ghana for two weeks, while Padmore stayed for two months. Back in London, James set to work on three projects at once: a revision of his 1938 *Black Jacobins*, a co-authored pamphlet with Grace Lee Boggs and Cornelius Castoriadis (Pierre Chaulieu) on the Hungarian Revolution, and the book on Ghana. The letters in appendix 1 show how these projects all collided in James's thinking.

In September 1957, James explained to Padmore that he hoped to return to Ghana in order to research some articles and possibly a book or pamphlet that would give the majority of "thinking people I meet" in England the information he believed they sought: "Many of them want to see [Ghana] in a better light. They are not deceived by the *Daily Telegraph* and the *Daily Express* any more."[13] Although James did not make the trip back to Ghana until 1960, he nevertheless set about writing his proposed book, which aimed to fan the spark of worldwide interest in Ghana as one of the first African countries to successfully negotiate independence from European colonial rule. The intention for James's *Ghana Revolution* came from a different time and place to that of Padmore's *Gold Coast Revolution*. Padmore's aim in 1954 was "to trace the evolution of Gold Coast nationalism from the foundation of the Ashanti Confederacy to the emergence of the Convention People's Party." *Gold Coast*

Revolution detailed the institutional and constitutional political history of the Asante and Fante in the Gold Coast from the sixteenth century, in order to set up the demand for self-government: "When the Gold Coast Africans demand self-government today they are . . . merely asserting the birthright which they never really surrendered to the British."[14] The point, for Padmore, was that Nkrumah's leadership of the CPP proved his "statesmanship." Padmore's book was a case for political independence under the terms that British "progress" toward self-government demanded. James's book set a different tone: to inspire postcolonial futures. *Nkrumah and the Ghana Revolution* never mentions Padmore's earlier book.

For both Padmore and James, independent Ghana seemed to demonstrate the possibilities for building socialism in societies and governments that were trying to forge a new path out of European colonial rule. By the end of the year, both men had departed London in order to involve themselves more directly in this task. Padmore and his partner, Dorothy Padmore (Pizer), moved to Accra in December 1957 and lived there until their deaths in 1959 and 1964. Dorothy, also an author and journalist, collaborated with Padmore on his manuscripts, and the couple coauthored some work together. Indeed, James's unfinished biography of Padmore always maintained that "Padmore was the man he was because of the tremendous assistance he had from Dorothy." She remained in Ghana after Padmore's death and worked for the Nkrumah government.

In early 1958, James accepted an invitation to participate in the opening ceremony of the British West Indies Federal Parliament in Trinidad. He also began to help draft party documents for the People's National Movement (PNM), a young political party founded by one of his former students, Eric Williams, whom James tutored in Trinidad in the 1920s and then mentored in London in the 1930s while Williams completed his doctorate at Oxford. Williams's dissertation became the basis for his groundbreaking book *Capitalism and Slavery* (1944), which set out to show how African slavery and the slave trade provided the financial basis for the development of modern industrial capitalism.[15] In 1956, Williams consulted both James and Padmore in London before founding the PNM. By the end of 1958, James and his wife, Selma James, were living in Trinidad and working together to edit and produce the PNM's official organ, which James renamed the *Nation*.[16]

The fact that James's return to Trinidad in 1958 coincided with the inauguration of the British West Indies Federation was not inconsequential. The idea of regional unification, and in particular plans for a federation of

British West Indian islands, had been debated since the nineteenth century by various interest groups both in the Caribbean and in metropolitan Britain. In the early twentieth century, proposals for regional cooperation and/or federation were championed by the Colonial Office and even the planter-merchant oligarchies as a means of coordinating administrative bureaucracies and combating the poor economic status of the region. Federation, in the minds of the Colonial Office, became associated with ideas of progress, order, and efficiency en route to modernization of the region.[17] After 1945, the Colonial Office began negotiations for a British West Indies Federation, ostensibly as part of a transition toward self-government.

Full independence, however, was not enshrined in the federal government that emerged in 1958 (an omission that served as a major, if not the only, factor that divided political leaders and interest groups in their commitment to the government). Yet while the West Indies Federation was fraught with tension from the early planning process in the late 1940s to its demise in 1962, it was also a serious attempt by many Caribbean leftists to plan a new and unified future for the Caribbean out of the division and destruction of colonial rule.[18] Some Caribbean leaders, like Richard Hart in Jamaica, looked toward federation in the 1940s and 1950s as a framework for developing the Caribbean along socialist lines and approached federation not as an ideal end point, but as a practical solution, whatever the difficulties. These small and underdeveloped islands faced even greater challenges if each island tried to tackle self-government on its own.

More than this, James conceived of Caribbean peoples as interconnected—the different sociohistorical context of their islands did not negate for him the fact that Caribbean peoples were knit together by a similar history and in a proximity whereby events impacted each other. James's 1962 letter to Nkrumah, printed in part II of *Nkrumah and the Ghana Revolution*, articulates this idea that Caribbean people held the tools to "establish themselves as a modern progressive people" (151). When James asked Nkrumah, in this letter, to intervene and encourage Caribbean leaders not to break up the federation, James directly connected Ghana, as a model for modern national development based upon human emancipation on a worldwide scale, with the fate of Caribbean cooperation.

When James took over the *Nation*, it provided a vehicle for his belief that building up knowledge within a people was essential to self-government. In the pages of this weekly newspaper, he promoted socialist planning and, crucially, the development of Caribbean identity as a unique and unified people. He also made it clear why he believed Nkrumah's project was relevant for Trinidad: "If we pay attention to India and to Ghana, it is because they are clearing the road which vast millions in our position are following. Our racial affinities with them give us an added interest but we know the degree to which we as a people . . . [are also] organically associated with British civilization."[19] In May 1959, the *Nation* reprinted a speech given by Nkrumah in Guinea for the celebration of Africa Freedom Day. And, in July 1959, contrary to James's later criticism of Nkrumah's treatment of the Opposition, the paper reprinted a series of articles supporting Nkrumah's strict policy toward the opposition and curtailment of the press in Ghana.

In March 1960, the *Nation* produced a special memorial number for the third anniversary of Ghana's independence. The front page was emblazoned with a message from now-premier Eric Williams, which praised the "progress" of Ghana as a "model which in our own way . . . we would do well to emulate." In contrast to this more general and nation-building oriented message, James's editorial offered a wider, more international, humanist interpretation: it was the "vision" and "courage" of Ghana "in the service of a better world" that "should be admired and studied by all." His editorial sent greetings to Ghana "in the name of our whole community," and the supplement reprinted a transmission by James about the West Indies delivered to Ghana and Nigeria via a BBC London broadcast. This special issue of the *Nation* included an essay by James entitled "The People of the Gold Coast: They Created Ghana," which contained elements of *Nkrumah and the Ghana Revolution*.[20]

In the *Nation*, James aimed to put forward "the problems of the people . . . as stated by the people themselves" rather than the "point of view of the government."[21] But as someone who had been away from Trinidad for more than a quarter of a century and in a subordinate position to Williams, his younger, former student, James walked a thin line while in Trinidad. He faced increasing opposition from within the PNM, and Williams began to distance himself from James. James was vocally critical of US military imperialism in Trinidad, a critique that in principle Williams also shared. But when it came to Trinidad's negotiation of the terms of the US lease of Chaguaramas, a military base occupied since 1940 under the terms of the Anglo-American Lend-Lease Agreement, the two men's approaches did not align in practice. After March 1960, James resigned from editing the *Nation*. In October 1960, the PNM voted to expel him from the party.

For the next six years, James moved back and forth between London and the Caribbean. In London he continued to write, deliver lectures, and run a study circle with young Caribbean radicals including the Jamaicans Richard Small and Norman Girvan, future sociologist Orlanda Patterson, and historian Walter Rodney.[22] In Trinidad he built up connections with the Oilfield Workers' Trade Union and its leader, George Weekes. In 1965, James cooperated to found a new political party, the Workers and Farmers Party, which contested Trinidad's elections at the end of the year. Unfortunately for James, the party was unable to win electoral support, gaining no elected seats and only 3 percent of the popular vote.[23]

Yet James also found inspiration from his interactions with a group of Caribbean students based in Canada. Between late 1966 and early 1968, James made several visits to Montreal, where he was invited to give public lectures as well as private sessions with a group of students who admired, but also prodded and challenged, James's thinking.[24] The group of students in Montreal had contacts in most other Canadian cities as well as in New York, and many went on to play prominent roles in the rise of a new left in the Caribbean. These students included future prime minister of Dominica Rosie Douglass, Anne Cools of Barbados, Franklyn Harvey of Grenada, Tim Hector of Antigua, Robert Hill of Jamaica, Alfie Roberts of St. Vincent, and Walton Look Lai of Trinidad.

Montreal thus served as an intellectual petri dish for a new phase of Caribbean radicalism. At the same time, events in Montreal reverberated outward into the Caribbean.[25] Two separate sparks from Montreal set off protests in the Caribbean that articulated a "regionally-linked, home grown Black Power movement."[26] In October 1968, Montreal hosted the Congress of Black Writers, which witnessed a convergence of US and Caribbean leaders including Walter Rodney, James Forman, and Trinidad-born and US-based Stokely Carmichael. James delivered two lectures at this event, but it was the ideas and leadership emanating from Carmichael in particular that impressed the audience and captivated James. When Walter Rodney attempted to return from the conference to his teaching post at the University of the West Indies Mona (Jamaica), the government denied him entry and deported him back to Canada. The Jamaican government's expulsion of Rodney set off the wave of "Rodney riots" that stimulated Black Power in Jamaica.[27]

The second spark from Montreal came months later. In January and February 1969, after university administrators at Sir George Williams University appeared to be stalling action in response to a complaint lodged by six black students from the Caribbean of racially biased grading by a biology professor, students and community organizers occupied the university computer lab. The "Sir George Williams affair" placed Canadian racism on stark display, with racist vitriol shouted at those occupying the building, police violence against demonstrators, and blatantly harsh legal punishment administered to black participants after the end of the occupation.[28] Once news of the treatment of those who participated in the Sir George Williams occupation reached Trinidad, people organized protests in front of the Canadian High Commission and the Royal Bank of Canada targeting Canadian racism. But the students who organized these protests also looked inward, challenging Eric Williams's government directly and initiating a wave of public protests and marches against the government that spread throughout Trinidad. The Sir George Williams affair was, according to Brinsley Samaroo, merely the "trigger" for an uprising in Trinidad in 1970, with origins in a longer historical struggle for "meaningful participation" since the nineteenth century.[29] These were, therefore, major internal uprisings organized by students and workers in the Caribbean. They also reveal, as Kate Quinn argues, "an interconnected network of activists . . . operating across a variety of geographical spaces, engaged in cognate struggles in which local and international concerns intersected."[30]

It was this frame, of internal self-organizing combined with international connection, that was also important for James's interpretation of Ghana's revolution. The growth of Black Power and James's increasing interest in these movements clarifies why James continued to view Ghana and Nkrumah as relevant. At the end of 1968, James returned to the United States for the first time since he had been deported in 1953. James again led discussion groups from his apartment in Washington, DC, alongside his formal teaching at Federal City College. He also worked with the Center for Black Education, an organization that founded a community school for youth and ran education forums. Activists involved in this center also set up the Drum and Spear Press, to which he offered his 1938 book, *A History of Negro Revolt*, for reissue. When it appeared in 1969 under its new title, *A History of Pan-African Revolt*, it included a long epilogue where James attended in particular to the new political thought of Julius Nyerere in Tanzania. Parts of this epilogue were also chosen by James for reprinting in part II of *Nkrumah and the Ghana Revolution*.

That James chose to focus on Tanzania in 1969, and to reprint these thoughts in part II of *Nkrumah and the Ghana Revolution* in 1977, is not surprising. After Rodney was barred from reentering Jamaica at the end of 1968, he made his way from Canada to Cuba and, from there, back to his old teaching post at the University of Dar es Salaam in Tanzania, where he had worked between 1966 and 1967, and then again from 1969 to 1974. Rodney's circuit between the Caribbean and Africa is just one example of a new phase of pan-Africanism that James also became involved in. Indeed, in the early 1970s James participated in the early planning sessions and helped draft the call for the Sixth Pan-African Congress (PAC), which eventually convened in Dar es Salaam in 1974.[31]

What is striking, however, is James's decision in 1977 to affirm his analysis of Tanzania from 1969 without qualification. We know that James drafted a different introduction to the one that appeared in 1977 (see appendix 2, "Africa: The Threatening Catastrophe—A Necessary Introduction"), which commented on the "paper-thin veneer of Dr. Nyerere." This draft covers a wider range of African politics and leadership but does not go much beyond this remark about Nyerere, choosing rather to comment on Jomo Kenyatta and to focus on a critique of Hastings Banda's Malawi. Yet the introduction James chose in 1977 makes no negative mention of Nyerere; rather, it simply affirms his analysis that "something new" had, as in Ghana, emerged out of Africa. James never attended the Sixth PAC and was fiercely critical of the conference as a failure but, as Monique Bedasse shows, he remained committed to Tanzania as a pan-African-oriented revolutionary state through his support for Rastafarian repatriation to Tanzania in the 1980s.[32] The draft "Necessary Introduction" strengthens Robin Kelley's observation that James never really responded in print to the corruption in Tanzania, nor addressed criticisms of Nyerere's policies in the 1970s.[33]

All of James's activity in the 1960s gave new life to his thinking. Appendix 2 contains a 1964 draft of a new "Necessary Introduction" on "Africa: The Threatening Catastrophe." In 1973 James shared an almost exact typescript of this draft with one of his students at Howard University in Washington, DC. It contains substantive sections that ended up in the final 1977 published version as well as significant portions of what became "Lenin and the Problem." The dedication "To Francis" in this version ends, however, not with any reference to failure but with "hope springing eternal of the things that you yet can do." There is also no final paragraph, of course, on Tanzania. But what this 1964 introduction means is that even before Nkrumah and the CPP were overthrown in 1966, James had already drawn his conclusions about the direction of Ghana and of the continent more generally.

In the time between James's first draft in 1958 and this 1964 draft with its added introduction, Nkrumah and the CPP had busily embarked on a project to transform Ghana into an internationalist, socialist state. This project sometimes pursued contradictory policies. Ghana became a beacon of internationalism and a haven for African freedom fighters, even as preventive detention measures silenced Togolese activists and forced deportations to rid the country of unwanted elements.[34] National cultural symbols were created that were conducive to CPP ideology and often intimately tied to images of Nkrumah as leader, while massive infrastructure and modernization projects resulted in a ballooning bureaucracy and large-scale population resettlements.[35] At the same time, the plans and projects of Nkrumah and the CPP could never be imposed unilaterally from above. They were built up, constrained, and negotiated on the ground by young recruits, elders, intellectuals, journalists, market women, and expatriate experimenters, as well as by Nkrumah and party officials.[36] In other words, Nkrumah-era Ghana was inspirational and aspirational, and it did produce results. But we should also see Nkrumah and the CPP for what the project was: a human and messy approach to nation-building.[37]

The other noticeable omission from revised drafts of the book is any substantial reassessment of Eric Williams. Not only was James expelled from the PNM, but his relationship with Eric Williams became increasingly acrimonious. When James returned again to Trinidad in February 1965, Williams, fearing unrest on the oil fields, used recently passed legislation to place James under house arrest for a week.

Thus James broke not only with Nkrumah in the first half of the 1960s, but also with Eric Williams. This is not inconsequential to *Nkrumah and the Ghana Revolution*. As I will discuss in the next section, Eric Williams's leadership in Trinidad in the 1950s was crucial to James's analysis of the uniqueness of the Ghana Revolution and the distinctive contribution of African and Caribbean leadership. James's decision to retain part I of *Nkrumah and the Ghana Revolution* in its original 1958 rendering, therefore, involved a decision to affirm not only what Nkrumah had achieved in Ghana, but what Williams had achieved in Trinidad, despite subsequent disagreements with the actions of both men. And it prompts anew my question at the beginning of this introduction. If James knew more about Nkrumah's revolutionary strategy in 1977 than he did in 1960, and if he broke so decisively from Williams's strategy for independent Trinidad, then why did he insist upon publishing the manuscript without revision? Why, if so much had occurred to change conditions between James's early draft of the manuscript and its publication, was he so sure of his original conclusions?

The answer to these questions is twofold. First, the structure and content of *Nkrumah and the Ghana Revolution* are driven by James's historical sensibility. When the pioneering publisher and editor Margaret Busby worked with James in the mid-1970s to bring out some of his unpublished work, James carefully discussed with her each piece selected. Her new publishing house, Allison & Busby, collected significant pieces of James's work and made them available in three volumes: *The Future in the Present* (1977), *Spheres of Existence* (1980), and *At the Rendezvous of Victory* (1984). James, she recalls, presented pieces to her in their discussions with a sense that "I wrote that, I am not changing it."[38] This was something more than a determined spirit. James was a chronicler of movements: rewriting something he said previously would change the impression of what he thought at a particular time and alter the record. Instead, James kept his first draft about Nkrumah and Ghana as part I and supplemented it with further material. As part II of *Nkrumah and the Ghana Revolution* shows, James read the movements in the Caribbean, the Americas, and Africa as interlocutors in understanding the significance of Nkrumah's Ghana. But what is crucial for understanding both parts of the book is precisely that these events and changing ideas were not revisions, but supplements. The structure of the book in two parts is key to James's method and approach as a political activist, theoretician, and historian.

The second answer lies in the fact that James was not simply writing a history of the transition to political independence in the Gold Coast/Ghana; he was writing a blueprint of a new revolution. *Nkrumah and the Ghana Revolution* is, ultimately, a contribution to revolutionary theory (see the letters in appendix 1). This is James's global thinking at work. It draws upon his knowledge of the French, American, Haitian, and Russian revolutions and applies these models to events in Ghana.

It is worth noting that comparisons with Russia in particular were not merely due to a personal interest on James's part. Nor were they simply part of a necessary attempt by James to address Nkrumahism in relation to 1950s Soviet politics and criticism of the one-party state. Certainly, the introduction to part I does this. But the strong emphasis upon the Bolshevik Revolution also suited the strategy of Nkrumah and the CPP; it was not alien to their own thinking. Thanks in part to the advice and influence of George Padmore in the 1950s, the CPP party structure and revolutionary program paralleled the Bolshevik vanguard model. Padmore involved himself with ideological training of CPP members and recruits, and the party emphasized disciplined internal party loyalty under the direction of a popular leader who could mobilize mass support for their socialist program.[39] This dynamic is important to keep in mind when reading the first item in part II, James's speech in Accra in 1960, in which he rather vigorously affirms the role of the socialist party and Nkrumah's place as a world historical figure. But it also means that in part I when James compared the CPP's effort to give the illiterate villager "the best that was being thought and said in the world" (103) with the first years of the Russian Revolution, and when he analyzed Lenin's two essential recommendations to the Bolshevik Party—reconstruction of the government apparatus and the education of the illiterate peasant—in part II, James was applying the terminology that the Ghanaian revolution also, if not exclusively, spoke.

Although there are only two brief mentions of the Hungarian Revolution in 1956 and the Montgomery Bus Boycott of 1955–56, these events were crucial for James's thinking about the self-organization of working people against state authority. As the letters in appendix 1 of this edition show, James put aside work on the Hungarian Revolution to prioritize the Ghana manuscript. And at the end of March 1957, James met and spoke with Coretta Scott King and Martin Luther King Jr. on two occasions. The second occasion took place over lunch at his home, where James was stirred by the Kings' account of the events in Montgomery.[40] It is therefore striking that although James proposed, in his letter on 21 March 1957 (see appendix 1), to do an entire section on Montgomery in order to draw the attention of shared struggle between Africans and African Americans, this was never completed. Two of his other manuscripts from the late 1950s, *Every Cook Can Govern* (1956), which analyzed slavery and democracy in Ancient Greece, and *Facing Reality* (1958), a manifesto in response to the Hungarian Revolution cowritten with Grace Lee Boggs and cosigned with Pierre Chaulieu (Cornelius Castoriadis) that linked Hungary with the "Gold Coast Revolution," show how James was thinking through all these movements together. Part I of *Nkrumah and the Ghana Revolution* draws from the model of the Greek city-state and revolutionary change from above as well as from below and argues that events in Africa cannot be understood without first understanding "the substantially documented and widely debated historical experiences of Western civilization" (9). This Western experience held value precisely because debate was captured and analyzed in documentation. To this same end, James aimed to show that events in Africa were not sporadic and unintelligible episodes but a "developing pattern" that could be discerned with reference to other patterns.

James is quite clear that his analysis is intended not as the application of revolutionary theory to Africa but, rather, as an explanation of how the work of Nkrumah and the CPP in Ghana in the 1950s pushed the strategies of revolution not simply onto a new geographic stage, in Africa, but into their next phase. "Every revolution must attempt what by all logic and reason and previous experience is impossible," he writes. "Like anything creative it extends the boundaries of the known" (107). Ghana had extended the bounds of the known by orchestrating a paralyzing economic boycott of the country in 1950. The planned character of the boycott, and the role of trade unions in particular, marked this revolution as "blood and bone of the twentieth century" (111). By linking an absolute threat (a general strike) to a sweeping demand (self-government), the Ghanaian revolution boldly pressed on into inconceivable territory. But this, James declares, was why it served as a blueprint for revolution: "That is what revolution is, reasonable madness" (108).

With this "reasonable madness" the Ghana Revolution overcame the potency of the colonial "myth"—a myth that is the organizing force of the entire book. As explained by James, all societies have governing myths, and the "greatest of modern myths" is that which justifies colonialism (James states clearly that colonialism is not dead). This myth is governed by two interlocking components: first, it holds that Africans are backward and barbarous; second, that through contact with Western civilization (via colonialism) they are brought into the modern, "unified world" (25). This second component consequently extended the first principle of the myth, which justified colonialism, to its perpetual maintenance: the myth of the primitive Africans became also the myth that colonialism was an ordered and "systematic advance" toward human development and freedom (27). The two components of the original myth thus mutate into a second myth: that colonialism is advancement, not expropriation and destruction. This myth is not exclusive to Britain, but James is concerned in particular with how the British version of the myth prescribed stages of training to a political program justified by the myth.

In chapter 7, James makes clear why the workings of the myth, which he has laid out in chapter 1, are so crucial to his explanation of the revolution in Ghana. The logic of the originary myth of the "primitive African" drove the tactical miscalculations of the colonial administration, who consistently underestimated the Ghanaian people, the CPP, and Nkrumah. By stretching their tactics and demands to the point of unreason, the revolution overturned the logic of the myth of colonialism as development. More than this, power was reversed. James writes, "The people saw in the party a government of their own. They were listening to it, and not to the one with the power and the police and the laws" (110). By overcoming the myth, power was no longer with the Power.

Part I of the book takes up several key themes in James's intellectual thinking, including the self-organization of the masses as a creative revolutionary force, transformative educational practices, and the value and limits of Western political thought. Part II engages with some of the resulting complexities of these issues, including the role of the party and the dangers of bribery and corruption.

For James, the relation between people and leader was the "recurrent problem" of revolution (88). Indeed, at least three of his previous books—*The Life of Captain Cipriani* (1932), *The Black Jacobins* (1938) and *Mariners, Renegades and Castaways* (1953)—were in many respects absorbed by a working-out of the relation between the individual leader and the people. The Ghana revolution, he believed, helped to "illuminate" this problem. Part I places great emphasis upon African intellectuals as the people "who will lead the continent" (11). But James ultimately concludes that the people of Ghana had demonstrated that it was the movement of the masses that came first. Through the general strike in 1950, the people learned their own power and capacity to work together. With Nkrumah and most of the CPP in prison, the people proved that "For a movement to be led it must exist" (115–16). In other words, despite the importance of the individual, the movement preceded the leader.

Taken together, *Nkrumah and the Ghana Revolution* and *Facing Reality*, the coauthored book written in the same period, demonstrate how James came to emphasize the self-activity of the masses as a revolutionary force. His political work in the 1960s and 1970s with the Oilfield Workers' Trade Union in Trinidad serves as one example of how he built this relationship into his own activity. Both texts give critical attention to independent labor organizing and show how the creative self-activity of the masses acts as a catalyst for revolutions to advance into new and unknown terrain. *Facing Reality* argues that in Hungary, a "total uprising of the people" had disclosed to the world a new political form capable of "destroy[ing] the bureaucratic state power." Independent Workers Councils demonstrated a mastery of production that would allow government "to be based upon general consent and not on force." Through the creativity of Workers Councils, Hungarian workers had reversed the revolutionary process of seizing political power in order to organize production by instead "seiz[ing] power in the process of production and from there organiz[ing] the political power."[41]

This was, of course, distinct from Nkrumah's campaign to "seek ye first the political kingdom." But the self-organizing of Ghanaian workers had also made its mark on CPP organizing. In Ghana, the independent activity of the Trades Union Congress resulted in the expansion of the Positive Action campaign to form two demands—full self-government and the reinstatement of dismissed government employees—instead of one demand, ensuring that organized labor "set their own proletarian mark upon the national revolution" (111).

Yet the "problem" of the leader and the people is never far behind. The next sentence after James's statement emphasizing the proletarian mark on Ghana's revolution alludes to another problem that it will face: "But dominant over all was the will of the people symbolised in the person of Nkrumah" (111). Thus leaders acquired their value not from exceptional skill or intelligence but from an ability to capture and then embody the impulses of the people. James repeatedly placed a great deal of confidence in Rousseau's concept of the general will. Not inconsequential to James's faith in his own ability to see with rapid clarity what was going on in Ghana (articulated in the letters in appendix 1), he argued that Rousseau's analysis of France was so sharp because he was an outsider who could look in. And James vehemently opposed, without a sustained explanation, any argument that Rousseau's ideas were "the ancestor of totalitarianism."[42]

Paget Henry has argued that James interpreted Rousseau's general will such that the "creativity of the public selves of polities" became the "primary engine of history."[43] Indeed, James argued that it was the Parisian masses' vocal application of Rousseau that made them the driving force of the French Revolution, and that he himself had seen this principle in action twice in his lifetime, with the movements surrounding Captain Cipriani and Eric Williams in Trinidad, when a "social conception" came into view and "something for the total benefit . . . is lifting the population to a higher stage."[44]

Is this interpretation by James, of Nkrumah as the symbol of the will of the masses, the reason he blamed Nkrumah's downfall on a personal failure to surround himself with the right people? James explained the political struggle in Ghana as a separation between the "native masses" and a Westernized elite whose social aim drove them toward government positions and thus state bureaucracy. Yet the role of the party in this relationship, and in particular the CPP, is somewhat shrouded in James's analysis of Ghana in part II. From the late 1940s, James began to question the idea of a "vanguard party" and argue instead that the end result of the labor movement must be the abolition of the party.[45] The article in part II, "Slippery Descent," first published in the

Trinidad *Evening News* in 1964, contends that he "hinted" in 1960 at the dangers of an urge to the one-party state and its inherent corruption. His warning against corruption in this article explains that because of the stage of material development in postcolonial states, the government becomes the most powerful determining economic factor: what should occur outside government, occurs inside government. But James's statements about the relationship between the party, the people, and the state were complicated. James's speech in 1960, reprinted as "Government and Party" in part I, places great faith in the CPP, arguing that the party must be the check on government by studying socialism and serving as an outside voice. His critique of how the party becomes the state—evident, for example, in *Facing Reality*—is absent. Rather, in James's 1964 assessment it is ultimately Nkrumah's failure to listen to what his people needed that was the downfall of the revolution.

James's lifelong project of wrestling with the "problem" of the leader in revolutionary politics came into sharp relief in *Nkrumah and the Ghana Revolution* with regard to his analysis of not only Ghana, but also Trinidad. In chapter 6 of part I, James turns to an extended analysis of the role of education in revolution, and the ways that a revolutionary leader can participate in an egalitarian sharing of knowledge with the people. To do so, he explains Eric Williams's "University of Woodford Square" in Trinidad as a model for a new and different approach to political education. In this model, Williams chose not simply to lecture in the halls of institutional universities, but to convene an assembly of people in a public square and engage in direct public education. This strategy was important because Williams, as an Oxford-educated university professor, did not deign to speak a different language or to separate himself from working people, but entered their spaces and engaged in thoughtful discussion.

Taking education as his example of the "organic unfitness of the Colonial Office" (100) to the task of social development, James showed how workers read differently from traditional intellectual models. Crucially, for James, it is not that semiliterate or working people do not think, but that they do so in a different environment, with different tools and at different rhythms to the "almost automatic acquisition of information" of traditionally educated intellectuals (101). Print and oratory gain power and authority among workers as items are passed around, repeated, discussed, and thought about over a period of days or weeks. James argued that Eric Williams's lectures in Trinidad, as well as the CPP's journalism in Ghana, showed that both movements understood the rhythm and the drive workers had for education.

James's analysis of the education strategy of Eric Williams and the People's National Movement in Trinidad, alongside that of Kwame Nkrumah and the CPP in Ghana, remains illuminating because it provides a concrete example of how postcolonial projects thought about social and political organization in alternative ways to the supposed European prototype. From the point of view of metropolitan colonial planners and African nationalist leaders alike, educational programs in the 1950s were intended to affect both material and psychological transformation. The CPP Plan for Mass Literacy and Mass Education, initiated in 1951, involved annual campaigns to eradicate adult illiteracy, small-scale self-help projects in towns and villages, and regularly scheduled instruction in the domestic "women's work" of hygiene, nutrition, and family care. By combining education with social and economic development projects in villages, this program always aimed at ideological reorientation of the population toward the goals of socialist reconstruction.

We now know that this presented a new set of problems after 1958, as the expertise of "knowing" the will of the masses also became entwined with Nkrumah's personal power and with the maintenance of CPP authority.[46] But, for James, at least, the CPP project still indicated a different approach to popular education. In contrast, in the 1940s and 1950s the colonial "welfare and development" strategy financed agriculture and education projects, which also aimed to change hearts and minds by, for example, training workers in the "appropriate" paths of professionalization.[47] This Colonial Office program faltered, James argues, because it calculated its strategy mainly in terms of "bums in seats" and built infrastructure. This was the conception of development that underwrote the gradualist rationale of modern colonial rule. And it was precisely this rationale that meant that the metropolitan Colonial Office and colonial administrators on the ground would never be able to achieve real "development." Something new was required.

Part II sees James wrestling with what Tony Bogues has rightly characterized as one of the most prevalent issues in the study of African political thought: the modernity/tradition paradigm.[48] The dynamic of this paradigm is suffused with a pervasive assumption that African "tradition" is static and unchanging—resulting, as Terence Ranger first enumerated and African historians have since expanded, in misreadings of African politics that cannot account for the flexibility of custom and values over time and space.[49] In his 1964 article on Nkrumah's "Slippery Descent," James insists that Africans have a "tribal way of life" that is in a sense inherent, that is "in the bones" of Africans for "hundreds of years" (154).[50] Here James only hints at this question of the role of tradition in African politics as he attempts to confront the withering of political life in Nkrumah's Ghana. But it follows that Nyerere's political thought and, in particular, his emphasis on an African "tradition" that could develop into its own form of African socialism based on the extended family, *ujamaa*, would capture James's attention.

Structurally, then, the inclusion in part II of James's 1964 criticism of Nkrumah, followed by Lenin's analysis of Russia's backward illiterate peasantry and then a comment on the Arusha Declaration, follows a sequence of thinking about African political theory and socialism. If James's analysis of the place of "tradition" in African political strategy was cursory and implied a static interpretation of "African" history, he was more direct in confronting the dichotomy of "backward" and "advanced" societies. James consistently articulates a Marxist developmental analysis of backwardness as the material and historical components of a given society. Russian illiteracy was the result not of the "psychological ... weakness of men, nor the vices of instincts" but of the "defects of a system" (166–67). Hungarian workers had "advanced" to the stage where power could be seized via the process of production "as a result of the stage reached by modern industry and its experience under the bureaucratic leadership of the Party."[51] Ghana's economy, infrastructure, and education were backward, but Ghanaians faced the task of modernization with their eyes open and in full understanding that the "advanced" societies of Europe developed over hundreds of years by taking advantage of outside territories and resources—a point that his then-future student, Walter Rodney, would confirm in *How Europe Underdeveloped Africa*.

For James, this historic relationship meant there was necessarily a double task of addressing difficulties and deficiencies while at the same time "throwing [Europe's advantages] back" at the developed world. Europe's development pattern, as James explains in his 1960 speech, was not an option for the underdeveloped world. But it is precisely this point that is important. Africans were demonstrating that they had all the capacity, the "ability to learn" and to invent. What they could not do was follow the exact same pattern as existing developed countries. They had to go beyond the known.

Parts I and II together articulate at least three ways that African movements had contributed something new to history. In the Convention People's Party, Africans had demonstrated a "creative adaptation" of Western political ideas to their own environment and needs, creating a political instrument forged out of contact between Europe and Africa (131). This something new challenged an insular logic to political theory and practice. Where Nkrumah's practice had truly stepped beyond the known, however, was in its pan-Africanism. "Never before," James writes, "has any state ever declared that it is ready to abandon national sovereignty in the interests of a continent" (136). In 1960, when James made this declaration, Nkrumah's willingness to give up state sovereignty for regional cooperation was an important model for the British West Indies Federation James worked for. In the late 1970s, when James made the decision to include this speech in the book, the appearance of a periodic dwindling of the Pan-African movement perhaps sharpened James's investment in Nkrumah.

Finally, the Arusha Declaration's creation of cooperative villages as the fundamental social unit, with the Tanzanian farmer as the nucleus of the education system, broke the bounds of the known again: "Not in Plato or Aristotle, Rousseau or Karl Marx will you find such radical, such revolutionary departures from the established educational order" (180). The first paragraph of " . . . Always out of Africa" makes clear that James is more interested in foregrounding the historical achievements of an African state than anything else. He exposes what he believes to be fraudulent African claims to build socialism, but the thrust of the work is clearly to identify a new stage of society produced in Africa. Nyerere's translation of socialism as a doctrine of human equality rather than class struggle, Tony Bogues argues, was a prominent interpretation of socialism within radical anticolonial thought of the era.[52] Whatever James's full view of Nyerere's interpretation, particularly with regard to the role of production in socialist and capitalist societies, we have already seen that human equality played a role in how he situated Ghana's importance for his Trinidadian readers in the *Nation* in the early 1960s. And it is ultimately the harmony between humanism and socialism, which Nyerere's thought had exposed, that James celebrates.[53]

James's description of what African leaders like Nkrumah and Nyerere were doing was an affirmation of experimentation that contained an unequivocal rejection of the status of lab rat: "To let other people stand aside and look upon us critically as if we were some experiment. . . . That we will not stand" (142). And its method, which involved multiple terrains of activity and thought, was fundamental to many of the thinkers and leaders James engaged with. Tony Bogues has argued that one characteristic of early postcolonial African and diaspora thinkers, including Nyerere, was that they directly engaged their political thought and theory with practice, a move that demands some sympathy: it required both "a willingness to question the orthodoxy of political thought and the capacity to begin to understand their own societies on their own terms." The questioning of political orthodoxy—the "throwing it back in their faces," as James put it—was in itself a complex task of critical and imaginative thought. Discerning exactly what "their own terms" were is another. It required the ability to operate "at the daily level of political life and also engage in reflection and political work." The result was a "political discourse [that] was being continuously reshaped."[54]

James believed that his conclusions about Nkrumah were still as relevant as ever two decades after he originally wrote them. They gain new life today. His concern that university training could "instil [a] poisonous medicine into the veins" (101) that would produce no new ways of thinking have been taken up by student movements in South Africa, Britain, Europe, and the United States. Current movements to decolonize the educational curriculum demand more honest intellectual tools from universities and thus reinvigorate James's attention to different modes of education. New ways of thinking about education, beyond the number of schools built or teachers counted, were "at the heart of the emancipation of Africa" (103). Across Africa political and intellectual agendas are asking critical questions about the trajectory of the continent after independence, demanding new political forms and ways of thinking about the relationship between politics and society. The questions of what it means to decolonize, and how that might be done, are being critically rethought not just in the former "Third World" colonies but, finally, in settler colonies and in the heart of the former colonizer.

The layers of time present in *Nkrumah and the Ghana Revolution* meant that James was constantly gesturing forward and backward on different scales. The present infiltrated his reading of the past, just as the past incited the future. "It is the present, and not researches into archives which determine our understanding of the past," he writes. "So it is our conceptions of what is going on around us that will enable us to renew ourselves at the richness of heart which was present in the people of the Gold Coast as it was in the people of France at the greatest moment of their national history" (88).

The fact is that James was never very far from his own work. In the 1964 draft of his introduction, James admitted that a publisher had read the manuscript and found it "dated," to which James replied, "I should hope that this history is dated."[55] He then proceeded to locate the book in his own personal history from the 1930s, which included his work with George Padmore and *International African Opinion* and their early belief in the coming African revolution. That historical explanation remained in the final published version in 1977.

This "dated" history was no mere aside or qualifier. It was, it could be argued, at the root of James's project. We can return again to the question, Why did James persist in his effort, over decades, to make his manuscript public? His corpus demonstrates a deep and long-standing commitment to serve as a spokesman for revolutionary change and as a chronicler of the "remarkable men" that Africa and the African diaspora produced. In a lecture on "The Old World and the New," James argues that "you cannot under any circumstances write the history of Western civilization without listing" the achievements of René Maran, George Padmore, Marcus Garvey, Aimé Césaire, or Frantz Fanon.[56] One of James's first published books was his biography of the Trinidad labor leader Arthur Cipriani. And if *Beyond a Boundary* was about Trinidad just as much as it was about cricket, it was also a record of the achievements of his friend Learie Constantine and James's fight for Frank Worrell to become the first black captain of the West Indian cricket team. If *Nkrumah and the Ghana Revolution* was a record of Nkrumah's achievements in spite of many mistakes, its preface was also an archive of George Padmore's work in Africa, and its postscript a commitment to Julius Nyerere and his project in Tanzania.[57] Padmore's death in September 1959 affected James deeply. If he remained committed to revisiting and publishing his book on Nkrumah throughout the 1960s and 1970s, he also continued to work on a biography of one of his earliest friends.

Unlike the Nkrumah book, James's book on George Padmore was, as far as we know, never completed.[58] But he was still researching it in the late 1960s, and the text of "The Old World and the New," which was delivered as a speech in London in 1971, paid homage to Padmore as one of the men produced by a particular Caribbean situation.[59] James's elaboration in 1971 of how and why these "remarkable men" emerged reads very much like a letter written in 1968 requesting research funding to write his book on Padmore.[60] Even if this drive was not entirely conscious, the publication of *Nkrumah and the Ghana Revolution* in 1977 realized another small archive of Padmore's work. Indeed, in a 1973 interview, James explained that much of his information about independent Ghana in the late 1950s, during the writing of part I, came from his direct correspondence with Padmore. Until his death, in September 1959, Padmore sent James frequent updates and documents of "everything that he was doing" in Ghana.[61]

James always identified his own position within a text and the history that informed that position. The author was never absent from his writing. I wish to do the same here. I write this introduction from Winnipeg, Canada, a settler colony only barely able to acknowledge that its policies of land and re-source expropriation, cultural genocide, and pass system instituted against indigenous peoples are not the distant past, but the lived history of the twentieth century. This is the country of my birth. It is a country that, in James's arresting prose, is so "choked and stifled by the emanations from the myth" (29) that in 2009 its prime minister could stand before a gathering of world leaders and state that Canada has "no history of colonialism."[62] In 2016, from the mouth of a new prime minister, and despite his personal admonitions against "colonial behaviours" toward Canada's indigenous peoples, Prime Minister Justin Trudeau still found it possible to paint Canadian government as a more benign form of rule that did not bear "some of the baggage that so many other Western countries have—either colonial pasts or perceptions of American imperialism."[63] The powerful ideas contained in what James has called "the myth" remain in our world today. James's careful delineation not only of the ideas but also the "politics that flow from the myth" make the first chapter of *Nkrumah and the Ghana Revolution* a productive resource "for all those seeking to lift ourselves from the parlous conditions of our collapsing century" (19).

NKRUMAH AND
THE GHANA REVOLUTION

| | | | |

TO FRANCIS

in never-to-be-forgotten memory.
Like Cromwell and Lenin, he initiated
the destruction of a régime in decay—
a tremendous achievement; but like them,
he failed to create the new society.

C. L. R. JAMES

In 1957 in Accra, I had long conversations with Nkrumah about the Ghana revolution. It was the revolution in the Gold Coast, ending in the state of Ghana, which had struck imperialism in Africa the blow from which it would never recover. I told Nkrumah that I thought it was one of the most significant revolutions of the century, and that there was still much of great importance to past and future history to be said about it. He said he had been thinking the same, and ultimately I willingly undertook to write a history of the Ghana revolution. I felt myself particularly qualified to do so. I had known Nkrumah in New York before he came to London to join George Padmore; Padmore was from 1935 the founder and guiding spirit of the African Bureau and today is universally known as the father of African emancipation. It was under the auspices of the Bureau that Nkrumah went from London to the Gold Coast in 1947 to begin his preparations for the revolution which was to initiate a new Africa. I went to work at once and completed the history by 1958. What I then wrote is the basis of Part 1 of this book.

I had been the editor of the journal *International African Opinion*, published by the African Bureau, and between 1953 and 1957 had seen a great deal of Padmore, not only a close political associate in the struggle for colonial emancipation but a friend from boyhood in the West Indies. During the struggle for independence Padmore had been Nkrumah's personal representative in London. Padmore stage by stage in articles and in books had publicly recorded the development of the African struggle for independence. He and I had been in Ghana together in 1957 when I was discussing with Nkrumah. We examined the African revolution in Ghana itself in 1957 and what I wrote in the history expressed, I believed, more or less what our circle, which had lived with the African question for over twenty years, thought of the future of the struggle for African independence at the time of its first success. By 1957 we had acquired great confidence in our own approach to these questions, for in the years before the second world war we had been the sole political grouping which not only foresaw the coming independence of Africa but under the guidance of Padmore worked unceasingly for it. We were not wrong in 1935, and events since 1958 give me no reason to modify and bring up to date what I wrote in 1958.

In that year I went to the West Indies. There, as Secretary of the West Indian Federal Labour Party which governed the now defunct Federation, I had a practical and illuminating experience of a colonial territory on its way to independence. I am now in a position to say that the political officials and pundits, especially the ones sympathetic to colonial freedom, illuminated their far less complicated bankruptcy over Africa by their miscomprehension of the West Indies. In 1960, on political business connected with the West Indies, I again visited Nkrumah in Ghana. We talked, not as much as in 1957, but this time I knew more about these matters and renewed acquaintances and friendships in Ghana. Ghana, from being the finest jewel in the crown of Africa, was obviously in a state of impending crisis. After getting Nkrumah's agreement as to what topics I should deal with, I addressed a meeting of his party in Accra. The speech was recorded and I have reprinted it here (135–48) without annotation or omission. Nkrumah learnt about the speech and its reception, expressed his approval and told me that he would get the text printed. I sent the script to him and it was never acknowledged, far less printed: Nkrumah was very acute and, knowing my general political ideas well, he must have recognised far more than anyone else what I was saying; without fanfare I had not modified the perils that I saw ahead. As I had occasion to say later, I was quite certain that my audience understood what I was talking about.

I nevertheless continued to consider Nkrumah one of the forward looking politicians of the day and the most important political leader in Africa. Against all criticism of the unquestioned anomalies of his régime, I stood firmly by the fact more important than all others added together that in a situation of enormous difficulty, on the whole he was not only doing his best but was, as politicians go, one of the most enlightened. As late as 1962 I had occasion to say so. Deeply disturbed at the impending collapse of the West Indian Federation and the effect of this defeat on his struggle for a United Africa, Nkrumah addressed a carefully phrased but no less powerful political letter to every head of government in the West Indies, pointing out what the collapse would signify for the public image of black men, and with firmness and sobriety asking them to reconsider. He also sent me a copy of the letter saying rather formally that he knew my interest in the subject. I was a little surprised, but not for long. No West Indian political leader allowed it even to be known that he had received such a letter. I therefore published it, and Nkrumah's régime then being under fire for its anti-democratic tendencies (putting the opposition in jail)[1] I took the opportunity to add to the publication a personal letter to him stating that then, in 1962, as over the previous twenty years, I had always found him a great African statesman and one who stood in general on what I can best call the progressive side of world politics. That letter I have republished here (149–51).

In 1963 I had occasion to write to him of my concern at a second attempt to assassinate him: I implied that something was seriously wrong with a régime in which there were two attempts at assassinating the political head of state: I knew that in 1957 over a large part of Ghana Nkrumah could have walked for days without a single attendant. His reply to this letter I found most lacking in his customary political sense. But I have always paid attention to politics in Ghana; I could see there was trouble ahead and I was deeply disturbed at the way things were going. For one thing I had always found that many ordinary people in the Western world looked hopefully at Africa on account of the impact upon them of Ghana. I therefore wrote a long memorandum to Nkrumah about the continuing and growing crisis in newly-independent African states. Unfortunately I never sent it—one has to be careful in relations with political leaders, especially leaders of new states. But shortly afterwards I had occasion bitterly to regret that I had not sent him the memorandum.

The continuous crisis in Ghana had reached a climax when Nkrumah dismissed his Chief Justice for giving a judicial decision of which he disapproved. I have to emphasise that, as the book will show, this act showed the degeneration not only of the régime but of his own conception of government. As usual most commentators seemed to believe that Nkrumah, an African inexperienced in the ways of parliamentary democracy, was drunk with the wine of power, and had once more proved the inability of Africans to govern except as some reactionary tribal chief in modern dress. I on the contrary realised at once that Africa had crossed a Rubicon. In order to drive home the significance of this dismissal I have gone to the length of saying to public audiences that an unscrupulous head of government might find it necessary to shoot his Chief Justice while trying to escape, arrange for him to be run over by an errant motor lorry, have a bunch of doctors declare him to be medically unfit and, Kremlin-fashion, put him out of the way in an asylum, send him on a long holiday and beg the British government to make him a life peer on resignation, even invite him to dinner and poison him. But what a head of state does not do is to dismiss his Chief Justice after he has given a major decision on a matter in which the whole country is interested. *The very structure, juridical, political and moral, of the state is at one stroke destroyed, and there is automatically placed on the agenda a violent restoration of some sort of legal connection between government and population.* By this single act, Nkrumah prepared the population of Ghana for the morals of the Mafia. Those learned societies which passed resolutions disapproving of his act should have known that Nkrumah could have said the most admirable things about the rule of law. It wasn't that he did not know. What was important was that he knew all the arguments against such a step and its inevitable consequences.

I wrote to him at once making clear the far-reaching consequences of the mistake he had made. I asked him to write to me or ask some trusted secretary to do so. I told him that if I had been able I would have come to talk to him: he needed as most of these leaders do some old associates who could talk to him without any sense of past obligation or future hopes. I suspected the pressures which had driven him to this fateful action. He never replied and after a month I wrote three articles in a West Indian newspaper using the situation in Ghana as a peg on which to hang my long-felt premonitions of the African degeneration. These articles are republished in Part II of this book. I have no need either to add to or subtract from them.

I had not come to an end of my relation with Ghana. In 1963 I was asked to write for a political journal to be published in Accra. I declined to write anything about Africa—I knew the hopelessness of the situation in which the African leaders found themselves, and knew that *all* that I had to say would not be published in any African paper. Ultimately I compromised by suggesting and agreeing to write a study of Lenin's final reflections on Soviet Russia, the first underdeveloped country to face the problem of the transition to the modern world. The book's penultimate chapter is a reprint of the article. It deals with Lenin's summation of what Soviet Russia had done and had not done by 1923. It could have been written with contemporary (and future) Africa in mind. As far back as 1958 I had sent a bound copy of these writings of Lenin to Nkrumah to mark his fiftieth birthday. But it seems that only after an ocean of blood, sweat and tears will African politicians be able to understand Lenin's prophetic warnings and drastic revolutionary proposals for solution.

The future of Africa will be rooted in the African experience of African life. Yet nobody, European or African, can make anything clear and consistent of the developing pattern in Africa unless upon the basis of the substantially documented and widely debated historical experiences of Western civilisation. That must first be established so that he who runs or merely looks at television may read. Modern Europe begins in France in 1848, and Karl Marx in *The Eighteenth Brumaire of Louis Bonaparte* pointed a fearsome finger at what he then saw as the dominating political reality of the age which was beginning:

> It is immediately obvious that in a country like France, where the executive power commands an army of officials numbering more than half a million individuals and therefore constantly maintains an immense mass of interests and livelihoods in the most absolute dependence; where the state enmeshes, controls, regulates, superintends and tutors civil society from its most comprehensive manifestations of life down to its most insignificant stirrings, from its most general modes of being to the private existence of individuals; where through the most extraordinary centralisation this parasitic body acquires a ubiquity, an omniscience, a capacity for accelerated mobility and an elasticity which finds a counterpart only in the helpless dependence, in the loose shapelessness of the actual body politic— it is obvious that in such a country the National Assembly forfeits all real influence when it loses command of the ministerial posts, if it does not at the same time simplify the administration of the state, reduce the army of officials as far as possible and, finally, let civil society and public opinion create organs of their own, independent of the government power. But it is precisely with the maintenance of that extensive state machine in its numerous ramifications that the *material interests* of the French bourgeoisie are interwoven in the closest fashion. Here it finds posts for its surplus population and makes up in the form of state salaries for what it cannot pocket in the form of profit, interest, rents and honorariums. On the other hand, its *political interests* compelled it to increase daily the repressive measures and therefore the resources and the personnel of the state power, while at the same time it had to wage an uninterrupted war against public opinion and mistrustfully mutilate, cripple, the independent organs of the social movement, where it did not succeed in amputating them entirely.

That is what I saw in Ghana in 1960 and this is what has been mounting in ever-widening circles as the outstanding social and political development in contemporary Africa. The African state enmeshes, controls, regulates, superintends and tutors civil society from its most comprehensive manifestations of life down to its most insignificant stirrings. At least it attempts to do so, and where it fails will compromise for static acquiescence. That is so and must be so. The contemporary state has not only a finger in every pie, it initiates the gathering of material for all new pies, and finds it necessary to claim at least a token share in all the old pies. This is so more particularly in underdeveloped countries and overwhelmingly so in dynamic underdeveloped countries determined to "catch up with and in time surpass" the advanced countries. Stalin, to whom we owe the phrase, at least caught up with and surpassed many millions of his own subjects.

The concentration on the one-party aspect of the term "one-party state" is a typical myopia of people who insist on looking for two parties and are horrified to find only one. In actuality they see none. In the African one-party state the term "party" is a euphemism. It is the state, that expanding source of dignities, wealth and power in countries and among people which have very little of these and are accustomed to being excluded from them.

Politically the people of Africa have gone through the initiation from puberty into manhood. Sometimes, though not always, the circumcision was rough: the physician was modern, but often a member of the Royal Family was the only anaesthetic. The great barrier in the way of grasping, of absorbing this simple but shattering new portent in contemporary history has been the defensive reiteration by the leaders of British public thought that the British government "gave," "handed over" independence for which (God save us) it had long been training them.

The truth is that the population was trained by two forces: imperialism, which exploited them with a brutal and horrible cruelty and shamelessness, and the concomitant violence adequate to ridding themselves of this burden grown intolerable. All politics in Africa today begins from there. As in independent India, the violence in face of which the imperialist power retreats can burst out after the imperialist departure.

Economic relations are the basis of any form of state and the colonialist states of Africa were from start to finish organisations for economic exploitation. Economic relations in Africa have not collapsed, although they were very near to collapse. Economic relations are relations between people. The economic relations in the African states have acquired new functionaries, that is all, but it is now that the total collapse is imminent, because *the people the new functionaries have to manage are not the people over whom the colonial power and its civil servants, its chiefs and its army, kept order.*

The whole of the Western world became poisoned by the fantasy of whether independent Africa could work the two-party system or not. And as the unreality of this has become manifest, there has been a spreading tendency to accept the one-party state as for the time being the next best substitute. The reality is that the new African states for the most part are bastard imitations of the Russian one-party state of Eastern Europe or headed for that haven by way of bastard imitations of the two-party state of Western democracy (with the opposition in jail, in exile or very conscious that that is the fate which awaits it unless by hook or by crook it gets hold of the power). Both cohorts in the manner of African chiefs are ennobled by a large new umbrella which they quite shamelessly dignify with the title of African socialism. Thereby they seek to do two things: sanctify the concentration of all available funds in the hands of the state, i.e. their own hands, and seek to build a wall of consciousness between themselves and the capitalist imperialism against which they mobilised the African masses in the struggle for independence. One feature is common to all these states. As I found in Ghana in 1960, and have verified on innumerable occasions for practically all of newly independent Africa, the population is convinced of one new inescapable feature of the new governments, the corruption of government and party officials from the highest to the lowest. Where the ordinary citizen does not find it he is uneasily aware that something is wrong. As Lenin said so clearly of the Russia of 1923, corruption is inherent in the system. The brutality which follows this corruption pervading any new sphere of government has been amply demonstrated for all the world to see and even officially acknowledged by the late Nikita Khrushchev at the Twentieth Congress of the Soviet Communist Party.

The man at the helm is the African intellectual. He succeeds—or independent Africa sinks: unlike Britain in the seventeenth and France in the eighteenth centuries, there is no class on which the nation falls back after the intellectuals have led the revolution as far as it can go. In the twentieth century it is quite impossible for Africa to develop the class of large-scale capitalists that followed the victory over the slave-owners in the Civil War: apart from the changed picture of the world view, there is not even the mercantilist base that America had. As in Russia after the 1917 revolution, it is the intellectuals who will lead the continent. Yet Western racial prejudice is so much a part of the Western outlook on life that the African intellectual continues to be looked upon as some kind of primitive barbarian climbing the sharp and slippery slope to civilisation. The Congo rebels against Tshombe, threatening and even shooting white prisoners, evoked a chorus from minds not merely tinged but soaked in the mire of racial superiority. The following from the *Evening Standard* was typical:

One of the many paradoxes of the violent and unhappy Congo is the part now being played by Mr Thomas Kanza, the Foreign Minister of the Stanleyville rebels who, according to one report, threatened to "devour" the European hostages.

Mr Kanza, a Harvard man, is well known in London, where he was Congolese Chargé d'Affaires from 1962 until last December. He is a sophisticated and amusing bachelor of thirty-one who is remembered as the host of some lively parties while he was posted here.

He played a leading part in lobbying against the Union Minière interest behind the scenes at Westminster. He resigned when Mr Adoula was succeeded as Prime Minister of the Congo by Mr Tshombe.

His father was Burgomaster of Leopoldville. After graduating from Louvain University in Belgium, he read psychology and education at the College of Europe in Bruges, won a scholarship to Harvard, joined the EEC in Brussels and returned to America as Congolese delegate to the United Nations. He is now negotiating in Nairobi on behalf of the rebels.

Personal political ambition and long-term opposition to Mr Tshombe no doubt explain his present loyalties, but many people who knew him in London find them a little difficult to reconcile with the memory of an urbane diplomat.

One would believe that the régimes of Hitler and Stalin had existed ten thousand years ago in the twilight dawn of history. In fact the African intellectual is a modern type, and will never be understood except as a type of Western intellectual. Luckily the type has been analysed and described with a clarity and force unsurpassed in modern history, literature or psychology. The author is Dostoyevsky, and the occasion is that supreme masterpiece of European criticism, his address on Pushkin, delivered in Moscow in 1880, a year before his death. The only thing to do is to quote various passages, and the reader is asked himself to substitute Africa wherever Dostoyevsky says Russia:

The character is true and admirably realised; it is an eternal character, long since native to Russia. These wanderers are wandering still, and it will be long before they disappear. In our day they no longer visit gypsy camps, seeking to discover their universal ideals and their consolation in that wild life, far from the confused and pointless activity of Russian intellectuals; now, with a new faith, they adopt socialism which did not exist in Aleko's day, and labour eagerly, thinking like Aleko that they may reach so their final goal, not for themselves alone, but for all men.

Dostoyevsky knew the origin of these socialists:

The greatest number of intellectual Russians in the time of Pushkin served then, even as now, as civil servants in government positions, in railways, banks, or other ways, or even engaged in science or lecturing—earning money in a regular peaceful, leisured fashion, even playing cards, without desire for escape, whether to the gypsies or other refuge of more modern days. They only played at liberalism, "with a tinge of European socialism" which in Russia assumes a certain benignity—but that is after all only a matter of time. One man is not even yet annoyed while another, encountering a bolted door, furiously beats his head against it. All men meet destiny in their turn, unless they choose the saving road of humble identification with the people. Even though some escape, this must remain truth for the majority.

Like the African, the Russian of Dostoyevsky's day yearns for truth,

yearns for the truth, somehow and somewhere lost, which he can nowhere find. He cannot tell wherein this truth resides, when this truth was lost, nor where it can be found, suffering nonetheless. Meanwhile a restless and fantastic creature searches for salvation in external things, as needs he must. Truth continues external to him, perhaps in some European country, with its more stable organisation and settled mode of life. Nor can he understand that truth is after all within him. How could he understand this? For a century he has not been himself in his own country. He has no culture of his own. He has forgotten how to work. He has grown up within closed walls, as in a convent.

Despite the consistently reactionary character of his politics, Dostoyevsky knew where only salvation could be found. He knew that

Truth is within them, not without. Find thyself in thyself. Humble thyself to thyself. Be master of thine own soul, and see the truth. Not without, nor abroad is this truth; not in things, but in thee and in thine own labour upon thyself. If thou conquerest thyself, then wilt thou be free beyond dreams, and make others free; thou wilt labour upon a great task, and will find in it happiness and fulfilment, and, at long last, understanding of thine own people and their holy truth. If thou art thyself unworthy, proud, and given to malice, if thou demandest life as a gift, without payment, neither with the gypsies nor in any other place, whatsoever shalt thou discover the "harmony of the spheres."

And the great master of fiction returns once more to the reality of the Russian intellectual:

In the remote heart of his fatherland, he is yet in exile. Conscious of his aim, he yet knows not where to turn. Later, he still feels himself in the midst of strangers, even more a stranger to himself, despite his brains and his sincerity, wherever he may roam. At home or abroad. He loves his country, but cannot trust it. He knows its ideals, but has no faith in them. He cannot see the possibility of any work in his own country, and he can feel only sorrow and derision for those few who can believe in it.

That is why African intellectuals kill. Perhaps we are watching in Dostoyevsky's pages the crisis of the intellectuals of all the underdeveloped countries and African peoples.[2] What Dostoyevsky feared more than anything else was their coming to power. He had died before the Russian proletariat appeared on the scene. Lenin unreservedly placed his faith in a new Russia upon the proletariat, small and inexperienced as it was. But as we shall see, before he died he was very much aware of what Dostoyevsky had divined, in fact seen. The African intellectual may even in times of stress revisit and consult the juju of his parents. That does not in the least alter the fact that if he is an educated person, he is a man of Western civilisation. The only advantage he has is that Africa is so backward that he will be guilty of violences far closer to Mussolini's cruelties than to the unbridled savagery of hitlerism or stalinism seeking "to catch up with and surpass."

The road out of this fearful morass which daily multiplies must of necessity be a simple one. A government must arise which will state publicly and officially what all the population knows. In Ghana in 1960 I found the educated section of the population seething with anger against this cancer. Ghanaians in 1960 were very proud of themselves. They felt that they had made history—which they undoubtedly had. And now corruption was eating away at the foundations of the new state they so proudly cherished. Under strong public pressure Nkrumah had appointed a government commission of investigation, but the opinions that I pertinaciously sought and found were that such a commission was bound to be powerless before so pervasive an evil. There was a sense that not a commission seeking wrongdoers but the whole function of government was involved. I did my best to let them see that I understood their problem. As best I could I indicated the way out. The problem is first and foremost an internal problem of the African state. That no outside body can fix for them. But the problem also lies at the nub of Africa's international relations. Without economic, technological and educational help and encouragement from the advanced areas of Western civilisation, Africa will go up and go down in flames, and heaven only knows when that conflagration will be halted. But the advanced world will hear and understand the need for aid on the scale and in the manner required only from a continent which has righted itself and registers across the skies that something and something new has again come out of Africa.

One definitive stage has been reached and passed. All, including the sycophantic rulers themselves, recognise the utter futility of constant begging for aid. They will never get it, and even if they get it they are in no position to make adequate use of it. At present they are allowed to create glittering units of foreign-owned exploitation, a token industrialisation which only places them more tightly and firmly in the shackles of the economic domination which they denounce and woo almost in the same breath.

The future of this vast continent and its millions lies in their making the advanced peoples realise that on the millions of Africans, as much as on any other section of modern society, hangs the real beginning of the history of humanity to which all that has hitherto taken place is only prehistory, more dehumanising and self-destructive in the twentieth century than ever before. But this embracing of the millions of Africa by the West can take place only on a clear recognition that they are an African people, with a way of life and a view of life and society thousands of years old. Tribalism is this way of life. Everything that does not begin there is for the Africans vanity and vexation of spirit. Tribalism in contemporary Africa has a fantastic and curiously modern history. I take leave to give some indications of it.

It is the practice of the contemporary African politician in power to denounce tribalism as the chief enemy of progress in Africa. By that he is usually defending the centralised power he wields (this he identifies with the nation) against trivial and unscrupulous politicians who, defeated at the elections, i.e. the struggle for the centralised power, find in their own tribe a basis for immediate partial and possible complete power. These quite unprincipled tribalists are not helped to see the error of their ways by a similar unscrupulous use of tribal connections, associations and rivalries by the very government which is denouncing tribalism. These unsavoury practices are a commonplace of African politics, and their superficies are quite often repeated by the liberal and socialist supporters and apologists of African self-government. Yet certain observers of African tribalism have claimed for it an integral place in any universal reconstruction of the modern world. It is a West Indian, i.e. a Western poet, direct heir of Rimbaud and Baudelaire, who is the creator of the concept of Negritude. In *The Black Jacobins* I have translated and published a review of sections of the now world-famous poem, Aimé Césaire's *Cahier d'un retour au pays natal:*

> My Negritude is not a stone, its
> deafness a sounding board for
> the noises of the day
> My Negritude is not a mere spot of
> dead water on the dead eye of
> the earth
> My Negritude is no tower, no cathedral
> it cleaves into the red flesh of the
> teeming earth
> it cleaves into the glowing flesh of
> the heavens
> it penetrates the seamless bondage of
> my unbending patience
> Hoorah for those who never invented
> anything
> for those who never explored anything
> for those who never mastered anything
> but who, possessed, give themselves up
> to the essence of each thing
> ignorant of the coverings but possessed
> by the pulse of things
> indifferent to mastering but taking the
> chances of the world

In contrast to this vision of the African unseparated from the world, from nature, a living part of all that lives, Césaire immediately places the civilisation that has scorned and persecuted Africa and Africans:

Listen to the white world
its horrible exhaustion from its
immense labours
its rebellious joints cracking under
the pitiless stars
its blue steel rigidities, cutting
through the mysteries of the flesh
listen to their vainglorious conquests
trumpeting their defeats
listen to the grandiose alibis of their
pitiful floundering.

The poet wants to be an architect of this unique civilisation, a commissioner of its blood, a guardian of its refusal to accept:

But in so doing, my heart, preserve
me from all hate
do not turn me into a man of hate of
whom I think only with hate
for in order to project myself into
this unique race
you know the extent of my boundless
love
you know that it is not from hatred
of other races
that I seek to be cultivator of this
unique race.

He returns once more to the pitiful spectre of West Indian life, but now with hope:

for it is not true that the work of man
is finished
that man has nothing more to do in the
world but be a parasite in the world
that all we now need is to keep in step
with the world
but the work of man is only just beginning
and it remains to man to conquer all
the violence entrenched in the recesses

of his passion
and no race possesses the monopoly of beauty,
of intelligence, of force, and there is
a place for all at the rendezvous of
victory.

Here is the centre of Césaire's poem. By neglecting it, Africans and the sympathetic of other races utter loud hurrahs that drown out common sense and reason. The work of man is not finished. Therefore the future of the African is not to continue not discovering anything. The monopoly of beauty, of intelligence, of force, is possessed by no race, certainly not by those who possess Negritude. Negritude is what one race brings to the common rendezvous where all will strive for the new world of the poet's vision. The vision of the poet is not economics or politics, it is poetic, *sui generis*, true unto itself and needing no other truth. But it would be the most vulgar racism not to see here a poetic incarnation of Marx's famous sentence, "The real history of humanity will begin."

In this poem Césaire makes a place for the spiritual realities of the African way of life in any review and reconstruction of the life of modern man. Césaire's whole emphasis is upon the fact that the African way of life is not an anachronism, a primitive survival of history, even of prehistoric ages, which needs to be nursed by unlimited quantities of aid into the means and ways of the supersonic plane, television, the Beatles and accommodation to the nuclear peril. Césaire means exactly the opposite. It is the way of life which the African has not lost which will restore to a new humanity what has been lost by modern life with

its rebellious joints cracking under
the pitiless stars
its blue steel rigidities, cutting through the
mysteries of the flesh.

These are poetic divinations of worlds to come. They are the waves of reality in which present-day Africa must live if it is to live at all.

One final word about the form the book has taken. Beginning with Kierkegaard and Nietzsche and reaching a completion in Sartre, modern philosophy expresses its modernity by assuming the form of a personal response to extreme situations, and is no less philosophical for that. I record here a sequence of political responses to an extreme political situation, the African situation, as it has developed during the last thirty years.

This book was concluded at a time when I feared for the future of Africa under African auspices, a fear which was immediately justified by the fall of Nkrumah. My bewilderment, however, was almost immediately soothed by the appearance of the Arusha Declaration of Dr Nyerere. Before very long, on my way to lecture at Makerere, I was able to pass into Tanzania and read, hear and see for myself what was going on. I remain now, as I was then, more than ever convinced that once again something new had come out of Africa, pointing out the road not only for Africa and Africans but for all those seeking to lift ourselves from the parlous conditions of our collapsing century.

PART I

| | | | |

Two forces met in the Ghana revolution. On the one side were the British colonial government, the local industrialists and merchants, and the City interests whom this government represented. Opposed to it were the vast majority of the people of the Gold Coast.

Behind the colonial government was the full power of the British government, its economic power, and what must never be forgotten for a moment during this struggle, its armed navy and air force. In addition, it enjoyed the moral and political support of the other imperialist powers, of all who believe in progress as it is defined and limited by "constitutional methods," and of those who believe in no progress at all. The people of the Gold Coast could count on no direct support from anywhere. But they had on their side the active sympathy of vast millions of colonials in Africa itself and in Asia, and intangible but no less valuable, the lack of confidence and latent hostility to the powers and claims of imperialism which could be found in Britain itself and in all the great metropolitan centres of the world. This last was perhaps the deciding external factor in the genesis of the revolution and its successful conclusion. Its full force, however, could only be appreciated since Eden and the British Cabinet made the mistake of ignoring it in their dealings with Nasser.

The colonial government, with the British government at its back, had enormous forces at its disposal. But political power never rests entirely on naked force. By the time it has reached that stage, it is already doomed. All political power presents itself to the world within a certain framework of ideas, and in any estimate of social forces in political action it is fatal to ignore this. Modern critics of literature and the dabblers of psychology lay great stress on the creation of myths and the great role that myths have played in the lives of early peoples, particularly the ancient Greeks. It is not sufficiently recognised that this creation of myths, universal throughout the ages, has never been more prevalent than at the present time. One of the greatest of modern myths has been the myth justifying and even ennobling "colonialism" or, as it used to be called, the "white man's burden." At present it is a common belief that colonialism in the modern world is dead or dying.

Nothing could be further from the truth. Colonialism is alive and will continue to be alive until another *positive doctrine* takes its place. From the very beginning of its negotiations for self-government with the leaders of the Ghana revolution until the very end the Colonial Office and those whom it represented were governed by the ideas of colonialism. They had and could have had no other ideas. They made adaptations, they discarded some elements of the myth and added others. They have given up positions that they could not hold, as the Greek myths were continually organised and reorganised to suit new situations, but the myth itself remains. It governs the relations of the British government with Kenya, Uganda, Tanganyika, Rhodesia and South Africa. French, Belgians and Portuguese have their own versions of the myth. The politics that flow from the myth can send the tortured continent of Africa up in flames from the Sahara to the Cape and from Dakar to Mombasa. The myth continues to govern the relations of the British government with independent Ghana as it governed the relations of the British government with the dependent Gold Coast.

On the night of the celebrations of independence, Nkrumah told a vast crowd that Ghana was "forever free," a sentiment excusable and under the circumstances legitimate. But in the event of, for example, a civil war in Ghana, British imperialism, disguising itself in the mantle of the United Nations, will go in again to protect British life and British property. British economic interests and a substantial section of the British press would subsidise and encourage armed rebellion against a Ghana government as they subsidised and encouraged Ashanti when independence approached. The British government did it in Egypt. No government (except Russia or China) would dare to do the same in Belgium or Holland or Portugal.

It is important to remember at all times that those who are administering in the spirit of the myth are not hypocrites or criminals, although the myth drives them often to commit hypocritical or criminal actions. They believe in it. A myth in which people do not believe is not to be taken seriously—it is mere political manoeuvre or vulgar propaganda. What is more catastrophic, the vast majority of the British people, having no other views placed before them and unable to investigate, do research, or to construct a theory of relations between advanced and backward peoples, have no other choice but to follow along the same lines of thought and to accept the actions of those who govern the relations between the European peoples and the colonies by these patently false, but nevertheless dominating, ideas.

Here is the myth in its elemental terms, the only terms in which it can be understood, because they form the unconscious premise of those who live by it, despite the intellectual structures, logical or illogical, which they build upon this instinctive basis.

Africans are, and always have been, a backward and barbarous people who have never been able to establish any civilised society of their own. Some of the more liberal would qualify this by saying that this backwardness was due not to any natural inferiority but to the circumstances of their environment, the climate or the soil or the forests, or something of the kind. These barbarous people were brought in contact with civilisation by the brutalities of the slave trade. However, the unhappy slave trade is happily behind us, and as a result of their contact with Western European civilisation, primitive Africans became a part of our unified world. The British government has by and large aimed at bringing these peoples to the stage where they would be able to exercise self-government, despite certain lapses from principle to which all nations, all peoples and all individuals are of course subject, human nature being what it is. It was always a *principle* of the British colonial system, but within recent years with the rise of the colonial peoples, it has been clearly understood and is being carried out. Ghana is the first example in tropical Africa where the British connection with Africans has had its first beneficent fruits in the establishment of self-government and parliamentary democracy. The experiment is to be viewed with the greatest interest, and the people of Ghana are to be assisted wherever possible. Upon their success depends much of the future of Africa.

It is quite true that there are a few scholars and a few educated people here and there who know differently. But this is the view of the large majority of modern people except in one particular section of the world. The American Negroes, faced with this view of the past of Africa which has been used not only to justify slavery but also to maintain segregation and oppression, found themselves driven to make the most serious studies of the past of Africa and to learn and to popularise the works of the great scientists and anthropologists who have worked on this question. The result is that among them there is a greater knowledge of the real history of the development of Africa than exists proportionately in any other sector of the world. But, as we have seen, they too have been contaminated by the prevailing myth and, try as they may, cannot rid themselves of it.

The British version of the myth expresses itself in a corresponding political programme, a programme which has been carried out in the past with the inevitable weaknesses and mistakes (that British governments, like all other ruling governments, are prone to) but nevertheless follows more or less the following pattern.

First of all, when the people are at a low stage of backwardness, the British government rules by means of a Legislative Council and government is in the hands of officials, white men appointed by the Colonial Office. At their head is the Governor, who rules with the advice of an Executive Council. These know how to govern, the primitive peoples don't. After a certain number of years (always vague) when the people have made a certain progress under this régime, a new step is initiated. The Colonial Office then nominates members to the Legislative Council. These are from the more advanced, i.e. the more educated members of the community; usually they also represent the richest. After a further period of training, the people are allowed to elect a few members. At a still later stage, the elected members can become a majority in the Legislative Council, and one or two of them are promoted to the Executive Council. When the elected members are granted a majority in the Legislative Council, the Governor on the Executive Council continues to maintain a majority of officials; and at a still further stage, if the elected members of the Executive Council should attain a majority, the Governor has at his command certain reserve powers, which enable him to override the elected majority in the Legislative Council, and the elected majority in the Executive Council. He needs this power to help train the people in governing themselves. The ultimate goal is reached when the people, having been trained by these stages, are considered fully able to govern themselves and the British government hands over to them complete control and the Governor becomes a Governor-General with no powers whatsoever. This is what is supposed to have happened in Ghana. The myth, however, prescribes yet another stage, the stage through which we are passing now: Ghana is now on trial to see if the decision to give Africans self-government was not premature.

The power of the myth will be appreciated by the shock many people will feel when I say that this elaborate theory so profoundly expounded by so many Secretaries of State for the Colonies, members of parliament, colonial governors, constitutional authorities and leader writers, cannot stand concrete examination for a single moment and is in reality a tissue of falsehood, hypocrisy and empiricism, all designed to present disorderly retreat as systematic advance. This must be proved.

Trinidad, the West Indian island from which I come, is an island with no background of native culture or native language and enjoys a standard of literacy, a highly qualified professional intelligentsia, easy communication, which as far back as 1900 was far in advance of where Ghana is today. Yet the Colonial Office governed the island with the help of nominated members until in 1919 a great strike shook the island. *As a result of this*, a commission was appointed and the rigmarole of a few elected members began. Further stagnation until in 1937, seven thousand oil workers stage a strike, practically the whole of the island follows, and a series of strikes runs from Trinidad up the islands to Jamaica. A commission is appointed. But the commission barely has time to report when another series of revolts runs through the islands. A new and larger commission is appointed. After the interval of the war begins the tragicomedy of majority of elected members, etc. Trinidad now enjoys ministerial responsibility and has a few more stages to go. Unless the Colonial Office claims that it trains the masses of the people to strike and revolt whenever a new stage of fiddling with the Legislature is reached, its elaborate claims for training colonial peoples is an elaborate fiction.

In colony after colony that is the history of this training for self-government. The Colonial Office rules, there is an explosion causing loss of life and property and then one stage is benevolently granted. If the colonial people organise themselves to demand political rights, they are met with government persecution, police violence and gaol (Gandhi and Nehru, Uriah Butler, Bustamante, Nkrumah, to mention only a few of the best known). As late as 1954 the Kabaka of Buganda was yanked out of Uganda by one of the most brutal, tyrannical and blundering actions of a colonial governor in colonial history.

The bland conviction of competence in colonial government can be sustained only because the judges of this competence are the culprits themselves. Look over the history of most colonies in recent times. There is a violent upheaval, a commission is appointed, after one year a constitution is promulgated. Often it is discarded before it is introduced, or having been gestated for ten years and taking two years to deliver, it lasts for one year. Or the people who are persuaded or coerced into accepting it use it for the sole purpose of breaking it up. In Kenya, we have seen thousands of dead, years of violence and disorder, commissions and goings and comings between the Colonial Office and Kenya, pacification, fifty thousand people in concentration camps, rearrangement of populations, voters to have certificates of good conduct in the Emergency—after these and other preparations the Lyttleton Constitution comes into being. But no sooner does the carefully screened African electorate elect its eight members than they refuse to work the Constitution and demand fifteen more members. Whereupon we read the following from the *Manchester Guardian* correspondent, 21 May 1957: "The Chief Secretary's reply to the African members' demand was by no means a flat refusal. He stated that the government did not believe that constitutional change was either impossible or undesirable." Only there must be inter-racial discussion. In other words, here is the Lyttleton Constitution just out of the womb dying before it has uttered a cry. This farcical history can be repeated seven times in the history of any ten colonies.

The more you examine the successive theories of British colonialism, the more it is seen for the genuine myth-making that it is. One more example must suffice—the test of literacy. Any colonial of the previous generation will remember the illiteracy barrier to self-government. It was repeated and repeated and expounded and expounded until even the colonials themselves grew to believe it: it stood to reason that until a large majority of a people were literate, the practice of parliamentary democracy was impossible, and it followed that self-government was out of the question until the population was literate. But now hundreds of millions of illiterate people in India, spread over a vast area, vote by means of symbols representing the different parties. The century-old literacy axiom is quietly dropped over the side. Why should anyone take seriously the remaining axioms of colonialism? The plain truth is that a colonial people gets self-government when the cost of withholding it from them is too much for Her Majesty's Government—usually because the people concerned are determined to have it and show that even if they have to be shot down in thousands, they will not be denied. A totalitarian government can do this. In the present international situation it is not too easy for a democratic government, though not at all impossible as Kenya and Cyprus show. And when this stage is reached, as it was reached in the Gold Coast, then, after making use of every conceivable obstacle for delay and obstruction, self-government is finally handed over. At this stage, illiteracy, literacy, semi-literacy, fully-trained, half-trained, all the solemn self-evident truths do not mean a thing. The only settled policy of Her Majesty's Government has been to get out where to stay any longer is impossible.

The colonial peoples are not fooled by all this deliberate myth-making. The real victim of it is the great masses of the British people and particularly those who try to take a serious interest in such matters. They are at the mercy not only of the actions but of the ideas so pertinaciously propagated by their governments. The booklets published by the Colonial Office on the occasion of the independence of Ghana, purporting to give an account of relations between Britain and the Gold Coast up to and including the achievement of independence, are full of characteristic suppressions and evasions and in the general impression they are intended to convey, are monuments of falsehood.

The British people as a whole are now ready for new relations, human relations, with colonial peoples for the first time in four centuries, but they are choked and stifled by the emanations from the myth. And this is particularly true in regard to Africa. Just below the surface of the British people is a deep vein of feeling for the people of Africa which they do not have for the peoples of, for instance, India or Burma.

It is doubtful if for centuries Britain was ever more deeply shaken, socially and morally, than by the struggle for the abolition of the slave trade in 1807 and of slavery in 1834. I have shown in *The Black Jacobins*, and no one has ever refuted it, that the success of this movement was due to the fact that by the beginning of the nineteenth century the rising industrialists of Britain were convinced that slavery and the plantation system, and the privileges it bestowed on West Indian planters, were now a handicap to British industry and had to be abolished. But this does not in any way alter the fact that among the great masses of the people, just feeling their way towards political and social emancipation, the abolition of the slave trade and slavery was a great moral issue. Not only in the recognised abolition organisations but in their churches and other religious bodies, they registered their protest with a passion that, like a similar movement in the United States, remains a mystery to all who probe into that period. Within recent years historians of these great mass movements suggested that they owed their power to the fact that in the shackled slaves, millions on both sides of the Atlantic saw an image of themselves engaged at the time in casting off the bonds of the eighteenth century which still encumbered the modern world and democracy. During the Civil War in the United States, when Tories and Liberals in the higher circles of government were partisans of the South or indifferent, John Bright was able to lead a movement in the North of England in which tens of thousands of cotton operatives suffered severe privation rather than accept cotton from the Confederacy. Despite the gross accentuation of racial prejudice which resulted from the division of Africa and the growth of imperialism in the last years of the nineteenth century, this powerful current among the peoples of Britain remained and is now once more emergent under the blows imperialism has been receiving and the discredit which now colours all colonial adventures.

But the myth does not die: whenever it is torn apart, it is hastily patched together again and reorganised to suit the new situation. The Ghana revolution which should have torn large and irreparable rents in the myth has been washed, dressed and tied with ribbons and the imperialists have actually succeeded in presenting it as a shining example of the settled policy of Her Majesty's Government. No more impudent fraud has ever been imposed upon the British people.

Why is the myth so powerful? Simply because after so many generations of indoctrination and its apparent truth as a reflection of reality, it is now an organic part of the thought processes of the nation and to disgorge it requires a herculean effort. It is not that the myth is not challenged. It is, but almost always on premises which it has itself created, premises which, as with all myths, rest on very deep foundations within the society which has created them. Many serious and well-meaning people are absolutely incapable of understanding another premise to the African question. In his autobiography, as elsewhere, Kwame Nkrumah constantly repeats in the most uncompromising terms that no people is fit to govern another people. "Freedom is not something that one people can bestow on another as a gift. . . . To assert that certain people are capable of ruling themselves while others are not yet 'ready' as the saying goes, smacks to me more of imperialism than of reason."

This is not an aberration or exaggeration. All the politics of Nkrumah, his whole success from start to finish, were built on this conception. Yet many people who hail him as a great liberator, one of the great political figures of the age, and study his work, turned pale when faced pointblank with the application of this principle to Kenya, Uganda, Tanganyika, Nyasaland. The myth holds them tight. Hundreds of millions of people in Asia are firmly convinced of this doctrine. The Western European, even when he accepts it in principle, proceeds at once to hedge its realisation with all sorts of impossible conditions.

There can be no hesitation. A myth that has lost all contact with reality is the direct source of immeasurable confusion, catastrophes and disasters. The plain truth is this, that the Europeans in Kenya, Rhodesia and other colonial territories, the people of European descent in South Africa, are not the guardians of civilisation, they are not those who are saving the contemporary African from barbarism. They are the ones who are creating disorder in the continent, they are the propagandists and architects of barbarism. The continent and the people of Africa today are a part of the modern world. The idea that Africans will sink back into barbarism unless they are governed as they are at present is as crude propaganda as any perpetrated by Hitler or Stalin. If, by some stroke of good fortune, the forty thousand European settlers were removed from Kenya, in twenty years the forces of progress in the world will have received a powerful reinforcement in economic development and social example; while the situation as it is, guided by the settled policy of Her Majesty's Government, holds no outlook but continuing strife, the intensification of every evil passion, and in the end, a conflagration spreading ruin throughout East Africa, if not the whole of the continent.

The myth cannot be modified. It must be routed, torn up by the roots, ridiculed.[1] Five million Africans in Kenya want progress, they want education, they want political freedom, they want to send their children to Europe and America and India to learn, they want European technicians and educators of all sorts to come to Africa. In a wide experience of African nationalists of every type, I have never met or heard of a single one who did not envisage a far wider contact with Western civilisation after independence than anything Africa has seen so far. All they ask is that this contact be established on the basis that they have primary and inalienable rights in their own country. And those who deny this to them and falsify history, elevate immorality to a guiding principle and rule by brutal force, lies and corruption, who suppress the aspirations of millions of people, who seek to create and maintain in the twentieth century social relations and forms of government that the world has left behind for centuries—what is the logic, the incredible coarseness of the values and social conceptions that sees in them and not in the aspiring Africans the protagonists of civilisation and the guardians of culture?

Under the best of circumstances, the future of Africa is a future of turmoil, of stress and strain, or revolution, of counter-revolution, of disputes between tribes and national units, complicated by the disputes between European powers and the Africans, and between the European powers themselves. It is a fantasy to believe that these European imperialist powers are the ones who will guide Africa safely through these troubles. They are the ones responsible for them. They are the ones who are making it more difficult than ever for the Africans to find their own way.

This is the question to which they will not, they cannot, give a clear answer. Who are the civilised, the builders of the future, the people of moral strength and endurance? The Strydom Government and the cowering liberals, or those magnificent Africans, undemoralised by a merciless and unceasing persecution, walking twenty miles a day to protest against the crimes committed against them and as a gesture of solidarity to their leaders, being tried for treason in a courtroom where they are caged like animals in a zoo? Yet faced with the fact that the only alternative is that these people must govern themselves, liberals and socialists and people of good will retreat into the myth and so leave the field to the uninhibited enemies of civilisation. All observers expect, if they do not actually predict, the inevitable explosion.

Myth-making conceals yet another virulent poison for the myth-makers. It insists that they see themselves always as the givers, and Africans as the takers, themselves as teachers and Africans as the taught. In the thousands of reports, articles, speeches, that I have read about events in Ghana, I have never seen a single word, the slightest hint that anything which took place there could instruct or inspire the peoples of the advanced countries in their own management of their own affairs, and this is as true of friends of Ghana as of its enemies. Yet I doubt if, with the single exception of the Hungarian revolution, any event since the end of the second world war has been so charged with symbolic significance for the future of Europe and America as what took place in the Gold Coast between November 1947 and February 1951. Information is not lacking, for the thing was not done in a corner. To indict a generation of people as lacking in reason and intelligence convicts the accuser, not the accused. There is only one tenable explanation, and that for want of a better word I have called "the myth."

In 1943 Sir Alan Burns, Governor of the Gold Coast, thought that the colony needed a new constitution to advance it a stage forward on the road to self-government in accordance with the settled policy of His Majesty's Government. Promulgated in 1946, this constitution introduced four appointed members into the Executive Council, of which three were Africans. The Governor retained a safe majority of seven. The Legislative Council consisted of a President either appointed by the Governor or the Governor himself as President. The Governor also nominated six members, including at various times representatives of the Chamber of Commerce and of Mines, the Chairman of the Methodist Church of the Gold Coast, etc.

Now for the representatives of the people. Of these, nine were elected by the Joint Provincial Council (chiefs); four were elected by the Ashanti Confederacy Council (paramount chiefs and native authorities); two represented the municipality of Accra and one each the municipality of Cape Coast, Sekondi-Takoradi and Kumasi.

The constitution was hailed by educated Africans, the British press and the Fabian Bureau as the most advanced constitution in tropical Africa and a great step towards self-government. But it was obvious that it was nothing of the kind. For in addition to a Legislative Council and an Executive Council loaded with nominees of the Governor, the Governor was able to pass any bill which he wanted and which the Legislative Council refused to pass by merely declaring it to be the law. The Governor claimed that in proposing such an advanced constitution, he was in advance of the people of the Gold Coast and he pointed out that the politically-minded African lawyers and merchants had made no political claim, which was perfectly true. But, alas, having welcomed the constitution in 1946, these intellectuals denounced it in 1947 as mere window dressing, designed to cover but not satisfy their natural aspirations. They organised the United Gold Coast Convention to use "all legitimate and constitutional means" to ensure that self-government should pass into the hands of the chiefs and people in the shortest possible time. The traditional game of colonial tag had begun.

These lawyers and middle-class intellectuals were men who were making money and enjoyed some social status in the colony among their own people and also, to some extent, with the governing officials. In the life that the merchants and lawyers lived, the vocal ones, and particularly the lawyers, had no serious rivalry from Europeans. The Chairman, Mr George Grant, was a prominent man of business and had been a member of the Legislative Council. The celebrated Dr Danquah was another prominent member and he had actually been appointed a member of the Legislative Council under the Burns Constitution by the Joint Provincial Chiefs. Political power for them was merely the crown of an already active and full existence. Their skins were black. But they had essentially the same attitude to the great masses of the African people that a liberal colonial official would have. Self-government for them meant the substitution of themselves and members of their caste for the colonial officials. And, like the colonial officials, they sought the support of the chiefs.

The chiefs, however, uncertain of where the power lay, wavered between the colonial officials and the local intelligentsia, leaning for the time being to those who actually had the power, the Colonial Government. The members of the United Gold Coast Convention could not, any more than colonial officials, see themselves as carrying on mass agitation, and that is why, towards the end of 1947, they sent for an African student and agitator who had made a name for himself in London, to come to the Gold Coast and popularise their organisation for them. So Nkrumah, after twelve years, returned to his native country.

The situation in the country was normal and the causes of any untoward events were apparently easy to trace. As a result of the war prices were high and growing higher. There was a shortage of foodstuffs. Thousands of returned ex-servicemen who had fought in various parts of the world were dissatisfied with the contrast between the reality of their lives and the promises which they claimed had been made to them.

There lived in Accra a sub-chief called Nii Kwabena Bonne III. He was also a businessman. He made a short campaign through the country enlisting the support of the chiefs. He then, on 11 January 1948, called a boycott on the purchase of European imported goods. The boycott was as complete as such an undertaking could be. It became general in the Colony and Ashanti and lasted until 24 February.

During the boycott events of immense symbolical significance took place. Native administrations, up to this point, like the chiefs, tools of the government, now used their legal position to impose fines upon those who did not co-operate in the boycott of European goods. Groups of young men went around the towns maintaining the boycott by force when necessary.

It was only on 11 February that the government intervened. There was a series of meetings between the Chamber of Commerce and Nii Bonne III, with the Colonial Secretary in the chair. It was agreed that prices should be lowered for a trial period of three months. Nii Bonne III then called off the boycott.

Meanwhile, the Ex-Servicemen's Union planned to present a petition to the Governor setting forth their grievances on Monday, 24 February 1948, but then postponed it until Saturday the twenty-eighth. On that day the Ex-Servicemen's Union began their march. In the course of it they changed the prescribed route and announced their determination to march on Christiansborg Castle, the residence of the Governor. They found a squad of police in their way and in the course of the dispute which followed, the superintendent of police, a white man, fired at the ring-leaders, killed two of them and wounded four or five. The news spread into the industrial district of Accra where the people for the first time in a month were buying European goods. They were already dissatisfied because they believed that the goods were not being sold to them at the prices stated in the published agreement which had preceded the calling off of the boycott. The news of the shooting precipitated an outburst of rage. The people attacked the European shops and looted them. The police were unable to restore order for two days, Saturday the twenty-eighth and Sunday the twenty-ninth. There was destruction of property by fire and in the two days fifteen persons were killed and a hundred and fifteen injured in Accra alone. There were other disturbances in various parts of the colony. The most important were at Koforidua where the outbreak began after the arrival of a lorry with men from Accra. They broke out in Kumasi and district on Monday 1 March, an hour after the arrival of the train from Accra.

Nkrumah says that he and his organisation, the United Gold Coast Convention, had nothing whatever to do with the disturbances, and, as we shall see, there is every reason to believe him.

These are the bare facts of the case. When, however, we look a little more closely in the light of after-events, an often-analysed logical movement discloses itself. These were no ordinary riots of a hungry populace over high prices. The first stage of every revolution is marked by a great mass movement of the populace, usually led by representatives of the old order. M. Georges Lefebvre of that great school of historians, the French historians of the French Revolution, has established that the bourgeois revolution in France in 1789 was preceded by what he calls the aristocratic revolution, the revolution of the nobles against the monarch which took place in 1788, one year before the popular eruption which captured the Bastille on 14 July 1789. In this case we are in the middle of the twentieth century. The first outburst takes the form of an economic boycott that lasted a month, but it is led by a chief and supported by the chiefs. The people of Accra follow exactly the course that the masses of the people have followed in every great revolution. The only organisation at hand was the organisation of ex-servicemen, and when they began their march they were at once reinforced by large numbers of spectators and sympathisers. Whatever had been the original intention of the ex-servicemen, these sympathisers encouraged them to take the road to the Governor's Castle. Anti-racial cries were frequently uttered. Among the remarks were such as: "This is the last European Governor who will occupy the Castle." (They were not far wrong; he was the last but one.) The crowd directed a heavy fusillade of stones against the police. When the police tried to stop them, they shouted insults at the European officers and invited the Africans in the ranks to abandon their duty. It seems that they were successful. For when the Superintendent finally gave the order to fire, the Africans did not shoot and he himself had to seize a rifle from the nearest man to fire the shots which caused the casualties. Superintendent Imray had with him at the time only ten men. The idea that a crowd of two thousand, many of them men who had seen battle, was cowed by the shooting is ridiculous. They could have swept the ten men away in ten seconds, and as there were only two officers and twenty men at Christiansborg, the Castle could easily have become another Bastille. In these situations you have to work by inference, similar conjunctures in previous historical situations and an absence of prejudice against crowds and against Africans. The crowd retreated because it realised that to sweep away the petty resistance which faced it would be to initiate a battle for which it knew it was not prepared. Therefore, as crowds will do under such circumstances, it preferred to retreat.

I am here using the report of the investigations made later by a Colonial Office commission, and it must be remembered first that at moments like these what the crowd is really thinking and the motives of its actions are profoundly difficult to recapture after the actions have taken place; and in any case, a government commission is not exactly the body which would know whom to question, how to elicit the answers that matter, and even to understand what evidence it does manage to collect. The commission calls the crowd a "lawless mob." That was precisely what it was not. It was acting instinctively according to certain fundamental laws of revolution and we shall see that it obeys these laws to the very end.

We should note these incipient actions carefully because, unless there is a great unsettlement of the settled policy of Her Majesty's Government and the other European powers, that is precisely what is going to take place over vast areas of colonial Africa. What has really taken place can be summed up as follows:

1. The people on a national scale had mobilised and organised themselves during the boycott and felt their power, and they had been able to do this so rapidly because the first step was taken under their traditional leaders, their chiefs.

2. The call to the African police not to obey their European officers and not to shoot was not an accident. It takes place at the beginning of all revolutions. Neither was it spontaneous. Already, during the boycott, at the trial of a local chief on a charge arising out of the enforcement of the boycott, posters had appeared in Accra calling upon the police to strike and to refuse to obey the orders of the European officers.

3. The march on Christiansborg Castle and the shouts that the Governor would be the last European governor show that out of the confidence built up in the month-long boycott, the people had proclaimed the ultimate slogan of the revolution, the end of imperial rule.

They knew what they wanted. If they turned aside from the direct march to the Castle and hesitated before sweeping aside the police, it was because they understood the consequences of such actions. They had been waiting for somebody to lead them and they welcomed Nkrumah as a person to do so. Lawless mob indeed. Within eighteen months Nkrumah was going to call a Ghana Constituent Assembly in Accra which would be attended by ninety thousand people. Within two years these people would carry out a policy of positive action in which the life of the whole country would be brought to a standstill with the utmost discipline and order. Within three years they would give Nkrumah a vote of 22,780 out of a possible 23,122.

No. The reader will not understand these events or what is taking place all over Africa today unless he makes a complete reversal of traditional conceptions as to where is law and where is lawlessness. The disciplined community obeying its own laws was the masses of the people in Accra. The mob was the heterogeneous collection of chiefs, government officials, merchants and lawyers. These were a mob because they were pulling in all directions and did not know where they were going. They were lawless because the laws that they were trying to administer had been rejected by the people and they had no force with which to enforce them. This is the great paradox of Africa and we shall meet it time and again.

The chiefs, like the aristocrats in France, had had their first and last adventure in revolutionary activity. The merchants and lawyers were quite prepared to claim power from the government because of the violence which had been unloosed. They did so in a telegram to the Colonial Secretary. Once they had been placed in power, they would have attempted to restore order with a ruthless hand. Dr Danquah gave it as his opinion that if there had been more shooting, there would have been less loss of property, a sentiment which we must remember. They did not seek to organise the masses in any way but sought to use the upheaval as a means of frightening the government with the necessity of sharing the power with themselves. In this they were playing exactly the same role as the French bourgeoisie in the revolution of 1789. The French bourgeoisie was quite prepared to try to extort concessions from the King, pointing to the spectre of the mass movement. Once the mass movement had organised itself under its own independent leaders, they followed the aristocracy into the counter-revolution. The difficulty that faced these Gold Coast merchants and lawyers was that they had no time to manoeuvre. The mass movement was organised even before the economic boycott.

In this organisation for immediate ends under leaders of the old régime, the spontaneous outburst of political action, and the statement of the most ulterior aims of the revolution by unknown elements in the crowd, the readiness of larger provincial towns to act as soon as they heard the news from the capital, the people of the Gold Coast were following a pattern we have seen repeated often enough for nearly two hundred years: Ghana from the very start takes its place in the very vanguard of the middle of the twentieth century, and the future is established without possibility of argument by the actions of Nkrumah.

Nkrumah had landed in the Gold Coast on 19 December 1947. For the next fortnight he was resting in the country. For the next two weeks or thereabouts he was organising an office in Saltpond. On 20 January 1948 he called a meeting of the working committee of the United Gold Coast Convention and laid before them a programme, written if we want to press the matter on the very day he presented it. This is *the* document of the revolution. The economic boycott had started only nine days before; the ex-servicemen's demonstration was over a month off. Yet Nkrumah divided the course of the revolution as follows:

Organisational Work

The organisational work of implementing the platform of the Convention will fall into three periods:

First Period

a. Co-ordination of all the various organisations under the United Gold Coast Convention: i.e. apart from individual membership of the various political, social, educational, farmers' and women's organisations, as well as Native Societies, Trade Unions, Co-operative Societies, etc., should be asked to affiliate to the Convention.

b. The consolidation of branches already formed and the establishment of branches in every town and village of the country will form another major field of action during the first period.

c. Convention branches should be set up in each town and village throughout the Colony, Ashanti, the Northern Territories and Togoland. The Chief or Odikro of each town or village should be persuaded to become the Patron of the branch.

d. Vigorous Convention weekend schools should be opened wherever there is a branch of the Convention. The political mass education of the country for self-government should begin at these weekend schools.

Second Period

To be marked by the constant demonstrations throughout the country to test our organisational strength, making use of political crises.

Third Period

a. The convening of a Constitutional Assembly of the Gold Coast people to draw up the Constitution for Self-Government or National Independence.

b. Organised demonstration, boycott and strike—our only weapons to support our pressure for self-government.

This was the programme as he saw it, before anything serious or violent had taken place. Within twenty-seven months he was to have carried it out just as written, to the last comma.

What is more, he took no part in the boycott, but having organised his office and placed the plan for the revolution before his committee, he turned aside from the boycott and set off to the country to start educating and organising the illiterates in the villages, while in between he continued his organisation at the centre. He knew exactly what he was aiming at and what was required to do it. In all the coming turmoil, ups and downs, the shifts and chances, the unforeseen and the confidently expected which did not take place at all, he was not thrown off course because he had known in advance where he was going and how he would get there.

This is revolutionary leadership of the twentieth century, standing on the shoulders of a long line of great revolutionary leaders and theorists whom Nkrumah studied and mastered without ever losing his strong grasp of the concrete reality before him. He found a substantial body of men and women whom he could train and inspire and through whom he succeeded in organising the vast majority of the nation to a pitch where it would act as a unit and over and over again show a complete, a perfect self-discipline. The story of the Ghana revolution is a tract for the times and not an episode in the history of backward Africa. There was nothing backward about the Ghana revolution. It was a revolution of our times. The backward, the barbarous, the politically ignorant, sat in the Colonial Office and in the Colonial Administration. There will be no compromise on this, for it is the shocking truth which will repeatedly force itself upon our attention in these historical events and will help us to free ourselves from the myth.

Let us try to form some estimate of the people in 1947. It is a necessary task even if at best it can only be an approximate one. The fundamental difficulty is that only after a revolution or at a certain definite stage in it, as for example in the 1951 elections in the Gold Coast, is one able to estimate what the people were like before the revolution began. The people themselves do not know. The process of the revolution is essentially the process of the people finding themselves. As they scale one height, that girds them to attempt another. It is sufficient to say that this rapid movement is contained in them before they move a step, though it may be only in vague aspirations and thoughts which they do not dare to think to the end. They think by acting.

In 1947 the Gold Coast was a model colony, and despite the upheaval in 1937 and some vigorous journalism by Azikwe and Wallace Johnson, it was agreed that for fifty years the relations between the colonial government and the indigenous population had been of the happiest. How to characterise this happy population in December 1947 when Nkrumah landed at Takoradi?

To begin at the most elementary level: it consisted of 327,800 persons directly engaged in labour of various kinds and farming. Of these, by far the largest number were cocoa farmers, for the greater part in Ashanti, 210,000. There were 38,000 workers in the mines, for the most part in the provinces. There were 23,000 workers in various small manufactures; 1,000 in building, 8,000 in transportation; 16,000 in commerce; 8,000 working in hotels and giving personal service. This is a very small number out of a total population of nearly five million.

Very small also was the town population in relation to the population in the country. There were about 135,000 in the municipality of Accra, the capital; in the Kumasi municipality, including suburbs, there were 77,000. In Sekondi-Takoradi there were 44,000 and in Cape Coast 29,000. For the rest there were a few small towns with about 10,000 people. This, in all, is about 300–400,000. Of the 100,000 wage-earners there were about 30,000 organised in thirteen unions under the general direction of the Trades Union Congress.

The great majority of the people therefore lived in native villages, scattered far and wide, many of them in remote parts not easily accessible.

There were less than five hundred miles of railway, and these had been built chiefly in the interests of the European traders, primarily to get raw materials to the coast, as is usual in colonies, such other benefits as the population got from them being quite incidental.

There were 100,000 children in some 700 primary schools, either government or assisted by the government. In the non-assisted schools, chiefly religious, there were the same number of children. In all there were 28 secondary schools with a total enrolment of 4,000 students. The total enrolment was about 4½ per cent of the population. Only 10 per cent of the population could read.

The central government was in the hands of the Governor and persons nominated by him to the Legislative and Executive Councils. But local government on a regional and on a village scale was in the hands of chiefs and their supporters who administered under the firm direction of a European representative of the colonial government.

By every settled standard of the government's settled policy, these people were totally unfit for self-government, and by these standards would continue to be unfit for another generation at least, which was as far as anybody ever cares seriously to think about. They were illiterate, they were tied to the family unit, they were hopelessly divided into tribes. There was a small population of educated people but between them and the mass in the villages there was a gulf which it would take the administration decades to bridge. Furthermore, the people were quite satisfied. If there was unrest, it was about such simple elementary things as high prices and shortage of goods.

It was the myth at its most mythical. When you examine this population of the Gold Coast on the eve of the revolution (and not purely in the light of after-events, though this cannot be entirely avoided), the first thing that strikes you is its essential unity.

The basis of this unity was not in its black skins, but the unity of the conditions under which it lived. The population is divided into various tribes, speaking different languages and guarding jealously their own traditions and customs. But these tribal divisions are grossly exaggerated and are not necessarily constituents of a permanent division. In any particular area they are a source of unity; the division which they represent on a national scale can be overcome or adjusted but for the fact that they were systematically fortified, fostered and encouraged by the British administration. Even when the administration was not doing this positively at all for self-interested purposes, it considered tribalism as a permanent feature of the social and political landscape. This was inherent in the situation, because the administration had no aim or purpose which could attempt to integrate the divisions of tribalism into a higher unity. Furthermore, the divisions of tribalism were an obvious argument for the settled policy of the government, which was to introduce self-government only when the people were sufficiently unified to act as a homogeneous body.

But transcending these tribal divisions was the essential unity of the Africans in their villages, whether Fanti, Ashanti, Ga or Ewe. There is absolutely nothing here of the caste system that exists in India. The people live in a unified poverty and squalor. Their chiefs, except for that small number who were big politicians by grace of the administration, were very close to the people, the majority of them as illiterate as their subjects, and governed by a long tradition of democracy in which the chief was no more than a representative of his people who could be, and often was, ruthlessly removed if his actions did not accord with their wishes. This was the condition of some 75 per cent of the population.

The workers, particularly in the mining industry and the railways, are united by the very mechanism of the process of production itself. That among the thirty-five thousand miners only three thousand were actually in the union is of far less significance than the fact that in the United States only fifteen million workers are organised out of a total working population of over sixty million. At any critical moment the large unorganised majority always follows the small organised minority.

The chief towns, Accra, Kumasi, Sekondi-Takoradi, Cape Coast, Koforidua and Tamale, were comparatively small but socially effective. Apart from the workers in manufacturing industries, the town population consisted mainly of the mass of unskilled and unorganised manual labourers, domestic servants, messengers, and casual workers of all kinds. But between 1926 and 1946 the numbers in the schools rose from sixty thousand to nearly two hundred thousand. Thus by 1947 there was a substantial body of young people, not only literate but of some educational attainments and occupying thousands of subordinate positions as teachers and clerical assistants of one type or another in government and business. In 1947 a great number of them were in their early twenties, and particularly in the colony were not only educated but Westernised, inheriting the century-old traditions and practices of Western civilisation.

The division between town and country did not, as is usual in more advanced and older civilisations, create a division in the population. On the contrary, these usually divergent elements were knit more closely together. The population in the six large towns had grown from less than 150,000 to over 300,000 since 1931. Thus the inhabitants of the towns were closely connected with the village population, a fact which had had an enormous influence in the Russian revolution. But in the Gold Coast this unity was reinforced by certain special features, and here we approach the specifically African.

The fundamental units of African life are the family and the tribe, and they persist under all forms of African life. The urban members of the family retain their intimate social and spiritual connection with the family left behind in the village. The family in the village retains its close sense of relation with the literate urbanised children in the town.

The sense of unity and common social purpose which for centuries has been imbued into the African by the family and the tribe is not lost in the city. In the older European countries the towns centuries ago created new forms and conceptions of social unity in the artisan guilds. Later, large-scale capitalist production recreated another form of unity in the labour process itself, which finally produced the unions and labour organisations of today. Yet in the United States, as late as 1935, one of the most powerful constituents of the meteoric rise of the CIO was the fact that scores upon scores of thousands of Southern workers, on the basis of the discipline imposed upon them by large-scale production, brought an energy which was rooted in their close sense of bewilderment in the big city, from which the union was a refuge. The urbanised Africans had found neither guild nor large-scale union to organise them. They created their own forms of social unification and they used what came naturally as a basis, the tribe. On a tribal basis they formed unions and associations of all kinds, mutual benefit associations, religious groupings, literary associations, a vast number of sports clubs, semi-political associations or associations which provide in one way or another for one or some or all of these activities. Sometimes, although some of the members are well educated, they conduct their business in the native language. They maintain close communication with their tribal organisation or village. They raise money and initiate schemes for education and social welfare in the village or tribe. The tribal bond unites both the literate and illiterate members of the town. They often act politically as a unity. Nevertheless these are not tribal organisations in the old sense. They are fundamentally a response to the challenge and the perils of town life in a modern community.

In their variety and multiplicity these organisations are unified by the fact that they serve the same purposes. And thus they make of the city a meeting place and solvent of the ancient tribal differences. It is in this way that, independently, by their own activities, energy and need for organisation, in response to their environment, and making use of their historical past, the basis of national unity between literate and illiterate, between tribe and tribe, between town and country was being laid. The administration babbled about training the people by stages in order to practise local government in the English manner. When they realised what had been happening, they, who had always claimed that tribalism was one of the main obstacles to the implementation of the settled policy of the government, at once began to do their utmost to stimulate and revive the ancient tribalism in its crudest form. But this is to anticipate.

There was yet another social feature of Gold Coast life, which was specifically African and was to prove of enormous importance to the revolution. For the great mass of the common people the centre of African life has always been the market. The Ewe week consisted of four days, the day before market day, market day, the day after market day, and stay at home day. The traders for generations have been the women (Nkrumah's mother was a petty trader), and this function has been maintained and developed until today a large proportion of the retail distribution of goods, and the main channel through which the distribution of commodities flows from the big wholesale importers to the private home is the market, in small villages as well as in the big towns such as Accra and Kumasi. Thus in Accra there are thousands of women in action in the market, meeting tens of thousands of their fellow citizens every day. European visitors and officials up to 1947 saw in these markets a primitive and quaint survival in the modern towns. In reality here was, ready formed, a social organisation of immense power, radiating from the centre into every corner and room of the town. Instead of being confined to cooking and washing for their husbands, the market-women met every day, dealing with the European and Syrian traders on the one hand and their masses of fellow citizens on the other. The market was a great centre of gossip, of news and of discussion. Where in many undeveloped communities the women are a drag upon their men-folk, these women, although to a large extent illiterate, were a dynamic element in the population, active, well-informed, acute, and

of Ghana's independence
he resulting formation of
1anchester Guardian in its
ı special supplement gen-
torial:

fields of Achimota more
ι. No men have deserved
ɛxander Fraser and James
cipal of this great school,
: drew the breath of finer
ɩer (now 83) has done, to

ɪ form. In the struggle for
ere were fifteen thousand
of them, was worth any dozen Achimota graduates. The graduates, the highly educated ones, were either hostile to Nkrumah and his party or stood aside. The social forces that made the revolution were the workers, the market-women and, above all, the stratum of youth educated in primary schools who had not been subjected to the influence of British university education. Aggrey understood his people and as far back as 1930 had made his celebrated prediction that a youth movement was coming in Africa which would astonish the world. These were the ones in which Nkrumah found his ablest, most devoted and most fearless supporters, and they remain the core of the party to this day.

This was the condition of the people in the Gold Coast in 1947, not in absolute terms, but as a developing process, the process of modernisation. Objectively the most effective single factor in the evolution was in all probability the lorry. Packed to the limit and beyond the limit of safety they sped along such roads as there were, opening up communities at a rate undreamt of in an earlier time. There were 200 licensed in 1923. The number of new ones licensed at the end of the war was 3,467. In the course of the next year it rose to 4,249. By 1955 it was 12,583. These did more to prepare Ghana for independence than all the graduates produced in Achimota during the same period. They reunited the common people.

These strictly objective processes, the movement of a people finding themselves and creating a new social order, were powerfully aided by certain subjective factors whose effect it is impossible to overestimate, once they are seen in relation to the response of the mass to the changing social environment.

The African is a black man, and centuries of Western domination and indoctrination, Western science and Western history, the material privileges and social superiority which those who embody the settled policy of the government have arrogated to themselves, these create in the minds of the great majority of Africans and people of African descent everywhere a resentment which is never entirely absent, may remain dormant for long periods, but can be depended upon, in a particular population at a particular time, to create and cement a formidable unity and determination, especially when the prospect arises of putting an end to the assumptions of superiority or particularly offensive manifestations of it. Imperialism created this feeling, it has paid and will pay dearly for it. It is a social and political force which seems to grow in power and refinement of expression, as the people of the world, and with them Africans and people of African descent, break down the barriers to racial equality. Thus in Harlem, New York, in 1943, the Negroes broke out in a long-smouldering resentment against segregation and discrimination in general, and against high prices and the brutal treatment of black soldiers in Southern camps in particular. With a systematic and relentless thoroughness they smashed the windows of every shop owned by a white man throughout the area, and it is an established fact that those who did the smashing did not loot—the looting came after and was done by the poor and the hungry and the lumpen-proletarians who could not resist the sight of goods waiting to be taken. But what was most remarkable was that though tens of thousands were in the streets participating or sympathising and encouraging, no single black person attempted any violence to any white person and crowds of white people, many of them from Manhattan, walked, watching and very often talking and exchanging cigarettes and lights with the Negroes in the most amicable manner. The racial consciousness which has been so mercilessly injected into the Negro is today a source of action and at the same time of discipline.

In Montgomery, Alabama, for one year a Negro population of fifty thousand decided not to travel in segregated buses any longer, organised transportation of their own in the form of a car pool, and from the first day of the boycott to the last it was maintained by well over 99 per cent of the population, undoubtedly one of the most remarkable manifestations of social consciousness and self-discipline in the long and varied history of revolutionary movements. The actions of the Africans in South Africa are sufficiently familiar.

Some such cementing power was most obviously at work during the Ghana revolution. When every objective social factor is analysed and weighed, there remains something over and beyond which alone can fully account for the incredible solidarity, endurance and discipline which was shown by the Gold Coast population between the years 1947 and 1957, and particularly between 1948 and 1951. Nobody expected it, the administration was specifically contemptuous of any such possibility, repeatedly the leaders were overcome with wonder and admiration at it, and as we have already seen, it nerved them for a political audacity which time and again seemed to tremble on the edge of a frightful catastrophe, but remained to the end under complete control. They were bound together by the bitter tie of centuries of racial humiliation, and it is to the eternal credit of themselves and their leaders that they were conscious of it, used it with extraordinary confidence, subtlety and finesse, and, despite the most extreme provocations, never abused it. The world of today, and still more of tomorrow, owes much to them.

Finally, and perhaps most important, the people had lived through the great experience of the second world war. Knit together by the objective environment, conscious in a thousand ways every day that they were in a stage of violent transition from the immemorial past to the modern world, they had heard around them the clash of world conflict, had seen the fall of mighty empires and had heard the slogans and the rhetoric, the promises of an end to age-old injustices, the facile promises of a better world without which it is impossible today to mobilise peoples for war. Particularly they had heard the ringing denunciation of all forms of racial superiority, the simplification of the slogans of democracy, the tears and prayers for national freedoms lost, the paeans of triumph for the national freedoms regained, the great liberation. Western politicians promulgated charters embracing an ocean and enumerated freedoms. Their populations listened with scepticism and fought as a matter of duty or to save themselves from concrete dangers which they saw as imminent and intolerable. Not so the colonial peoples. They took them seriously. For them the post-war world had to be a new world. It would be new only if they were free. The war being ended, there followed in rapid succession the freedoms of India, Ceylon, Burma. Thousands of Gold Coast soldiers fought in the Far East and brought home eye-opening information about countries that were on the high road to independence and were not in any way superior to the Gold Coast in literacy and all the other shibboleths

of the Colonial Office. What they had done, the Gold C₍
right to do, owed it not only to themselves but to the wo₍

The Western world as a whole, blinded by the myt₍
what all this means in Africa, and it must. The people
their own freedom within the context of themselves as
tropical Africa, and as part of a worldwide revolutiona
world. It is in every line of the record. But even if the ₑᵥᵢₑ
in such profusion, knowledge of all previous revolution would show that ₜₕₑy
always find strength and wisdom and perspective in the most advanced actions and ideas of their time. They always see themselves as leading humanity.

Such in outline were the forces at work, though as late as December 1947
they had not yet overtly manifested themselves in the Gold Coast. The Colonial Office and the administration knew nothing about all this until it had
hit them two, three, a dozen times across the face, sent them reeling again
and again, never giving them a chance to recover. The idea that they trained
the people of Ghana for self-government and independence is the literal reverse of the truth. Here again is the paradox. It is the people of Ghana who
trained, bludgeoned the Colonial Office into the meaning of self-government
and independence.

Such then were the people. They produced from themselves and their own resources the great body of their leaders. These were native-born and native-taught. Their very backwardness mobilised the people for the mighty self-propulsion forward. But to do this they needed all that the modern world had to teach them. This is what Nkrumah brought, and again I recommend that advanced peoples pay attention, with the necessary humility, to what their backward brothers are doing, so as to learn how to help themselves in their own difficulties. What other language is it possible to use to bring to his senses a writer like David Apter who spent a period in the Gold Coast, is profoundly sympathetic to the people, is anxious to pass on his information to the people of the West, entitles his book *The Gold Coast in Transition*, and spends fifteen pages out of more than three hundred on the actual revolution? He spends precious pages on native institutions and the Colonial Office use and misuse of them, he analyses at length the debates in the local assemblies and is happy to report that they compare favourably with parliamentary discussions elsewhere. Yet his greatest discovery is that in Nkrumah the people of the Gold Coast found the authority of an individual as substitute for the lost authority of the chiefs—*charisma* he calls it, borrowing from the sociology of Max Weber.

To put it briefly: he examines the political development of the Gold Coast as a botanist examines a new specimen. The reader closing his book will feel that he had added to his store a new and very interesting political experience, he will very likely be filled with good will, but that the experience matters to him personally, that it imposes upon him a revaluation and reorganisation of his own political ideas and perspectives, as every great political experience must do, that he will never get from this and a dozen similar books. In the end these books only reinforce the myth.

Nkrumah is the exact opposite, antithesis, negation of a tribal chief. In actuality and symbolically he fulfills and completes the strivings of the Ghanaian people to become a free and independent part of a new world. He could lead the people because his genealogical tree is to be found not among Africa flora but because he is the fine flower of another garden altogether, the political experiences and theoretical strivings of Western civilisation. The people heard of him as such, worked for him as such, followed him as such, and expect him to continue in the same way. Anything else is mythical and mischievous.

Nkrumah helped to develop and has most fully embodied in action an independent current of Western thought, the ideas of Marx, Lenin, and other revolutionaries worked out chiefly by people of African descent in Western Europe and America, to be used for the emancipation of the people of Africa. These ideas were developed in conscious opposition to both stalinism and the social democracy. Charisma indeed! It is precisely this task to which revolutionaries in the East and West are now slowly awakening.

The Ghana revolutionaries, including Nkrumah himself, take a great and natural pride in recalling that the national movement for independence was not born with Nkrumah and the Convention People's Party, but has a long and honourable ancestry, beginning with the Fanti Confederation in 1871. That is undoubtedly true. Writers in the West, on the other hand, are apt to stress Nkrumah's experiences in the revolutionary and socialist movements in Britain, where he is supposed to have learnt the principles of what they call "party organisation." But both these views are superficial and do not touch the heart of the question.

The first and ever-to-be-remembered name in the history of the body of political ideas which went to the making of Nkrumah is that of George Padmore, an extraordinary man and a Trinidadian known to me from my youth up. He was a journalist in the West Indies and in the twenties went to the United States. As usual with the young West Indians of that day, he had ideas of qualifying for a profession, but he was drawn to the ideas of communism and, while at Howard University, threw a bunch of revolutionary leaflets into the face of Sir Esme Howard, the British Ambassador, at some university function, and finally joined the Communist Party. He worked with the Communist Party in the United States and ultimately became head of the Negro Department of the Profintern, the Communist Trade Union International, with an office in the Kremlin. In the course of this work he was constantly in contact with African nationalist revolutionaries all over the world and himself visited and helped to organise revolutionary activities in various parts of Africa, acquiring an immense practical and theoretical experience. In his relations with Stalin, Manuilsky and the other leading figures in the Comintern, he devoted himself to African and Negro problems and studiously avoided being involved in the great conflicts of Russian politics.

In strict theory it was a mistake. You cannot divide the colonial struggle and the metropolitan struggle into separate compartments. In actual fact it turned out well, for it almost certainly saved Padmore's life, and in addition to his own unique personal qualities enabled him to preserve for future use much that was valuable in the Comintern of those days. The inevitable break came in 1935. In that year Stalin, seeking the alliance of the democracies against fascism, decreed that henceforth the colonial peoples of Africa and elsewhere should support the democracies. But it was the democracies and not the fascists who held the greater part of Africa. The international policies of the Stalinist régime had caught up with him at last, and Padmore broke decisively with the Comintern. He came to live in London permanently in 1935, and to continue his work for the freedom of colonial peoples there upon a new basis: he would collaborate with any or all of the metropolitan revolutionary or socialist movements, but he would never again submit himself to any of them.

At that time in London the leading African politicians were Jomo Kenyatta and Wallace Johnson, afterwards collaborator with Azikwe, the Premier of Eastern Nigeria, in the publication of the first revolutionary paper in West Africa, and now a member of the Legislative Council in Sierra Leone. Both Kenyatta and Johnson had had experience with stalinism and had revolted against it. I was at that time a trotskyist, and though I looked askance at the practical separation of the colonial movement from the struggle for the socialist revolution in Europe, I was able to work with them without friction. What united us was not only the cause of political freedom for the colonies but our common repudiation of stalinist policies in the colonies. Padmore (in *Pan-Africanism* [*or Communism*]) gave an accurate, though condensed, account of the Ghana revolution. The theory as developed and carried out by Nkrumah in my opinion is of immense importance for political theory in general, and will play a great role not only in the colonies but throughout the world in the twentieth century. It is not only that Nkrumah carried it to the Gold Coast, it is that the people of the Gold Coast accepted it so completely that gives it international significance.

The first move in London in 1935 was the formation of the International African Friends of Ethiopia in response to the Italian invasion of Ethiopia. It was a body formed to educate British and international opinion and to agitate against the imperialist plans for Africa. Padmore had not been very long in Britain at the time and I was therefore the chairman of that body, Padmore serving with Kenyatta and others as members of the committee.

The International African Friends of Ethiopia fulfilled its purpose, and when for the moment the Ethiopian question was over, the question arose as to what next was to be done. Padmore now formed the International African Bureau, an organisation that devoted itself to the study of the colonial question and the spread of propaganda and agitation all over Britain, in Africa and in the territories inhabited by people of African descent. Of this new organisation Padmore was the chairman. I was the editor of the paper and was responsible for the most part for its literary publications. Padmore himself carried on an unceasing correspondence with people all over the world. He made a precarious living by being correspondent for a great number of papers in the United States, in the West Indies, in West Africa, in East Africa, everywhere, and, though limited by the political opinions of his employers, he gave his readers a steady stream of information about European matters that affected them. The Bureau published a journal in which it was free to say what it pleased and this was sent over the world. We carried on agitation and propaganda in England whenever we got the opportunity, speaking in Hyde Park regularly and addressing meetings of the Independent Labour Party, the Labour Party, attending all the front organisations that the communists organised. Articles and letters were written for papers that would publish. Members of parliament were kept informed on questions that would be or might be raised in parliament.

The basis of that work and the development of ideas was Padmore's encyclopedic knowledge of Africa, of African politics and African personalities, his tireless correspondence with Africans in all parts of the continent, the unceasing stream of Africans who made the Bureau and its chairman their political headquarters when in London. Revolutionaries and bourgeois nationalists all came, and not only programme and tactics for the revolutionary nationalist movement in Africa but many a tactical approach to the Colonial Office by bourgeois African politicians were worked out with Padmore's advice and not infrequently under his direct inspiration. He kept a strict eye on all colonial struggles, maintaining contacts with movements, organisations and individuals in the Far East. At the same time he published for general reading *How Britain Rules Africa* and *Africa and World Peace*, for which Sir Stafford Cripps wrote an introduction.

My own approach was different, and although I was immersed in the British revolutionary movement I worked on the application of marxist and leninist ideas to the coming African revolution, and for this purpose wrote *The Black Jacobins*, a full-scale study of the only successful revolution of people of African descent that the world had yet seen—the revolt of the slaves in the French colony of San Domingo during the French revolution, which ended in the establishment of the state of Haiti. Nkrumah and other revolutionaries read and absorbed the book. In the French edition it has been studied and referred to in the French press of the left, for the light which it throws on the relations of French imperialist policy and North Africa. It is treasured by most African nationalists and is widely known among Negro leaders in the United States. Historical in form, it drew its contemporaneousness, as all such books must, from the living struggle around us, and particularly from the daily activity that centred around Padmore and the African Bureau. It represented in a specific form the general ideas that we held at the time, and it is still the only book of its kind, perhaps the most direct attack on the myth that has yet appeared in England.

The theoretical basis of the book, amply demonstrated, is that in a period of world-wide revolutionary change, such as that of 1789–1815 and our period which began with 1917, the revolutionary crisis lifts backward peoples over centuries and projects them into the very forefront of the advanced movement of the day. The slaves in San Domingo were two-thirds raw Africans from the Guinea Coast in a strange country, many of them not knowing the language. Yet with the example and slogans of the French revolution, these for the most part illiterate blacks organised themselves in a manner fully comparable to the great achievements of the same movement in France, produced a body of great leaders in politics and administration, differentiated among themselves in clear alignments of right, left and centre, and all in all showed themselves immensely superior in every human quality to the highly educated colonial officials and ministers in France who ruled them. The final conclusion must be given here:

> These black Haitian labourers and the mulattoes have given us an example to study. Despite the temporary reaction of fascism, the prevailing standards of human liberty and equality are infinitely more advanced and

more profound than those current in 1789. Judged relatively by these standards, the millions of blacks in Africa and the few of them who are educated are as much pariahs in that vast prison as the blacks and mulattoes of San Domingo in the eighteenth century. The imperialists envisage an eternity of African exploitation: the African is backward, ignorant. . . . They dream dreams. If in 1788 anyone had told the Comte de Lauserne, the Minister; the Comte de Peynier, the Governor; General Rochambeau, the soldier; Moreau de Saint-Mary, the historian; Barbe de Marbois, the bureaucrat, that the thousands of dumb brutes who were whipped to labour at dawn and whipped back at mid-night, who submitted to their mutilations, burnings and other savageries, some of whom would not even move unless they were whipped, if these fine gentlemen had been told that in three years the blacks would shake off their chains and face extermination rather than put them on again, they would have thought the speaker mad. While if today one were to suggest to any white colonial potentate that among those blacks whom they rule are men so infinitely their superior in ability, energy, range of vision, and tenacity of purpose that in a hundred years' time these whites would be remembered only because of their contact with the blacks, one would get some idea of what the Counts, Marquises, and other colonial magnates of the day thought of Jean-François, Toussaint, and Rigaud when the revolt first began.

If I show scant respect for the British colonial ministers, governors and other officials, it is because I have met them before and have unimpeachable knowledge of how they think and act.

The book concludes:

The blacks of Africa are more advanced, nearer ready than were the slaves of San Domingo. . . . Imperialism vaunts its exploitation of the wealth of Africa for the benefit of civilisation. In reality, from the very nature of its system of production for profit it strangles the real wealth of the continent— the creative capacity of the African people. The African faces a long and difficult road and he will need guidance. But he will tread it fast because he will walk upright.

This was not directed only against the imperialists. We had learnt from hard experience that, in those days in particular, not only socialists of the right and of the left needed to have this placed before them in unambiguous terms. The communists of the metropolitan countries were all for the

African revolution (until the Kremlin changed the line), but they continually wrote and spoke in terms of "giving" freedom to Africans. In time I was to learn that the trotskyists also saw revolutionary politics as the giving of leadership to masses who were otherwise helpless without it, and the Africans (and American Negroes) being the most backward, of necessity needed the most leadership. But the reader is asked to note the complete confidence in the self-emancipation of the African people from imperialism as a contemporary political issue that imbued everything we did, and if he is interested, to compare it with the dreary repetition of percentages of literacy, centuries of barbarism, centuries of training, and all the rubbish now in the dustbins that characterised the official attitudes and pronouncements of the time. Colonial politics is not a parlour game, and it is a duty not to give but to remind all concerned of the blindness and folly of many of our present-day colonial pundits and their immediate ancestors.

But the book had other premises, raising urgent questions which had to be readily revised and are by no means settled. It took armed rebellion for granted as the only road to metropolitan and colonial freedom, and from this premise flowed certain theoretical perspectives. The San Domingo revolution had been directly inspired by the French revolution, had developed side by side with it, and had had an enormous influence upon the course of that revolution. The book therefore constantly implied that the African revolution would be similarly contingent upon the socialist revolution in Europe. It did not envisage an independent movement of Africans as being able to succeed in face of the enormous military power that a stable imperialist government would be able to bring to bear. This has been apparently contradicted by the experience of the Ghana revolution, but conversely reinforced during the same period by the experience of the revolt in Kenya. If a British government had been unable to send assistance to Kenya, or a revolutionary British government had been in a position where the success of the Kenya revolt against the counter-revolution was necessary for its own preservation (this is what happened during the French revolution) the revolt in Kenya, though made by the same people, would have been entirely different. It would have had socialist allies and would have been made under socialist slogans, representatives of the British government would have taken part in it and guided it, and the result, particularly in the modern world, would have been an African government under which (of this there can be no question to any who have studied the San Domingo revolution) white settlers, once they saw no other way out, would have fraternised, male and female, with General Kimathi,

General China and their associates and successors. This has happened before and will happen again, and we must not be too surprised if from limbo querulous voices assure us that this too was the settled policy of the government. Whatever the future of tropical Africa will be, one thing is certain, that it will not be what the colonial powers are trying to make of it. It will be violent and strange, with the most abrupt and unpredictable changes in economic relations, race relations, territorial boundaries and everything else.

The work of the Bureau continued all through the war and in 1945 there came a sharp break with the theory outlined above. The Bureau changed its position from the achievement of independence by armed rebellion to the achievement of independence by non-violent mass action. But to say that is one thing, to carry it out in practice is another. The problem has never been treated fully even in the publications of the Bureau, and it is time that this was done.

No serious politician is unalterably opposed to a policy of armed rebellion. The question is always armed rebellion by whom, against whom and for what. A great number of people in the world were for the armed rebellion of the Germans against Hitler, especially during the war. It is a significant testimony to where our society has reached that thousands of dyed-in-the-wool conservatives found themselves urging on and cheering the rebellion led by Hungarian workers under the leadership of workers' councils against a totalitarian government. Against a revolutionary dictatorship in Britain, the supporters of the Establishment would most certainly plot an armed rebellion. Against a fascist dictatorship the workers of Britain most certainly would do the same. Political thought today is in no sphere lower, and nowhere more than in the United States, than when it seeks the condemnation of armed rebellion in the fact that the rebels' forces have only 49 per cent of the votes.

When the revolution and the counter-revolution in any country are approaching an ultimate crisis, it is usually the supporters of the existing régime who raise the question of armed rebellion by constituting themselves into all sorts of military or semi-military organisations which enjoy the protection of the government. Central Europe was full of these before Hitler came to power. In the United States today, in the Southern states, the defenders of segregation have formed themselves into White Citizens' Councils. In response to these, the revolutionary forces—especially if the military forces of the counter-revolution begin to attack them, break up their meetings and murder their leaders, and feel that the government in power has no firm foundation—in their turn begin to form extra-legal organisations. Thus both sides move to the ultimate climax, and the question of 49 or 51 per cent of the votes fades into insignificance except as propaganda. Elections then become merely a means whereby each side can draw its own conclusions as to its own strength and the strength of the opposing side. Under these circumstances public warning of the necessity for armed struggle and open and secret military preparations are taking place on both sides.

In a colonial country and especially in tropical Africa, these moves and counter-moves are impossible. The colonial government in power can call upon the power of the metropolitan country as soon as it is aware of any dangerous movement against it. To stake independence upon armed rebellion was therefore to have as a precondition the collapse or military paralysis of the metropolitan government. It was in other words to place the initiative for African struggle upon the European proletariat. In *The Black Jacobins* are the words: "Let the blacks but hear from Europe the slogans of Revolution, and the Internationale, in the same concrete manner that the slaves of San Domingo heard Liberty and Equality and the Marseillaise, and from the mass uprising will emerge the Toussaints, the Christophes, and the Dessalines. They will hear." Those were exactly the ideas that we had had.

But by the end of the war the proletariat of Britain and France had not spoken. Imperialism still held sway at home. Only a radical alteration in theory could form a basis for action. The perspective of armed rebellion was abandoned (though held in reserve) and non-violent mass action was substituted.

Both the advocates of armed rebellion and of militant nonviolence follow the same road up to a certain point, and that point is the general strike. A marxist revolutionist uses the same means as the militant advocate of nonviolence to mobilise the population. He uses all grievances, demonstrations, mass rallies, an unceasing attack upon the government, exposure and denunciation of the timid or reactionary elements in the mass movements whose vacillations might weaken the will and sense of solidarity of the masses; and ultimately, when the movement is ripe and the occasion presents itself calls the population out in a general strike and faces the government with the unified opposition of the people. It is here, however, that the problem begins. Lenin, and after him Trotsky, summing up the lessons of their own tremendous experiences and studies, laid it down categorically that it is adventurism of the worst kind to lead (or sometimes to follow) a population to the stage of the general strike against a government without at the same time openly warning the people and making armed preparation for the fact that you cannot stop at a general strike. It is the ultimate challenge to the ruling powers. Either you go on, and that means taking the power from them by force, or you retreat. And if, after having taken the people so far, you retreat, it is certain that the ruling powers will recognise your weakness, recognise the demoralisation that is likely to set in within the revolutionary forces, and most certainly counter-attack with all the armed force at their disposal and crush the movement for a long time to come. This does not mean to say that there are not general strikes for a brief period, say, twenty-four hours or even for less, one day, which do not immediately involve the movement towards the seizure of power by force or the immediate resort to arms by the government. But these brief general strikes are merely stages in the mobilisation of the people for the ultimate challenge to the government. The general strike poses the question: "Who is to be master in the house?" Furthermore, the great marxists denounced social democracy for playing with the general strike, hoping to bring down the government by the mere threat of force. By this means one reactionary government might be replaced by another. But they considered it criminal not to be prepared for the fact that ultimately the decision would be made with arms.

But the situation was not quite the same in the colonies. The colonial government forces consisted of soldiers and police who were able to deal with a riot or a demonstration of a few thousand people. They could easily shoot down demonstrators, very often they would provoke them in order to put a quick end to a movement which threatened to involve large masses. But colonial governments had neither the forces nor the experience to deal with a general strike of the great body of the people who refused to be provoked.

It was calculated that the organisation of the masses, in trade unions, co-operatives, political organisations, those that existed and new ones, in whatever form they presented themselves, strikes in industry, political demonstrations, etc. were all constitutional, and therefore, in theory at least, could be carried out with a fair chance of being able to avoid cruel reprisals. By the time the masses were organised, it would be possible then to challenge the government. This also was constitutional in that it did not involve armed rebellion.

But it was just here that the theory was skating on very thin ice indeed, because a general strike and an economic boycott which threatened or could actually bring the whole social and economic life of a colony to a standstill could not stay there. Either the government would have to give way or it would be compelled to mobilise forces at its disposal or send to the home government for larger forces, in order to intimidate or to crush the total disruption of society with which it was faced. Risk though it was, a colonial territory, particularly a territory where the government had a very slender basis in the population, was a territory where the risk could be taken. It required that the organisation of the masses should be complete, a gigantic task, and that further, the control of the leadership should be such as to prevent sporadic or partial violence, particularly at an early stage which would give the government an excuse or an opportunity to act.

Changes in political strategy are often motivated by appreciations of deep social changes which have not been fully formulated but of which all involved are very much aware. The war had seen, in Britain in particular, an immense objective growth of the power of the proletariat in the social structure. On the other hand, as a result of the war, of revolutions and crises which had shaken contemporary society to its foundations for almost forty consecutive years, the bourgeoisie had lost its self-confidence in the face of a united mass movement. It had lost the confidence of large sections of the population on whom formerly it could rely. It had been accepted on all sides in the period previous to the war that in the face of a Labour government with a substantial majority which attempted to put its hands upon the sources of economic power, the bourgeoisie would most certainly reply with an attempt at armed rebellion. Lenin and Trotsky believed this and John Maynard Keynes also believed it. It was an axiom in the revolutionary movement in all branches that India could not gain its freedom except by armed rebellion, and this rebellion would have to be led by the proletariat.

By 1945 it was clear that the bourgeoisie in Britain could not attempt extra-legal action against a legally elected Labour government; it was fairly clear in 1945 that it would never be able to carry out military action against India in revolt. The relation of forces had changed and changed decisively to the increase in energy and audacity of any colonial people determined to revolt. Undoubtedly the influence of Gandhi's non-violent campaigns played a great role. But in 1945 when the change was made, India was not yet free.

Marxism is a guide to action in a specific system of social relations which takes into account the always changing relationship of forces in an always changing world situation. But political analysis and political directive can only go thus far. They are a guide, not a blueprint. It took the revolution in the Gold Coast itself to make possible a true evaluation of this policy elaborated in 1945. So it always is with a theory. What is written here does not embrace all that is involved and it is certain that it could not have been written at the time nor was there any need to do so. But when all is said and done the new political directive, breaking with the well-established ideas of the prewar period, is one of the great theoretical achievements of the present age, perhaps the first real break towards what the marxist movement requires today, the application of the traditional principles of marxism in complete independence of the stalinist perversion. It is to be noted that the theory did not reject armed rebellion, but held it in reserve in the event that the political and moral pressure envisaged failed to influence British imperialism.

Where the new theory comes from is only less important than the theory itself and in fact you cannot separate the two. First of all, there was the work of Padmore and the Bureau he founded, as I have described it over the ten years that followed his break with the Comintern in 1935. The second influence was the work of another man of African descent, this time from America, the celebrated Dr W. E. B. Du Bois. Du Bois was writing authoritatively on the American Negro in the Home University Series even before World War I. By 1945 he had taken always a prominent and often a leading part in all types of efforts in the United States to bring home to the American people the need to cut out the national cancer of racial segregation. Before Padmore organised the Bureau with its concentration on day to day problems, Du Bois had educated a whole generation in the more literary and historical manner that was characteristic of the period, and he reached the climax of his theoretical work in 1935 with *Black Reconstruction*, a history of the American Civil War written from the point of view of the Negro slaves and the Negro people as a whole. Though limited in scope, he approached his subject broadly, and this book is still incomparably the best account of that great event in the development of the American people. Despite his preoccupation with the Negro question in the United States, Du Bois had for many years devoted immense time and energy to the problems of Africa, its past history, its present problems and its future emancipation. He organised a series of world conferences to bring together the peoples of Africa and the people of African descent with the aim of organising a united movement for the emancipation of Africa as an indispensable step in the achievement of freedom and equality for people of the coloured race everywhere. To this movement he gave the name Pan-Africanism. His actual political programme was a programme of militant non-violence. In 1945 Du Bois and Padmore merged their ideas and influence to hold the fifth Pan-African conference in Manchester, and it was at this conference that the resolution analysed above was produced. Du Bois, then seventy-three years of age, flew from America to attend.

This conference, however, was unlike all other previous conferences of the kind. It was attended by over two hundred delegates from all over the world, the great majority of them engaged in trade union work or other type of work connected with the organisation of the masses of workers and farmers in Africa. Nkrumah had landed in Britain in June 1945. By October he was joint political secretary of the conference with Padmore, and he made the report on the problems of the West African colonies and European domination. The merging of the two currents represented by Padmore and Du Bois and the entry of Nkrumah signalised the ending of one period and the beginning of another.

Until Nkrumah came, it is true to say that despite the faithful work of some Africans and a few Negro workers, the moving spirits in this work were West Indian intellectuals living in England. The Bureau needed money and organisation in order to live a material existence at all. This had been supplied in the first case by Makonnen, another West Indian, a man of fantastic energy and organisational gifts who found the money, found the premises, kept them in order not only as an office but as a sort of free hostel for Africans and people of African descent and their friends who were in any way connected with the Bureau or needed assistance, organised meetings, interested people and did his share as propagandist and agitator. When during the war he was able to run a successful restaurant business in Manchester, he devoted most of the money he made into furthering the interests of the work and helping to finance the fifth Pan-African Conference. Chairman of the conference was another West Indian, this time from British Guiana, Dr Peter Milliard, who had had experience in the United States and had practised for many years in Manchester. Many gifted young West Indians, though not organisationally connected with the Bureau, were under its influence and shared its emphasis on the importance for all peoples of African descent of the emancipation of Africa. It would be beyond the scope of this book to explain why West Indians devoted themselves with so much energy and single-mindedness to the African question. But they did so. They had had the benefit of the excellent, if rather academic, system of secondary education which existed in the islands. Having no native culture, no native language, no native religion and being raised entirely in the British tradition, they mixed easily in English intellectual and left-wing political circles. In the political thirties they participated fully in the intense discussions and activities of the time, and few in England, except European refugees, had had more actual inside experience of revolutionary politics than Padmore. It was to this circle with its accumulated knowledge, experience and wide contacts that Nkrumah was introduced in June 1945. Nowhere in the world could he have found a better school. For two years and a half he worked and lived in the very closest association with Padmore.

Nkrumah not only took. He gave. This large body of active workers in Africa who attended the Manchester conference symbolised a new stage of the work in England. Nkrumah brought to this work what had never been done before. To theoretical study, propaganda and agitation, the building and maintaining of contacts abroad, he added the organisation politically of Africans and people of African descent in London. He helped to found a West African National Secretariat in London for the purpose of organising the struggle in West Africa. The leading members of this were Africans, and thus Africans with roots in Africa began to take over from the West Indians who had hitherto been the leaders. Most important of all, he was the leading spirit in the formation of the Coloured Workers' Association of Great Britain. Through this organisation he linked together the students and the workers from Africa and the people of African descent living in England, organised them and carried on political work among them. The Bureau had never done anything like this.

It is now possible to form some estimate of what Nkrumah represents. An African whose mother was a petty trader, he received his early education in the Gold Coast. But at the age of twenty-five or thereabouts he went to the United States and lived there for ten years. His academic education and his reading should not be allowed to take a preponderant place in this development. This African had lived an intensely active life among all classes of the coloured people in the United States, and that life is the life of a very advanced and highly civilised community, sharpened and broadened by its incessant conflict against the domination and persecution of official society. Not only in books but in his contact with people and his very active intellectual and political life, he was the inheritor of the centuries of material struggle and intellectual thought which the Negro people in the United States had developed from all sources in order to help them in their effort to emancipate themselves. Nkrumah had an astonishing capacity to learn, and there was much to learn in the United States that has not yet found its place in books. At the University of Pennsylvania he worked with students who were for the most part white.

After this shaping experience, in London he found himself at the centre of the highly political consciousness of post-war Europe within which had grown ideas and organisations for years specifically devoted to the cause which had always been the centre of his life. Thus the man who landed at Takoradi in December 1947 was, in the most precise sense of the term, a unique individual. In his elemental African consciousness of centuries of wrong and an unquenchable desire for freedom, there had met and fused, by theory and practice, some of the most diverse, powerful and highly developed currents in the modern world. He was a man strong enough to embrace them and be expanded by them, yet always keeping them disciplined and subordinate to his particular purpose. To this day the Colonial Office and the government have no idea of what hit them, and if they haven't now, it can be imagined how blank they were in 1947. While they were meditating on how to restore order after the economic boycott and the shooting of the ex-servicemen, Nkrumah sat alone and wrote out his precise plans for what they would have considered stark insanity, their final and irrevocable ejection from Ghana.

The administration and the government had been made aware in no ambiguous fashion that something was wrong, far beyond their own conceptions, and, with the leaders in gaol, they hastily appointed a commission from England to enquire into the causes of the economic boycott and disturbances and to make recommendations. Repeatedly in the history of the colonies a commission composed of citizens uncontaminated by colonial administration has shown far greater understanding of a colonial people than the whole Colonial Office put together. It was so in this case. The Commission got to work rapidly and though the shooting had taken place on 28 February, its report was ready on 9 June. It told a gory story.

The most serious problem, it said, was the suspicion that surrounded government activity of any kind. This suspicion did not attach to persons or individuals in government services. It was general. It was not based on any specific grievance. Its underlying causes were political, economic and social. Yet the causes were not purely political nor social. The "distrust and suspicion with which the African viewed the European" was "poisoning life in the Gold Coast." The situation was so urgent that only by some "far-reaching and positive action" in each field could the "unreasonable suspicion" be removed. They proposed what they considered far-reaching "positive action." The phrase "positive action," either noted from the Commission's report or discovered independently, was taken over by Nkrumah and became one of the great slogans of the revolution. That the Commission should call the total distrust and suspicion of the Africans for Europeans "unreasonable" is a striking example of how the myth can cloud otherwise trained and lively intelligences.

The Commission dealt exhaustively with all aspects of life in the Gold Coast. Its opening statement of the relations which had developed between the government and the people was indictment enough. It repeated the charge, familiar and yet incapable of correction by any European administration in the colonies, that the government had focused its interest on administration rather than on the balanced development of the people. This is the vicious reality that makes all colonials so contemptuous of the incessant repetition by colonial apologists of the high standards of administration which the British colonial rulers have given to the colonies. The Commission recognised that the desire for change had reached the remotest villages. Above all, it said that though the policy of rule through the chiefs had great advantages, the educated Africans looked upon the chiefs and elders as instruments used by the government to delay if not to suppress the aspirations of the people. It said that much of what was thought in the towns reached an ever-widening circle and that a great questioning had risen everywhere among these classes with little or no say in affairs. It showed a real anger at the inaction of the government during the crisis which led to the boycott, and condemned what it thought to be the reason for the inaction: the government's belief that the Africans were unable to combine and that the boycott would therefore end in failure.

All in all, the Commission's report was a creditable piece of work, and if it did not understand more fully the mighty effort at self-realisation that the Gold Coast people were already engaged upon, the Gold Coast people themselves were not fully aware of it. Only the course of the revolution itself would teach not only others but themselves where they had reached and what they were capable of. It is the abiding vice of colonialism that an alien administration, not only from its mentality but from its very position in the social structure, must obstruct the people at these moments of intensive growth. The more efficient an alien administration is, the more it obstructs.

The Commission could not escape the conditions of colonial administration. It saw the solution in giving to every African of political ability an opportunity to help govern the country, so as not only to gain political experience but also to experience political power. Where I have sketched a whole people in violent motion from one stage of social existence to another, it saw only the extension of the forms of government to include educated Africans so as to train them, etc. etc.

It therefore proposed a new constitution. The Executive Council should consist of a board of nine ministers. Five of them should be Africans nominated by the Governor, though requiring the approval of the Assembly. These Africans would be full-time and salaried. The Assembly should be elected by

Regional Councils, a Council for each region. These Councils would consist of the existing chiefs and native authorities modified by provisions to give representation to a specified proportion of adult males not now eligible for membership. Their reasons for this they made the mistake of stating unequivocally:

> The moral justification for Britain remaining in the Gold Coast lies in this: out of a population of approximately four and a half million Africans, on a fair assessment, barely ten per cent is literate. We have no reason to suppose that power in the hands of a small literate minority would not tend to be used to exploit the illiterate majority in accordance with the universal pattern of what has happened elsewhere in the past throughout the world. His Majesty's Government therefore has a moral duty to remain until:
>
> a. the literate population has by experience reached a stage when selfish exploitation is no longer the dominant motive of political power, or
>
> b. the bulk of the population has advanced to such a stage of literacy and political experience as will enable it to protect itself from gross exploitation, and
>
> c. some corresponding degree of cultural, political and economic achievement has been attained by all three areas now part of the Gold Coast.

Here was the settled policy of His Majesty's Government, put forward in all its arrogance, pompousness and absurdity not in 1848 but in 1948. It was no wonder that the Commission proposed that a constitution along such lines should be frozen for ten years. The mountain had produced a mouse, and sought to ensure that the mouse should have a long and untroubled tenure as ruler of the people of the Gold Coast.

The report duly went to the Colonial Office, but long before the time the Colonial Office could take action the initiative had passed from its hands and it was never to recapture it again.

The ever-recurrent astonishment with which anyone familiar with the history of revolutions reads or listens to the story of Nkrumah's leadership of the Ghana revolution is not at his energy, his tenacity, his capacity to act in every new and diverse sphere as if he had been training to do that and nothing else all his life. Rare though they are, historical circumstances and responsibilities develop such qualities in gifted men. The miracle is that, from the solitary drafting of his memorandum to the working committee of the United Gold Coast Convention to the final achievement of independence, *he knew exactly what he was doing*, in spite of the innumerable twists, turns, accidents, and catastrophes, large and small, inevitable in all politics, multiplied a thousand-fold in revolutionary politics. This, like any creative activity, consists in equal measure of careful preparation and leaps into the unknown. The word "miracle" is a metaphor. His unprecedented precision, in what is of its very nature imprecise, marked him as being predominantly of the twentieth century. But the proof of this must wait on the facts.

His first procedure was to organise and concentrate the people of the Gold Coast, and the Gold Coast meant first of all the villagers. The frail skeleton of the United Gold Coast Convention was the instrument to hand, he was the Secretary and for the time being he used it. He scoured the country. He explained the economic nature of imperialism and its relation to its colonies. He did not speak down to them. He traced the history of the connection between the British traders and the Gold Coast from early times. He told of the political struggles of the people of the Gold Coast for freedom over the past centuries. He put before them the United Gold Coast Convention as the continuator of that struggle. He put forward the programme, explaining in detail the meaning of the terms universal suffrage, an elected assembly, ministers responsible to the Assembly. He called for the subordination of tribal rivalries and the formation of a unified national state. This was to be the foundation of the effort to rid them of ignorance and poverty. The imperialists were the sworn enemies of these proposals and only the organisation of the people, the common people (those were the villagers standing before him) could defeat them. They must organise themselves for the struggle. It is safe to say that during the century of British occupation no educated man, white or black, had ever visited many of these villagers at all to speak to them, except perhaps for a few missionaries talking about God and morals, and European officials talking about the King and taxes. Here was an African like themselves introducing them to the most advanced ideas of the modern world and calling upon them, placing the responsibilities upon them, to take action for these ideas. Had the Colonial Office trained men, white and black, and inspired them to perform precisely this task, then it could rightly have talked about preparing Africans for self-government. Its settled policy when such men did appear was to persecute them and railroad them into gaol at the first opportunity.

The reactionaries sneered at the hero-worship and idolatry of Nkrumah by the African village masses of Ghana, comparing him to Christ, and even the liberals and socialists found it unfortunate and voiced their regrets, uttering solemn warnings and speaking of backwardness and dictatorship. If villagers looked upon him as a sort of Christ, they showed a far better understanding than the highly educated, not only of what should be the function of legitimate disciples today, but also of the historical Jesus.

The African, like most common people everywhere, and without the parade of sophisticated rigmarole with which his betters elsewhere disguise from themselves the fact that they do exactly the same thing, sees his aspirations and hopes embodied best in a single figure. The chief represents him in politics, in religion, in art. But more than that, in the psychological state to which European domination has reduced him and his instinctive but suppressed rebelliousness against that state, one single individual quickly becomes the focus of an immense mass of needs, hopes, aspirations. It is said that the fact that the illustrious Aggrey, an African, had shown himself capable of acquiring a number of learned degrees, proved to thousands of young Africans of the Gold Coast that they could do the same and broke the last barrier between them and the pursuit of higher education—a pitiful example of what European domination does to a subject people. Furthermore, the educated colonial of previous generations for the most part, even when he vigorously and altruistically espoused the nationalist cause, had imbibed with his Western education its contempt for uneducated and still more, for illiterate people. More often, the educated African used his education to advance himself, and his highest aspiration was to win a place among the Europeans or in the orbit of their functions. Here was someone entirely different. He was obviously an educated man with an imposing list of scholastic attainments. And he had travelled all that distance to speak to them. Often, his old car having broken down, to reach them he had had to sleep by the roadside. He carried his luggage in a small suitcase. He slept in their mud huts and ate yam and fufu with them.

Nkrumah's party was not built one by one. It was a crusade, a revivalist campaign and the villagers joined in thousands. This was politics in the Greek-city sense of the word. It embraced the whole man, symbolised the beginning of a new stage of existence. These people stepped over centuries. The action was no mere flash in the pan, like the sudden descents, capers, and as sudden disappearances of Billy Graham. Rapidly party organisers followed on foot, then in motor vans, distributing leaflets. The party organised village units, city units, regional units. Pedantic statisticians sneer at the figures, but by 1950 the party claimed that it had between a million and a million and a half members out of a total population of five million and had every right to do so. The villagers did not pay regular subscriptions, but when the party van appeared, and called for a rally, they came from far and near and, poverty-stricken as they were, could be depended upon to raise on the spot what were sometimes astonishing sums of money. I have personal experience of sharecroppers, black and white, in the Southern part of the United States who joined and considered themselves members of a trade union in precisely the same way, and turned out in force when the time came for action. The later structure was built upon the foundation laid by Nkrumah. In six months after his landing, despite six weeks spent in gaol and the work in the towns, he had personally or under his personal direction created five hundred and thirteen branches of the United Gold Coast Convention where only thirteen had existed before, including branches in the remotest villages of the colony and Ashanti. The nation of Ghana was taking form.

In that same June when the five hundred branches had been established, the Watson Commission, after its quite different labours, presented its report with its dictum that the moral justification of Britain's continued occupation of the Gold Coast was the need to protect the illiterate 90 per cent from the exploitation of the literate 10 per cent. His Majesty's Government, the Colonial Administration, the Watson Commission, saw the 90 per cent as the medieval clergy saw their flock. Nkrumah saw them as people only needing the call to embark upon the great sea of contemporary politics. I keep referring to the paradox. Isn't it legitimate to say that in Nkrumah and his party the twentieth century and the future were battling with the middle ages and the past?

In the towns it was easier. The youth, the teachers, the lower middle classes, mainly those who had been educated in the colony, flocked to join the United Gold Coast Convention under the inspiration, the guidance, and the insistence upon systematic organisation, of [the] new leader. Yet the slogan "organisation is everything" which he used so often has misled many. It had little in common with the organisation for which the stalinist parties are notorious or the organisation Lord Woolton applied to the Conservative Party after its defeat in 1945. The ultimate aim was to challenge the colonial government with all the mighty power of Britain behind it, to drive it out of the Gold Coast by sheer political and moral force without the use of arms. To achieve this almost insuperably difficult and frightfully dangerous objective, systematic organisation of a party was only the means to an end, a necessary means, but only a means. What he was doing was to lay the rails by which the whole nation could give to its hitherto inchoate strivings concrete forms, to make it fully conscious of itself. To do this required that the people should be stimulated to act to the utmost extent of their powers. And the only way to do this was to give it a vision of itself as being in the vanguard of a new world and to begin the process of self-government immediately, to take upon itself the responsibility of action as a free people in defiance of the British government.

This is not and cannot be a final history of the Ghana revolution. It can only point out certain things which have not been said, and are in danger for the moment of being swamped by deliberate and systematic lying and the all-pervading influence of the myth. There is room for only one statement among many recorded, and a multitude of others that were delivered and lost to posterity though engraved in the hearts and minds of those who heard. On Christmas Eve 1948 Nkrumah, as promoter of the Committee on Youth Organisation, sent a message to the Youth of Ghana, as the people were already calling themselves:

> In the spirit of the season, I send you a word of hope and cheer. As never before, the Gold Coast of today stands on the threshold of a new era, new era that bids the youth of this country, even the youth of West Africa, to take up their political responsibility. This era demands of the Youth of the New Ghana that they should be up and doing. In this sense, my message to the Youth of the Gold Coast in particular, and West Africa in general, is simple and direct.
>
> Stand firm: be vigilant and resolute. In a humble way, I would quicken in you thought of action. I would inspire in you the love of one's country above everything else. The future is in your hands; out of you must come thinkers; yes, thinkers of great thoughts; out of your rank and file must emerge doers; yes, doers of great deeds. You cannot think great thoughts and do great things by fear and cowardice. You must be prepared to face the shackles of imperialism with an unflinching courage. You must fight to destroy the doctrine of imperialism and colonialism, whether direct or indirect.
>
> Youth of Ghana, the future of this country is in your hands. Emulate the youth of other countries. Learn from the youths of Burma, India, China, Russia, Ceylon, Britain and the new democracies of Europe. God and nature did not intend you to be forever slaves to the diabolical machinations of imperialism and foreign rule!
>
> Youth of Ghana, be up and doing. This is the hour; this is the era; this the new days! The generation of tomorrow are looking up to you. Only you

the Youth—dynamic, volatile, fearless and daring—can carry on the struggle for freedom and emancipation to its logical conclusion. This is the age of action, and only the youth with their sagacity and impulsiveness can act.

Yes, fellow youth, the hour of liberation not only for the Gold Coast but for West Africa, is at hand. Go forward in Unity. Let not detractors, traitors, cowards, quislings, and opportunists get the better of you. Yours is a righteous cause. You fight for the cause of the right with the free people of other nations to rid this world of the pest of imperialism, tyranny and colonialism. You fight for peace, democracy and socialism!

In the higher reaches of our endeavour, I bid you rise above criticism, keep on building and lay solid foundations—foundations of thought and action. Let your watchword be: In all things national, Unity; In all things political, Self-government; In all other things, Action.

At this season I can only conclude this message by joining the chorus of the multitude: "Glory to God in the highest and on earth peace, and goodwill towards men."

That international note was never absent. It was the framework of the appeal, not to wait, not to be given permission, but to act. Without it the energy, the strength, the endurance, the discipline, and above all the creative audacity, would have been impossible.

The self-government was based upon the organisation of the people. To be addressed as they were addressed, to have full responsibility placed upon them to organise the party, to hold local, regional and national conferences and all with the one over-riding purpose of creating the nation by driving out the British government, this was training in self-government. Nkrumah stretched the process to the limits of audacity and creativeness.

In the schools many pupils and some teachers had responded to the arrests of the six United Gold Coast Convention leaders by strikes. The authorities expelled them. The parents, distracted at the loss of the now doubly precious education, came to Nkrumah. Nkrumah proposed to start a secondary school, independent of the British colonial government. A hall was hired in Cape Coast for eight shillings a month. With ten pounds he and his friends bought kerosene tins, packing cases and boards to serve as seats and desks. The dismissed teachers became the staff. There were only ten students to begin with but the school was entitled the Ghana National College. One year later the school had two hundred and thirty students and there were over one hundred students on the waiting list.

This was the beginning of the Ghana National Education Movement. At news of the foundation of the school requests poured in to Nkrumah from all over the country, and new schools were founded, sometimes within a few days of each other—a dozen schools and colleges, technical schools, elementary schools in the colony, in Ashanti and in Togoland. The people subscribed money. Chiefs appropriated land, teachers taught for small salaries and the consciousness for national self-education was established. This was the deepest meaning of the slogan—organisation decides everything. In the Gold Coast of 1947–1951 organisation, and particularly the organisation of the party, was the creation of the nation.

A stage further along the same road was the establishment of the press. With the use of the same primitive type of equipment as was used in the founding of the Ghana National College, in September of this same year, 1948, Nkrumah founded a one-sheet evening paper, the *Accra Evening News*. In January 1949 a daily, the *Morning Telegraph* of Sekondi, followed, and in December another daily, the *Daily Mail of* Cape Coast. The population of Sekondi was 44,000 people and of Cape Coast 23,000. These papers, the *Accra Evening News* in particular, attained a fabulous reputation and circulation. The *Evening News* sold all the copies it could print, 16,000; its offices were besieged by news vendors, and its editors of those days claimed that if they had had the facilities to print them, they could have sold 50,000 copies a day in Accra, a town of 135,000 people, of whom a large proportion was illiterate. Copies passed from hand to hand at increasing prices. They spread all over the country, one African reading aloud to a circle of those who could not read. The enemy was one, the British colonial government and all who, directly or indirectly, supported it. The style was an immense, un-inhibited vigour, and reminds one of nothing so much as the Leveller pamphleteers, with the same rapidity, the same single-mindedness which saw in the cause the truth, the whole truth and nothing but the truth; the same mercilessness in denunciation, both general and particular, especially particular. On the one side was the scrupulous calculation of illiteracy percentages; on the other the creation of organisations and instruments for the national dissemination of information and ideas among all sections of the population. Who was training whom, and for what?

Once the organisation got going there was a continuous round of public meetings and conferences on a local, regional and national scale. Nkrumah's plan was that all the various organisations of the country, the trade unions, the dozens of youth clubs from all parts of the country, the Taxi-Drivers' Association, the Ex-Servicemen's Union, all should be incorporated or affiliated with the United Gold Coast Convention. In addition, inside the United Gold Coast Convention, he began to build a mammoth youth organisation. [...] to join the youth organisation one had to become a member of the United Gold Coast Convention.

Nkrumah launched this new party on 12 June 1949 before a mass meeting of 60,000 people, up to that time the largest rally ever held in Accra. The slogan was "Self-Government Now." That was too much for the leaders of the United Gold Coast Convention (we shall come to them in a moment), and they decided either to get rid of Nkrumah or to circumscribe his activities. The struggle came to a head at a special delegates' conference at Saltpond in July, by Western standards a fantastic conference for it was attended by 40,000 people. There the split became definitive, and the Convention People's Party stood at last firmly on its own feet and under its own banner.

Meanwhile a government committee, through the greater part of 1949, had been working on one of the innumerable constitutions by which the Colonial Office carries out the settled policy of the government. Nkrumah had warned the committee that it was not representative of the vast majority of the Ghanaian people, and if ever a man had the right to say this, he had. The party press and publications had ceaselessly trumpeted the national demand for self-government and had gone into great detail on the kind of constitution wanted. When the government constitution was finally published in October 1949, the Convention People's Party denounced it as a mockery and Nkrumah carried the process of the formation of the nation and its self-government as far as the circumstances allowed. For 20 November, he called together the Ghana Representative Assembly in Accra.

Except for the leaders of the United Gold Coast Convention, the chiefs in their government-controlled councils, and the Aborigines' Rights Protection Society, now a moribund organisation, every organisation in the country, seventy-two in number, was represented. The total attendance was 90,000 people. If they had all turned up, said not a word and gone home again, the mere gathering of these people would have spoken loudly enough. This was the nation in political arms.

The Assembly declared that the constitution and the statement of the government on it were unacceptable. It demanded immediate self-government within the Commonwealth, based on the Statute of Westminster. It published a memorandum stating the constitution it wanted. What it did was necessary and useful and even important. But far transcending what the Assembly said or did was the fact that it had met. The people of Ghana, now organised and conscious of themselves as a self-created independent nation, with the most advanced ideology of the day, stood face to face with a government, not only alien but determined to use its immense power to obstruct this nation's further advance. Before these forces were finally defeated and driven out they set themselves to obscure, bury and even vilify the truth. But the truth in the end will prevail. And the truth is this, that in the long and brilliant history of revolutionary organisation, of that great moment in history when a nation comes of age, none exceeds and few equal the creative force, the intellectual power and the elevation of spirit which marked the people of the Gold Coast and their leadership from 17 December 1947, the day when Nkrumah landed, to 29 November, two years later, when he addressed the Ghana Representative Assembly. Scholars, revolutionaries, people concerned with the future of a world in decay, should tear away from their eyes the bandage of African backwardness and see and learn from this work of a vanguard of the twentieth century.

It would be unhistorical now to blame the Watson Commission for not seeing in 1948 what no one except Nkrumah even suspected, that the people
of the Gold Coast were taut as a bowstring stretched to its limit. It is to the
substantial credit of the Watson Commission that it had called for "positive
action." If I have emphasised the mythical elements in its report, it is because
the most positive action that can be taken against the myth is to pursue it to
every nook and cranny and hold it up to the light whenever possible. The
weak parts of the Watson Commission should not be held against it for another reason. We should not presume that if it had been made responsible for
affairs in the Gold Coast, it would not have rapidly shed some, if not many,
of the illusions which it held. The Watson Commission comes best out of
the whole record of governmental blunder and crime, and it is important to
recognise once again that it is Englishmen who had had nothing whatever
to do with the Colonial Office, or in fact with government of any kind, who
are best able to deal with the by no means easy problem for the metropolitan
power—the transition from one stage to another of a colonial people.

The statement of the British government on the Watson Commission report is a document that the curious will be able to read with the same interest
that archaeologists read painfully deciphered scripts of long-forgotten civilisations, were it not for the fact that the same mentality is at work in Africa as
if the experience of the Ghana revolution had never been made. The government said that the recommendations of political advance proposed by the
report were not to be considered as anything new or radical. The tone of the
Watson Report might imply that the Gold Coast government in the past and
the present has shown tardiness in meeting popular demands. No such thing.
"It is an axiom of British colonial policy. . . . The position[s] of the chiefs were

not fully appreciated. . . . All proposals must meet with the substantial acceptance of the people. . . ." It droned on and on.

In fact, for its pains, the Watson Commission was roundly abused by almost everybody. Nevertheless, its sense of impending crisis did have some effect. The Secretary of State for the Colonies appointed a commission to prepare a new constitution and made what was, for the worshippers at the shrine of the myth, the supreme gesture. The constitutional commission would be composed entirely of Africans. Africans themselves would work out their own constitution. It is not too much to say that in appointing all Africans and thus leaving Europeans out, these pathetic racialists believed that they were shooting Niagara or, more precisely, leaping into the dark. We must see what the stars of the All-Blacks did before pointing out the fallacies which the black skins of the commissioners concealed and which were pointed out from the start.

Appointed in December 1948, they reported in August 1949. The commission used some contemptuous language about the Burns constitution and its revolutionary introduction (the phrase is its own) of an African unofficial majority. "It is clear to any student of recent history that what might have been ideally suited to the conditions of 1943 was wholly out of place in 1946, so rapidly had the forces released by a global war changed men's outlook and aspirations." What it had not changed was the outlook and aspirations of the commissioners. They refused to give the people universal suffrage. Outside of the existing municipalities there would be a primary election by universal adult suffrage of delegates to an electoral college. These delegates would then elect a candidate for membership of the Assembly. The vote was restricted to males and females over twenty-five years. This damned the constitution from the start.

The great "step forward" was to propose to add five African ministers to the Executive Council consisting of the Governor and three of the colonial administration, all appointed by the Governor. The Executive Council, however, would be responsible to the Legislative Assembly. There would be a leader of government business elected by the Assembly, and the Executive was to be responsible to the Assembly. But here the commissioners pulled themselves up short. How could an Executive Council, presided over by the Governor with a chief secretary, financial secretary and legal secretary, all colonial officials responsible to the Secretary of State for the Colonies, be at the same time responsible to an Assembly? The commission proposed a neat solution. The Parliamentary Under-Secretaries of these officials would be elected members of the Assembly and therefore responsible to it. When the prince misbehaved, his playmate would be whipped. It could not work and it never worked—despite the all-African composition of its authors.

Why? The commissioners were without exception members of the lawyer-merchant class or chiefs. There were members of the clergy, over a dozen honourables, sometimes members of the Legislative Council, there were OBEs, CBEs and MBEs; there was Hon. Nana Sir Tsibu Darku IX, Knight, OBE; the Hon. Dr. J. B. Danquah, late deportee, was also a member, and the Chairman was Mr Justice J. H. Coussey.

Here was Africanisation complete. Yet to read their reasons and conclusions, except for a few preliminary flourishes, you could not find any difference between them and a report that had been written by some mild English liberals. They reasoned exactly like more authentic representatives of the educational system and social attitudes which have produced the British colonial official. At the opening session, the chairman struck the key-note:

> It should be unnecessary for me to state that this committee does not meet to form a ministry composed entirely of Africans to assume, immediately, power and responsibility for the government of the country.
>
> That is not within the recommendations of the Watson Report, nor of the proposals of His Majesty's Government nor of our terms of reference. Although it is the cry of some, who have not considered fully its implications, that self-rule should be granted at once, it must be obvious to those who place foremost the true welfare of the masses, that a system must be created, flexible and progressive enough to permit the orderly evolution to responsible government within the shortest practicable time.
>
> The objective is to be achieved by constitutional means, by fostering public spirit, promoting national unity, developing the intellectual and moral gifts, organising the economic resources of the country, educating the people in the grammar of democracy and studying urgently the complex machinery of government.

India, Ceylon and Burma already had full self-government with universal, adult suffrage. Literate or illiterate, whoever had ears in the Gold Coast knew it, for Nkrumah and his followers repeated it morning, noon and night. By the time the commission reported, Nkrumah had established his hundreds of branches, had founded a dozen schools and established two daily papers. The CPP had been founded before sixty thousand people. The commission, in its analysis of telegrams received and references made to them, reported that on a bicameral legislature there were three, on universal adult suffrage four, on full self-government eighty-seven; on the constitution drawn up by the Committee on Youth Organisation (later the CPP) published in the *Accra Evening News* of 29 December 1948 there were no fewer than one hundred and ninety-one references. But to the example of millions in India and scores of thousands of people around them bursting with energy and hope, these faithful products of the British system were completely blind. The CPP from the start made one accusation against them which was unanswerable and became more so with every succeeding day—they were unrepresentative of nine-tenths of the people of the Gold Coast.

Nkrumah called his Ghana Representative Assembly, which demanded a constituent assembly based upon universal suffrage. Meanwhile it published its own constitution, in my view under the specific circumstances in which it was produced, and the purpose for which it was written, as good a piece of political thinking as Ghana has yet produced. It must be seen for what it was, a basis for discussion.

It proposed a Legislature of two houses: a Senate for chiefs and elders, and a House of Assembly. The Assembly would be composed of seventy-five members. The vote would be by universal suffrage, the minimum age of voters twenty-one.

The Senate would consist of thirty-six members, nine elected by each of the four regions, not less than one-third being non-chiefs elected by the territorial councils.

The Executive Council (Cabinet) would be formed by the members of the Assembly who commanded the majority votes in the House. There would be a Minister without Portfolio from the Senate. The only ex-officio minister would be the Minister of Defence, appointed by the Secretary of State upon the advice and consent of the Executive Council. The Senate could not reject, amend or delay a money bill for a period longer than a month.

The constitution had two distinctive features. The first was that it was completely democratic in the parliamentary sense, *everybody to vote*, ministers to be responsible to the Assembly. That the colonial administration would have been able to recognise this and begin discussions was too much to expect. But was it too much to expect that a Labour Secretary of State for the Colonies should have seen this for what it was, a constitution that the people wanted? The heads of the colonial administration should have been asked to leave the Gold Coast (promoted preferably), new sympathetic people appointed, discussion opened. At one stroke the people of the Gold Coast would have been won over to the view that the British government was ready to work with them and not against them.

What really made the constitution remarkable was the place allotted in it to the chiefs and elders, and this brings us to one of the fundamental questions for the future development of Africa. I can only begin the discussion here.

The Watson Commission had written a few paragraphs on chieftaincy which show clearly the limitations of the liberal outlook and its pernicious effects when it attempts to deal with an alien people. This is what it said about the chiefs:

110. Among Africans with modern political outlook we found that their conception of the place of the chief in society was ornamental rather than useful; a man not necessarily of any particular ability, but of good presence, expressing in his person but never in his voice the will of the people; exercising the office of pouring libations to ancestors; remaining always among his people and never speaking save through his linguist; he must either remain on his Stool and take no part in external politics or forego the office—he should not attempt a dual role.

111. That such a one must speedily become a mere puppet in the hands of politically astute subjects admits of no denial, even if not conceded by those who advance this thesis.

112. Needless to say, the chiefs whom we had the pleasure of meeting both publicly and privately did not conform to this conception.

113. While for ourselves we are unable to envisage the growth of commercialisation in the Gold Coast with the retention of native institutions, save in a form which is a pale historical reflection of the past, we do not think we are called upon to make any immediate recommendation for the solution of a matter upon which Africans themselves are not in agreement. Our sole concern is to see that in any new constitutional development there is such modification as will prevent existing institutions standing in the way of general political aspirations.

114. To that end, in the recommendations we are about to make, the door is left open to any chief to climb the political ladder to a seat in the legislative chamber. But whether he does or not will clearly be by the

will of his people expressed through the regional council and not by the positive act of the government. Therein in our view lies the true democratic approach to a difficult problem.

These "Africans with a modern political outlook" were the lawyer-merchant caste with their basically Western intellectual outlook. Nkrumah and the CPP were more modern than these, and yet they were ready to give chiefs and elders an assured place in the constitution. Chieftaincy was not a hereditary anachronism as the House of Lords in Britain. The chief was not an Indian maharajah, a medieval despot maintained by British arms. He was not the representative of what all have agreed was on the whole a profoundly democratic institution until the British government perverted it. Whether it was visible or not in a modern form no one could say. The only thing to do was to discuss the question *in a constituent assembly* and thus begin the process of evolution by a nationwide discussion in which other areas of Africa could well have joined. But there was one indispensable condition of success. The people and the chiefs had to be under no doubt as to where the power was going to be. The mischief of the British administrators was to continue a desperate battle to maintain the power. They seemed to have all the basis for victory. Thus the chiefs, instead of being forced to recognise that their future depended upon an acceptance of the power of the democratic majority, chose to side with the British government and so ruined themselves for good and all.

Perhaps this rejection of the chiefs was inherent in the forward movement. I beg leave to think differently. Nationalism, in its old age when its crude and narrow conceptions of man in society are being more ruthlessly exposed every day, makes more fantastic claims for itself than ever it did in its more ebullient youth, and the more blows it gets, the more deeply it hides itself behind universal suffrage, elected assemblies and a loyal opposition. There are far greater deeps in the contemporary political psyche than were suspected even a generation ago. Investigations in sophisticated England as to why people act as they do and the discovery that they create images of their own and the opposing party; the totalitarians with their brutal, vicious and temporarily successful perversion of the instinct for a sense of community, for symbols, even for a figure as representative: all this is utterly lost upon rationalists, or they recognise it only to bewail it as a retreat from reason.

The African chief in the village fulfilled many functions which are seen to be increasingly necessary in the most highly developed modern community. There was possible an evolution of chieftaincy in a national legislature, a meeting of traditional and modern culture, the maintaining of the sense of community, the local and national continuity in the midst of the most violent transition. The possibility of this was to be utterly lost.

Nkrumah did not want to abandon this precious possibility. Having achieved the mobilisation of the people in political form, and made clear by the publication of the constitution that he was ready to recognise chieftancy as an integral part of the political life of the country, he then sought the support of the chiefs for the Ghana Representative Assembly. Confident that the British colonial administration would win, they not only rejected his advances but abused him.

There are exceptionally percipient and sympathetic Europeans (and more than might be thought) who can give precious help to an African people in this, one of the gravest problems of the transition. To this problem the contribution of the Colonial Office and its fellow-rulers was most instructive. All, whites and Africans, professed, and no doubt sincerely, the greatest respect for the traditions represented by the chiefs. This is what they did. They began by giving the chiefs a percentage in both the local and national legislatures, but the chiefs themselves had to choose their representatives. And by this they renewed the sole condition of any successful evolution—the control of the chiefs by the people. The African Commission, however, had offered as an alternative, a Senate of chiefs. This the Secretary of State rejected on the ground that there were not sufficient able men among the chiefs to fill posts both in the local councils and in the central legislature. The ablest men would be isolated in a Senate which did not have much power.

It would be impossible to find a more illuminating example of how organically unfitted is the official mentality to help the African people. The Secretary of State for the Colonies was concerned with administration and the ability of chiefs to legislate. That was not the issue at all. The question was whether the chief could bring into the government and integrate with it, modernise, the functions that he represented in the village and the tribe. With the movement to modernisation in the country as a whole, the educational level of the chiefs would naturally arise. The future would shape itself one way or another: the nation was in movement and would find its way. But in their movement towards creative self-realisation under the leadership of modern men, the people of the Gold Coast were checked and obstructed, their natural development violently distorted and directed into unhistorical and therefore unnatural channels. Within a few years they were to pay heavily for this, while on the historic scale incalculable mischief was done and a great opportunity lost for the education of the rest of Africa and the people of Western civilisation.

I have spoken repeatedly of the people of the Gold Coast. Modern rationalists tend to distrust the term, but despite the indisputable fact of social layers in any population and the absurdity of expecting all layers to arrive at the same pitch of political consciousness at the same time, enough has been said to show that such is the social structure of the Gold Coast and so great was the national awakening that it is legitimate here if anywhere to speak of the people.

I emphasise this term for two reasons. First, in any great revolution the people always lead, and to this the Ghana revolution was no exception. Secondly, our age has lost contact with the genuinely revolutionary process. It has been corrupted both by parliamentary fetishism and the falsifications and bureaucratisation of the concept of leadership by stalinism. The concept of the people, the concept of leadership. Unless the leadership of the people is clearly and decisively shown, not only the customary official falsifications but the political aridity of our age will obscure one of the most instructive political experiences of our time. The thing is usually difficult to do, and it is lucky that we have an unimpeachable witness, Nkrumah himself.

He arrives in the Gold Coast on 16 December 1947, unannounced, solitary and fearful that he will not be allowed to land. When the immigration officer, an African, asks him for his passport, he believes that his case is lost. But the African, after guiding him out of range of passengers and officials, shakes him enthusiastically by the hand. He gives Nkrumah the unexpected news that the Africans had heard so much about him, they rejoiced he was coming back to their country to help them, and they had been waiting for his arrival day after day. The future split in the national movement is unmistakably posed. The people had at their disposal the United Gold Coast Convention and its lawyer-merchant leaders, but they had heard of Nkrumah and his work among the sailors and the down-and-out Africans in London and it was he they were waiting for. The African, though a functionary of the government, had made Nkrumah, the outsider, understand that Africans, whether government officials or not, were solid against the alien government.

There was more to it. This African told Nkrumah to leave the passport with him, he would see about all the details and send it on to Nkrumah. To a man so sensitive to ordinary people and with his type of ordinary mind, an incident of this kind would convey more than a hundred pages of an official report.

His first public meeting is among the miners at Tarkwa. Nkrumah's biographer reports that an elderly miner interrupted the speech by walking through the crowd with a clenched fist pointing towards Nkrumah exclaiming: "This young man is God's greatest gift to the Gold Coast, hear ye him." Nkrumah writes of these miners: "From their absorbed interest and their acclamation I sensed that they, a representative gathering of the working class of the country, were indeed ready to support any cause that would better their conditions."

On the occasion of his first speech in Accra, he was very late and he was a little anxious that the crowd might have gone away. But they had waited in their thousands, "curious and expectant." The description is almost pedantically precise. As for himself, "After I had finished I realised more fully than ever before, from the reaction of the crowd, that the political consciousness of the people of the Gold Coast had awakened to a point where the time had come for them to unite and strike out for their freedom and independence." If we take that sentence, especially the first part, in its most literal sense, we get close to the relationship which was established always, and from the beginning, between Nkrumah and the people, who became more closely a unit with every succeeding stage of the revolution.

During the speech which launched the Convention People's Party, before sixty thousand people in the Arena, he asked them if he should break away from any faltering leadership and throw in his lot with the chiefs and the people for full self-government now. The question was not in the least rhetorical. The issue was whether the party should go ahead in defiance of the leaders of the United Gold Coast Convention and so take the serious step of splitting the national front. Nkrumah notes: "The unanimous shout of approval from that packed Arena was all that I needed to give me my final spur. I was at that moment confident that whatever happened, I had the full support of the people." It is rare to find anywhere in the history of revolutions, particularly after the event, this meticulous registration of the distinct stages by which the people mould the perspectives and will of the leader. Although he is writing many years after, he seems here as elsewhere, to remember the emotional reactions of his audiences as if they were outstanding historical events. Perhaps they were something like that to him.

The applause which had been tumultuous eventually died away and a deep silence followed. It was a most touching moment for each one of us there. We had decided to take our future into our own hands and I am sure that in those few minutes everyone became suddenly conscious of the burden we had undertaken. But in the faces before me I could see no regret or doubt, only resolution.

This resolution is transferred to the leader. He would need it soon, all they had to give him.

There followed the Special Conference at Saltpond, where the split became definitive and the CPP emerged on its own. In an appendix I have tried to reconstruct this unique event. Nkrumah has one characteristic which is found in all the great revolutionary leaders. The revolutionary leader finds his own sure foundation in the popular masses and organises them with the utmost thoroughness. But, contrary to the common view, he is never eager to split away from his hesitant, faltering or even treacherous associates, particularly if they have played a role in the beginning of the movement. This is true of Lilburne, of Cromwell, or Robespierre, and Danton, and of that most ruthless and realistic of all revolutionaries, Lenin. Nkrumah did not want to split from the UGCC. He spent long hours in working at a compromise with the UGCC and finally accepted one. The compromise had been accepted in the hall of the delegates and one reasonably authoritative account goes so far as to say that while Nkrumah was to resume his post as general secretary of the UGCC, the CPP was to be disbanded. But the youth and the thousands of people outside were shocked at the news. The delegates were surprised at the decision. Details are obscure, but the following facts are certain. From the crowd outside came a message to Nkrumah in the conference hall asking him to come out to them. Only his own words can do justice and every sentence is worth the most careful study:

"Resign!" they shouted, as soon as they saw me, "Resign and lead us and we shall complete the struggle together!" I realised at once that they were sincere and determined. Above all, I knew that they needed me to lead them. I had stirred their deepest feelings and they had shown their confidence in me; I could never fail them now. Quickly I made my mind up.

"I will lead you!" I said. "This very day I will lead you!"

Hurriedly I returned to the conference room and announced that I had decided to resign, not only from the general secretaryship, but also from membership of the UGCC. The delegates were then as jubilant as the crowd outside.

Standing on the platform surrounded by an expectant crowd, I asked for a pen and a piece of paper and, using somebody's back as a support, I wrote out my official resignation and then read it to the people. The reaction was immediate and their cheers were deafening. . . .

The overwhelming support I had received from the masses had prompted me to act, and so I had struggled to . . . the conflict which could only end with the fulfilment of my promise to my people, who had shown so readily their implicit trust in my leadership. . . . Standing before my supporters I pledged myself, my very life blood, if need be, to the cause of Ghana.

This marked the final parting of the ways to right and left of Gold Coast nationalism; from the system of indirect rule promulgated by British imperialism to the new political awareness of the people.

The people showing the way to the leader, the leader shaken to the core and rebuilding himself on a larger scale to raise himself to the boundless confidence and aspiration he could feel in the people: "I could never fail them now. . . . The overwhelming support I had received from the masses had prompted me to act. . . . I pledged myself, my very life blood, if need be. . . ." Nkrumah is not ashamed of the fact that at every decisive stage the mass drove him on and at this, the most decisive stage of all, roughly told him what it wanted. There were fifty thousand people there. How pitiable are the wearisome phrases of His Majesty's Government and the (all-African) Commission solemnly weighing whether the people were intelligent enough to vote directly or not and deciding in the negative. One who participated in all this from the very beginning says that by the time of the Saltpond Conference "even the villagers and the illiterate had understood why he formed the Convention People's Party." Nkrumah, it seemed, no doubt confident that the villagers were with him and his party, did not want to take the responsibility for the break. The people, however, decided that the time had come and by so doing forged a far deeper unity between himself and them and inspired him with their confidence and their will.

What we are witnessing here is a close approximation towards the solution of a very difficult historical question, the relationship of the leader to the mass movement in a revolution. The present writer once asked Leon Trotsky how it was that over and over again Lenin showed himself the first to see the need for a new turn in the policy of the revolution. Trotsky replied instantaneously and briefly: Lenin was always the first to understand what the great masses of the people were thinking or wanting. And the statement coming from him is doubly significant because in his superb history of the Russian revolution he shows himself much inclined to over-emphasise and indeed misunderstand the question of leadership.

M. Georges Lefebvre, the leader of the school of French historians of the French revolution, in his most mature work, writes repeatedly that as to the real leadership of the revolution in France, especially on the great decisive days, we have only a few indications of the unknown men who really organised them; we do not know who they were and we shall never know and we cannot know. It seems that in every generation historians seeking the truth of revolution find themselves ultimately face to face with this question and how to discover or rediscover an answer. In the preface to his *History of the French Revolution*, Michelet has told us in his finest manner of his discovery of the people in the French revolution. Michelet says:

> Another thing that this history will bring forward into the bright light of day and which is true of every party, is that the people generally speaking were far superior to their leaders. The more I have dug into this history, the more I have found that what really mattered was below, in the obscure depths. I have seen also that these brilliant speakers, powerful men who have expressed the thought of the masses, are wrongly looked upon as the chief actors. They received the impetus far more than they gave it. The chief actor is the people. To find them once more, to replace them in their role, I have been compelled to reduce to their true proportions the ambitious marionettes, of whom the people pulled the strings, and in whom, up to now, we thought we could seek and find the inner movement of history.
>
> The recognition of this, I have to confess, has struck me with astonishment. To the degree that I have entered more profoundly into this study, I have found that the party leaders, the heroes of conventional history, have foreseen nothing, have prepared nothing, that they did not take the initiative in any of the things that really mattered, and particularly of those which were the unanimous work of the people at the beginning of the revolution. Left to themselves at these decisive moments, by its pretended leaders, it worked out what was necessary to be done and did it.

The truth is wholly on the side of Michelet, though in the twentieth century the relations are a little more complicated and intricate than he states. What it is exactly is always a matter of the concrete analysis of the concrete facts, but these facts are usually difficult to get at. It is true to say of Nkrumah that as far as was humanly possible he foresaw everything and prepared everything. But it is equally true that at every stage the people either reassured him or showed him the way.

Michelet continues: "These are great and astonishing matters but the heart of the people which accomplished them was infinitely more great! . . . The acts themselves are nothing compared to their nobility of soul. This richness of spirit was such at that time that posterity is able always to renew itself from it without ever exhausting the source. Every human being who approaches these events will, as a result, feel himself more human than before."

I have said earlier and the whole tone of this book shows my conviction that the Ghana revolution is not some striking episode in the history of backward Africa upon which we must look with, at most, benevolence. Thanks to Nkrumah's unselfconscious autobiography, the Ghana revolution shows us the relation between people and leader in a manner that should help to illuminate this recurrent problem, both for previous revolutions and for ourselves, which in the end is the same thing—it is the present, and not researches into archives which determine our understanding of the past. So it is our conceptions of what is going on around us that will enable us to renew ourselves at the richness of heart which was present in the people of the Gold Coast as it was in the people of France at the greatest moment of their national history.

A revolution is first and foremost a movement from the old to the new and needs above all new words, new verses, new passwords, all the symbols in which ideas and feelings are made tangible. The mass creation and appropriation of what they needed is a revealing picture of an African people on its journey into the modern world, sometimes pathetic, sometimes vastly comic, ranging from the sublime to the ridiculous, but always vibrant with the life that only a mass of ordinary people can give.

If one song characterises the CPP it is the hymn "Lead, Kindly Light." Cardinal Newman's plea for help in his solitary intellectual communings becomes the battle-cry for the party at its most militant, and yet there may be affinities. It will be remembered that at the Saltpond Conference in 1949 the turbulent CPP crowd outside called Nkrumah from the UGCC Conference inside and insisted on his immediate resignation. When the letter of resignation had been written and sent inside, all present realised that a definitive step had been taken—henceforth it was either victory or destruction. An orator, sometimes a speaker of quite ordinary calibre, can at times find the words which will express and preserve for the future the feelings of the moment. But Nkrumah was in tears, as were most of those around. A woman jumped upon a table and led the assembled thousands in "Lead, Kindly Light." It struck some chord in the people, for it became a part of their ritual and to this day meetings usually begin with a singing of this hymn. So much was it associated with the struggle for independence that there were times when to sing it carried the risk of beating-up by the police, arrest, and gaol. At the same historic moment that the "Lead, Kindly Light" was sung, a libation was poured.

Christianity was an unfailing source of inspiration. They used the Lord's Prayer:

O Imperialism which are in Gold Coast,
Disgrace is thy name. . . .

The Apostles' Creed:

I believe in the Convention People's Party.
The opportune saviour of Ghana,
And in Kwame Nkrumah its founder and leader. . . .

The Beatitudes:

Blessed are they who are imprisoned for self-government's sake; for theirs is the freedom of this land. . . .

The pious held up their hands in horror, forgetting or ignoring the fact that the early Christians who laid the foundation of their religion had done exactly the same thing, and that many of the most cherished Christian rituals are appropriations from paganism.

"Lead, Kindly Light" and the libation—if their use of Christianity was often to turn it against those who preached it to them and so besmirched it by their practice, at grave moments they could turn back to their own religion in a manner that, here as so often with them, throws great light on many an ancient civilisation, particularly that of the Greek city-state.

The régime to which Governor Arden-Clarke subjected Nkrumah and the executive committee of the CPP when in prison was one of the most shameful and degrading of all the barbarities of the colonial régime. In the ordinary Western mind it leaves a memory of disgust, not at the perpetrators in particular, but as so often when elementary decencies are publicly outraged, at human nature in general. On the day that Nkrumah was released, women in the crowd fanned the released prisoners with costly white cloths, a symbol of victory. In the Arena before the assembled thousands a sheep was sacrificed and

Nkrumah stepped seven times with his bare feet in its blood. This, he says, "was supposed to clean me from the contamination of the prison." The word "supposed" implies some scepticism and may be due to Nkrumah's claim that he is a Christian. What it did to Nkrumah I cannot say, but I would hazard that the ceremony expiated the people who witnessed it and heard about it from a filthy, degrading memory. I for one, who have been for decades impervious to all sorts of blessed waters, wines and oils, would have been glad to be present at this particular ceremony. I feel strongly that, in company with all the others, the result would have been a psychological purge, a release from what otherwise would have remained in the mind to embitter it and clog it in the flights it had to make. Mrs Elspeth Huxley is welcome to make all that she can of that. They borrowed and transformed the song "John Brown's Body":

> Kwame's body lies a-mouldering in the cell,
> But his work goes prospering on.
> Kwame's body is behind the prison walls,
> But his soul goes marching on.

And with delicate sensibility they would walk along outside the prison at nights, singing it so that he and his fellow-prisoners could hear it and be strengthened. It is not the sort of action that is conceived or carried out by the highly literate.

A favourite quotation in the CPP paper was from the Greek philosopher, Epicurus:

> The greater the difficulty
> The more glory in surmounting it;
> Skilful pilots gain their reputation
> From storms and tempests.

The CPP songsheet contains the following verse from a hymn:

> The cocoa, diamond, gold and wood
> Thou blest us with for our own good
> Help us protect from alien might
> Give us the wisdom how to fight.

Another song begins:

> Sons of Ghana, arise and fight
> Girls of Ghana, arise and shine.

Unliterate as some of these verses are, this much is immediately obvious, they carry very concrete meanings to the tens of thousands who sang them, hallowed doubtlessly by association with some historic event or personal association in the revolutionary struggle. Unfortunately, the same cannot be said of the Ghana national anthem the words of which were written by an English MP—a pale imitation of traditional Western national anthems. It is a pity, for in the celebration of the national struggle, the Africans and the people of African descent had something of their own to say. Kitchener, the West Indian calypso singer, has composed a beautiful calypso:

This day will never be forgotten,
The sixth of March, nineteen fifty-seven,
When the Gold Coast successfully
Got their independence officially.

Ghana—
Ghana is the name,
Ghana—
We wish to proclaim.
We will be jolly, merry and gay,
The sixth of March, Independence Day.

As we have seen earlier, West Indian calypso, not American jazz, is the Western popular music to which the West Africans feel the closest affinity, and both words and music (despite some absurdities) get very close to a native celebration of the independence victory.

The last word, however, rightly belongs to the African. A native popular band, Dan Acquaye, has recorded the following, with E. T. Mensah and his Tempo Band:

Ghana, we now have freedom,
FREEDOM,
Ghana, land of freedom,
HALLELUJAH.
Toils of the brave
And the sweat of their labours,
Toils of the brave
Which have brought results.
Kwame, the Star of Ghana,

FREEDOM,
Nkrumah, Star of Ghana.

Chorus: Toils of the brave
And the sweat of their labours,
Toils of the brave
Which have brought results.

Gold Coast will thank
Nananom and Elders,
The late Caseley-Hayford,
Mensah-Sarbah,
Pa Grant,
Sergeant Adjete,
And all who fought for freedom.

Chorus: Toils of the brave
And the sweat of their labours,
Toils of the brave
Which have brought results.

The verse has a simple and rugged strength. The music is African in origin, magnificently arranged and played in the Western manner with Western brass and African drums. "Lead, Kindly Light" and the pouring of libations are here fused. Only the association with dancing and gaiety prevents this and music like this from being recognised for what it is, a truly national expression of the struggle for independence and victory. The masses of Ghana know this already. Their more highly educated countrymen and friends will in time arrive at the same understanding.

This role of the people being understood, we are better able to estimate in due proportion certain aspects of the role of Nkrumah, the political leader, up to the calling of the Ghana Representative Assembly, the moment before the revolution takes its final leap. We have seen the precision with which he planned the different stages of the revolution, the way in which he called upon the people to build their own schools, their own press, to summon their own version of a constituent assembly. We have seen the energy and the will.

There are certain other aspects which must be noted. He gave a philosophical education to the people of the Gold Coast. The actual activity, the building of the party, the creative projects: these were education in the truest sense of a word that the nineteenth and twentieth centuries have abused more than most. But every emergence of a people needs, a people cannot emerge without, a new ideology. Sometimes it has to be created as Lilburne, Walwyn and Overton created it. Cromwell got his philosophical ideas from Ireton and from the political philosophers of the Leveller Party, who are only now coming into their own. Lenin also was a politically creative mind of the first order. Nkrumah did not create. He did not have to. What he did was take all that he had absorbed during the years in Europe and America, and translate it into terms of the Gold Coast and the struggle for the freedom of Africa but without ever degrading or emasculating it. As early as June 1948 the Watson Commission had commented on his powers as a mass orator. It is unlikely that they understood his secret. Anatole France says somewhere that an orator gives himself to his audience and a great orator is one who gives himself fully. Nkrumah gave his audiences all he had, and he had a great deal.

But it is not enough to say that he gave. Rather, his mind was so charged with advances and varied revolutionary conceptions, and yet so open to the tumultuous national development around him, that he was able to give the unverbalised desires of an unexpressed people a concrete form which could satisfy their highest aspirations and open out always widening vistas. There was nothing inevitable about this. Engels says that the revolutionary crisis always finds the man. But he was referring to crises which produced a Luther, a Cromwell, a Robespierre. On a smaller scale the levels at which the revolutionary leader must operate will vary widely. The level on which Nkrumah operated was objectively of a very high order by any standards. He says himself that he did not need to prepare for a speech before a mass audience; the very sight of them brought the ideas and the words, but this was only because all his life had been a preparation.

The Watson Commission, even while acknowledging his power as an orator, added the sneering qualification "among Africans." What mass oratory could Nkrumah practise among the Europeans? Or was he to go to China? I have already given an example of his inspired rhetoric in the Christmas message to the youth on 24 December 1948. That was at a mass meeting in the Arena. This is how he addresses less than a dozen students, two or three members, and a few friends at the founding of the Ghana National College:

In establishing the Ghana National College, we have taken upon ourselves a grave responsibility. The times are changing and we must change with them. In doing so we must combine the best in Western culture with the best in African culture. The magic story of human achievement gives irrefutable proof that as soon as an awakened intelligentsia emerges among so-called subject people, it becomes the vanguard of the struggle against alien rule. It provides the nucleus of the dominant wish and aspiration, the desire to be free to breathe the air of freedom which is theirs to breathe. If we cannot find breadth of outlook and lofty patriotism in our schools and colleges, where else, in the name of humanity, can we find them?

The African today is conscious of his capabilities. Educational and cultural backwardness is the result of historical conditions. . . .

In spite of the humble conditions under which we have started, I bring you a message of hope and inspiration. I bid you shake hands with yourselves and your teachers over your study tables and before the blackboards. I look forward to the time when there will be a chain of Ghana colleges in all the four territories which make up the Gold Coast—leading up to the founding of the University of Ghana.

In the name of the people of the Gold Coast, in the name of humanity and in the name of almighty God, I bid you go forward till we realise a new and United Gold Coast in a United West Africa!

It is rhetorical but only people who are unattended by the vision fear to be rhetorical or shrink from hearing it. The ring is as authentic as anything in John Bright. And it is many years now that in vast areas of the most highly civilised people in the world, orators (and very few even of them) dare to touch that note only when calling upon the population to exert themselves for the national defence against a foreign enemy.

To anticipate a little, I shall give one more extract of a speech delivered to a vast crowd of ninety thousand people. It is a most critical moment. Nkrumah is preparing to call upon the people to embark on a general strike with the openly-avowed intention of forcing the government to grant self-government:

In our present vigorous struggle for self-government, nothing strikes so much terror into the hearts of the imperialists and their agents than the term "positive action." This is especially so because of their fear of the masses responding to the call to apply this final form of resistance in case the British government failed to give us our freedom consequent on the publication of the Coussey Committee report.

The term positive action has been erroneously and maliciously publicised, no doubt by the imperialists and their concealed agent-provocateurs and stooges. These political renegades, enemies of the Convention People's Party and for that matter of Ghana's freedom, have diabolically publicised that the CPP's programme of positive action seems riot, looting and disturbances, in a word, violence. Accordingly, some citizens of Accra, including myself, were invited to a meeting of the Ga Native Authority and the Ga State Council on Thursday 20 October at 1 pm "to discuss," as the invitation stated, "the unfortunate lawless elements in the country and any possible solution."

At that meeting, I had the unique opportunity of explaining what positive action means, to the satisfaction of the Ga Native Authority and the Ga State Council, and the meeting concluded with a recommendation by them that I should call a meeting to explain to the members of the Convention People's party as I did to them, what I mean by positive action, in order to disabuse the minds of those who are going about misinterpreting the position action programme of the Convention People's Party....

Party members, imagine the wicked misrepresentation, chicanery, falsehood, the untruths, the lies and deception, in such news.

This is the way our struggle is being misrepresented to the outside world; but the truth shall ultimately prevail.

It is a comforting fact to observe that we have cleared the major obstacle to the realisation of our national goal in that ideologically the people of this country and their chiefs have accepted the idea of self-government even now. With that major ideological victory achieved, what is left now is chiefly a question of strategy and the intensity and earnestness of our demand. The British government and the people of Britain, with the exception of diehard imperialists, acknowledge the legitimacy of our demand for self-government. However, it is and must be by our own exertion and pressure that the British government can relinquish its authority and hand over the control of affairs, that is the government, to the people of this country and their chiefs.

There are two ways to achieve self-government; either by armed revolution and violent overthrow of the existing régime, or by constitutional and legitimate non-violent methods. In other words: either by armed might or by moral pressure. For instance, Britain prevented the two German attempts to enslave her by armed might, while India liquidated British imperialism there by moral pressure. We believe that we can achieve self-government even now by constitutional means without resort to any violence.

Here there is scarcely any rhetoric at all. The occasion itself is so momentous, fraught with such dangerous consequences, that rhetoric would be out of place. The facts of the case are sufficient, and the simplicity of the exposition has an inner strength which excludes the emotional heightening from which sincere rhetoric flows. The references to enemies have a controlled but all the more sinister venom. The greatest task has been accomplished, the achievement of self-knowledge and inner conviction by the people. The rest is strategy.

> We live by experience and by intelligent adaption to our environment. From our knowledge of the history of man, from our knowledge of colonial liberation movements, freedom or self-government has never been handed over to any colonial country on a silver platter. The United States, India, Burma, Ceylon and other erstwhile colonial territories have had to wage a bitter and vigorous struggle to attain their freedom. Hence the decision by the Convention People's Party to adopt a programme of nonviolent positive action to attain self-government for the people of this country and their chiefs.
>
> We have talked too much and pined too long over our disabilities—political, social and economic; and it is now time that we embarked on constitutional positive steps to achieve positive results. . . .
>
> The majority of the people of this country cannot read. There is only one thing they can understand and this is action.

The speech did not, as do the greatest speeches, open up new perspectives for world civilisation, or give new meaning and urgency to beliefs and ideals which henceforth would bear that stamp. Such speeches are rare. Yet this one could have been delivered in any senate or any constituent assembly at any period that you can choose. To the market women, the youth and the massed thousands in the Arena of Accra, this was not merely a summons to action. To these people, literate and illiterate, these speeches were a liberal education; the mere fact of their delivery disclosed a new world, not in the distance but one which was actually taking shape as the orator spoke and they listened. How dreary and bleak are the platitudes, the worn-out phrases, the flat cadences of the prime minister of this highly advanced country and the president of that one. They dare not awaken enthusiasm for anything in particular. If they do, they will unloose passions and desires which may lead God knows where. That is the true backwardness, the backwardness in relation to one's own potentialities, the retreat into fear and cowardice, the gross materialism which is strictly confined to rising and falling graphs of the standard of living. In these years it was in the backward Gold Coast with its overwhelming majority of illiterates that words were said in English which could bring some quickening of the blood and broadening of horizon to highly literate and therefore all the more starved English-speaking peoples of the world. It is only the myth which prevents this. In only one other English speaker of this generation could one escape the smell of stagnant waters and hear again the call to manners, virtue, freedom, power. That was in the speeches of John L. Lewis, leader of the American miners, only but always when the miners found themselves in embattled isolation against the whole of American official society. Why did the Watson Commission believe Nkrumah was an orator of attainment only "among Africans"? I have given the answer in the chapter on the myth.

Like most men in his position Nkrumah had the gift of the pregnant phrase, the few words that take wing among a people attuned to hear them.

Seek ye first the political kingdom and all else shall be granted unto you.
We prefer self-government with danger to servitude in tranquillity.
We have the right to govern and even to misgovern ourselves.
We are determined to be seditious and more seditious by continuing the fight to its logical conclusion. The only thing that will stop our being seditious is the grant of self-government to our chiefs and people.

Sometimes he can give rise to a truly noble rephrasing and development of an idea:

There come in all political struggles rare moments hard to distinguish but fatal to let slip, when even caution is dangerous. *Then all must be on a hazard, and out of the simple man is ordained strength.*

It must not be believed that his attack was continually philosophical. If it is impossible to get records of the full ferocity of his speeches to audiences up and down the country, his journalism gives us some idea. The misguided authorities, either in London or the Gold Coast, must have thought it a good idea to send Sir Sydney Abraham to the Gold Coast to build some good will among the sports-loving people. The people of Accra believed this to be an attempt to divert them from politics. A public meeting Sir Sydney attempted to hold broke up in disorder. Nkrumah wrote a blistering editorial entitled: "Good-bye, Sir Sydney":

Did Churchill send round Lord Burghley or other athletes to go round Britain and to organise sports when the war with Germany was at its height? Perhaps you do not realise that we are in a comparable situation. The British fought to prevent Germany from enslaving them; we are fighting to liberate ourselves from colonial slavery imposed on us by British imperialism!

. . . Instead of your coming here to advise the British government to remove the blot on her colonial administration by providing proper education, ample employment and better social services, or instead of advising the British government to grant us a new democratic self-governing constitution, you have come here at this time to "organise" us for sports!

We like sports, but we want self-government first so that we can be masters not servants in our own country. When we get self-government, you will be amazed at what we can put into the field at the next Olympic Games; and you will also be amazed at the stadiums that will glorify sporting activities in the new Ghana.

But first things first, Sir Sydney! Please go back and tell Britain that we are ready for full self-government now; anything short of that will be unacceptable to us. We are in earnest; our "eyes are red," and we shall not rest until we have attained full self-government for the people of this country, this year.

Yen wura Sydney, Nantsiw yie!

Yours sincerely,

Kwame Nkrumah.

On Empire day, the colonial administration was wont to loose all its loudest and most bombastic armoury of empire upon the colonial peoples, especially the children:

It has been variously explained that Empire day was instituted to commemorate the birthday of Queen Victoria. In that case should not the people of Britain, whose Queen she was, celebrate it with their characteristic pomp and pageantry, in grateful commemoration of what their good Queen was able to do for them, rather than that we should make such fuss over it here?

The reader must constantly bear in mind that the audience was a colonial people, to whom only yesterday such remarks were sedition and would make the authors marked men. Now they were being said and written every day. Many of them had a local application which had to be explained to people from outside but were instantly savoured to the full by thousands and would run like wild-fire to all parts of the country. Here is one such. The African chief is a man of great ceremonial dignity, with his huge umbrella, his linguist who relieves him from the task of speaking, and his enormous ceremonial sandals which are built large so that the dust may not touch his feet. If for any reason a chief had to make a quick getaway, he would be encumbered by this ceremonial footwear. This is what gives the point to Nkrumah's remark that if the chiefs continued to support the British government and fight against the wishes of the people, the time would come when they would have to run away "and leave their sandals behind."

In the end what matters most is Nkrumah's sympathy for the ordinary people, his intuitive understanding of them, his respect for them. The colonial administration either ignored him or abused him as a demagogue, or at best an agitator, though what exactly is the crime of being an agitator, it is impossible to say. Such is the cynicism, the deep inner despair of progress that hangs like a load of lead in the heart of the modern men of progressive views that he often can see in Nkrumah a man mobilising the masses for a political purpose, using them as means to an end, even though they accept the end. The narrowness is in the limitations of the age. Only a large humanity and a deep respect for every human being as a human being could have sustained those tireless trips to the remotest villages to talk to the illiterate villagers by the roadside. No great revolution was ever led by men who sought only to use the people. Venal and corrupt as was Danton, some who have studied him most closely have recognised the human sympathy and the warm idealistic convictions from which sprang the great speeches and actions which so shaped the course of the French revolution. Lenin has told us how one of the most critical problems of the revolution was solved for him by the remark of a workman's wife: "They dare not give us bad bread now." He used to sit in his office in the Kremlin listening for hours to delegations of peasants telling him what he had already heard dozens of times and in any case knew beforehand. From the same magnanimity came the political wisdom which prompted him to say in 1920: we cannot incorporate the trades unions into the state; our workers' state is full of bureaucratic deformations and the workers need their unions to protect them from the state. No mean or calculating spirit can ever mobilise masses of people for a revolution. Western civilisation has forgotten or learnt to distrust the revolutionary temper, the revolutionary spirit, the revolutionary personality built on the grand heroic scale. It was on view in the Ghana revolution. It is everywhere in Africa, and Hungary has shown that contrary to all the defeatist lamentations, it burns in Europe still in millions of ordinary people. If it did not, civilisation would be at an end, destroyed not by hydrogen bomb explosions from without, but by the congealing within.

I have given much space to Nkrumah. And I have not mentioned his lieutenants, some of them like Gbedemah and Botsio, well known today, and the group of young men, barely out of their twenties, locally educated, of whom Kofi Baako, editor of the Cape Coast *Daily Mail* at twenty, and Eddie Ampah, chairman of the Cape Coast Municipal Council, are characteristic representatives. They wrote and spoke and travelled with a boundless energy over the country, went to gaol, came out and continued the struggle as did hundreds of others. More detailed, more intimate, more searching accounts will be written in time and I do not know these men sufficiently to do otherwise than give impressions which I have done earlier. But the history of revolution shows, and any examination of the material easily available for the Ghana revolution confirms that in these crises a single leader embodies in himself, the main strategic levels and demonstrates in person, either directly or indirectly, how they should be carried out. In a revolutionary crisis these are seminal and the ablest supporters find all their energies fully occupied in developing tactically the strategic ideas. It is not a one-sided process. The leader is nourished not only by the people, but knows the strengths and weaknesses of his closest associates, catches the slightest hints and overtures in their advice, information, judgements, eagernesses or reticence and thus bases his policies on the collective wisdom of his party and the people. All accounts agree, and a few moments spent socially with Nkrumah and the leading members of his staff show that the deference they pay to him is not that given to a holder of a traditional post, such as prime minister or president, but that given to a man who founded the movement and around whom it has grown. Others will do historical justice to them.

It is very difficult for even a sympathetic European or American of some education, without long experience of a colonial people, to grasp the relation between a colonial revolutionary of the first order and the masses of the people. The revolutionary will give unreservedly to the masses of the people all the knowledge and the ideas that he has gained from wide education and experience in the more cultivated parts of the world. I must make some final attempt to convey this because it embodies in yet another fashion the organic unfitness of the Colonial Office for the work to be done. In Trinidad the Chief Minister, Dr Eric Williams, conducts what is known as the University of Woodford Square and regularly delivers to anywhere between fifteen to thirty thousand people political disquisitions which with little change he could have delivered to students at the American university at which he was formerly a professor. The only contact a colonial official can have with this is to become one of the people and stand in the crowd and listen. Either directly or indirectly he must oppose this. He begins from the premise, his sole justification (even to himself) for being in the position that he holds, in that the people are backward, and being backward must be brought forward in graduated stages. His conception of education is in numbers of schools and teachers, of politics in carefully graduated initiation into the suffrage and the manipulation of nominated, elected legislative and executive counters in two or more colours, European and native. What is worse, the universities which bred him instil this poisonous medicine into the veins of many colonials whom they educate. The Ghana revolution, carefully studied, can blast this obstructiveness out of the way.

To an intellectual in a highly developed country, an article in a newspaper is just another article. He usually looks at two or three or more daily newspapers, and at the end of the week a similar number of reviews. A pamphlet he takes in his stride. Whereas the intellectual's habit of mind and his mode of existence are the constant, the almost automatic acquisition of information, working people do not read that way unless they are, as a few of them undoubtedly are, highly politicised. With the ordinary working man a good article in the paper, a pamphlet, is an event of some significance in his intellectual life. Workers think over it, pass it around, they remember it, they check events by it and it by events.

Intensify this relation to the twentieth power and you get some idea of the power of print and the educational and self-developing power of oratory and journalism among a colonial and largely illiterate population so long as that journalism is devoted to a cause they feel is their own. Nkrumah writes:

GBEDEMAH MARCHES TO CALVARY

Fellow Country and Party Members,

In the struggle for the liberation of our fatherland, Komla Agbeli Gbedemah has followed the imperishable footsteps of renowned martyrs for their country's freedom. . . .

That is why the struggle for the liberation of Ghana must be waged in a vigorous, relentless and uncompromising manner by people who are devoted to the cause and are prepared to suffer, and if need be, to die for it.

You remember the historic words of Churchill during the last war when Britain almost lay prostrate before the barbaric hordes of Hitler and his satellites. Thus said he: "I have nothing to offer but blood, toil, tears and sweat." Let us also remember the words of Garibaldi in his famous retreat from Rome: "Fortune who betrays us today will smile on us tomorrow. I am going out from Rome. Let those who wish to continue the war against the stranger come with me. I offer neither pay, quarters, nor provisions; I offer hunger, thirst, forced marches, battles, death. Let him who loves his country in his heart and not with his lips only, follow me!"

Do you remember the hectic days of the Battle of Britain? Do you remember the East African campaign and the battles in the jungles of Burma and India? Why were they fought, and where do we stand today?

Who is a bondsman that would not join in the liberation of his country? This is the question that Agbeli is asking the youth of this country from behind the prison bars. . . .

"Imperialism is at bay" and bestirring itself with the vain frantic fury of a drowning man, but its liquidation is surely drawing nigh and Ghana will be liberated. Agbeli has marched boldly to Calvary, but the day of resurrection, yes the day of the redemption of Ghana approacheth. Long live Agbeli Gbedemah; Long live the CPP. Long live the Ghana that is to be.

There is the central idea of being ready to suffer, even to die for the cause. There is the defiance of the overwhelming material power of imperialism. These are enough to hold the attention and lift not only the hearts but the minds of any people. But in addition there are the following windows to new worlds: fatherland; blood, sweat, and tears; Calvary, Garibaldi, Battle of Britain, campaigns of East Africa, Burma and India, Shakespeare's *Julius Caesar*, "Who is a bondsman that would not . . ."; the day of resurrection, the day of redemption. There is here a mass of ideas, facts, avenues for further exploration. One man reads and the others who do not read listen. Then would come the elucidation of the various points and references. It can last for days. Jomo Kenyatta has vividly described to the writer how in the early twenties when Garvey was a great name in the world, Africans would meet in the bush in Kenya, one of them would translate two or three hours over an article of Garvey to which messengers listened. When they had learnt it, they speeded off in different directions to repeat the article in various centres miles away.

Garvey wrote a vast deal of nonsense and many lies, but at any rate with a phenomenal energy he conveyed the idea that Africa should belong to the Africans. On this the illiterate Kenya native nourished his soul and his mind. Nkrumah was saying essentially the same, but in a style and manner that could compare with anything that was being said anywhere at the time in the English language. Thus stimulated, tens upon tens of thousands were driven to learn to read, to wish to learn a little and to know more. This is at the heart of the emancipation of Africa, in literacy, in politics, in economic and social development. On this foundation the rest can be built. At his best, the Colonial Office administrator with his statistics of literacy, his two schools built where there was only one before, cannot but be overwhelmed at the immensity of the task before him. He does the best that he can and thinks in terms of centuries, sometimes in terms of hopelessness.

Nkrumah's work is not known, it is not understood if seen only in terms of a political agitation. One must bear constantly in mind the ordinary man of Ghana, the immensity of the ground to be covered by the newly urbanised worker, the illiterate villager, and precisely for that reason the need to give them the best that was being thought and said in the world. This is the work that was done and magnificently done, and nothing like it has been seen anywhere since the first years of the Russian revolution.

In reply to the above, the colonial administration and the British government, these self-appointed trainers, had but one response. If any education for self-government was going to be done in the Gold Coast, it was going to be done by them and in their way, and this required first of all the destruction of the movement by the traditional method: smashing the leadership. We need spend only a little time on this familiar ground. The colonial administration initiated an unending series of prosecutions for sedition and libel which sent the editors of various newspapers to gaol and made the party pay thousands of pounds in fines—the chief of police alone got and enforced a judgement of £1,500. The money was usually paid by public subscription. They banned conferences on the grounds that these would provoke breaches of the peace. When the party wished to send cablegrams of protest to the Secretary of State for the Colonies, they recognised that no telegraph office in the colony would send them and travelled three hundred miles to French Togoland, only to find that the government had anticipated them and they could not dispatch cables from there either.

No detail was too poor or too mean to be overlooked. There was a housing shortage in Accra, and Gbedemah, a man with a family, had rented a house from an African. He spent much time and care in making it habitable. Given sudden notice to quit, he protested and was told by the owner of the house that he had no wish to throw Gbedemah out but that he had had orders from above and he did not want to get into any conflict with these people. Government officials similarly stimulated all sorts of minor people to pile up libel actions against the party newspapers. This is not unusual behaviour by reactionary party politicians in many countries. But when those who are carrying it out claim their privileged position and authority on the basis of higher civilisation, superior morality, and the moral duty of educating a backward people, these primitive cut-throat politics, and especially the abuse of the machinery of the government, and the legal system, can have only one result—the complete discredit of the government and the loss of all authority among the people. This is what happened.

The organisation and activity which had led up to the Ghana Representative Assembly left the government and the Europeans cold. Incredible as this may seem, they believed or pretended to believe (how can anyone tell?) that this was mere African drum-beating and dancing in the dust, and in this foolishness they were encouraged by the lawyer-merchant caste and the chiefs. The UGCC Committee denounced Nkrumah with such violence and pursued such a pro-imperialist policy that it was the people, as we have seen, who forced the split at the Saltpond Conference. The very circumstances of the split showed how completely they had exposed themselves to the population at large. Dr Danquah indeed not only won one of the customary libel actions against the *Accra Evening News* but tried to buy out the paper altogether (so great were its debts), and only alertness in effecting a legal transformation of name saved it. They denounced Nkrumah for starting the Ghana National Colleges. If there were not at all unbased rumours that the government seriously considered deporting Nkrumah from Accra to his birthplace, the UGCC tried to rid themselves of him altogether by getting him to return to England.

Against Nkrumah, the CPP and the Ghana Representative Assembly, the two rivals for power, the All-Whites and the All-Blacks, were one. And this was as it should be. The eyes with which these Africans looked upon the masses had learnt to focus in English universities and law-schools, their ears were attuned to parliamentary debates, their conceptions of political activity began from a clear differentiation between the classes and the masses, and inasmuch as they had no economic basis in the productive forces of the country, they attached themselves to the class in power, the European officials and men of business. The chiefs, closer to the people of the country, were not so uncontrolled in their denunciation of the party. But though with some wavering, they followed behind the imperialist power and the lawyer-merchants.

After the Ghana Representative Assembly, there was no way out but the head-on clash. To have expected the government officials to clear their eyes and understand the significance of the Assembly is not realistic. For them this grandiose spectacle, a people and an African people, striding over decades in a day, this was rebellion, crime, treason, and irresponsibility, and at the very best in direct contravention to the settled policy of the British government.

Perhaps the Secretary of State for the Colonies himself, or some other person, officially or unofficially connected with the colonies, might have read between the lines of despatches, or called for a file of newspapers and memoranda and sensed behind the cold print the human passions and aspirations in the country that were expressing themselves in this concerted sequence of events and demonstrations? The enquirer draws a blank. All that is to be found is a total incomprehension, we see only a lion-tamer with his whip and some intractable animals.

As for Nkrumah, as we know, his course had been set a few weeks after he landed in the country. The Ghana Representative Assembly, the tone and temper of the people showed that two-thirds of the original programme had been as far as possible fulfilled. But there remained the final third, the total economic boycott and general strike against the government itself. Nkrumah could not have been eager to embark upon this. It was a colossal step. But precisely because of that he had to be sure that everything else had been tried. Retreat now was out of the question—it would demoralise the people and could destroy the organisation for long years to come. He sought a round table conference with the government. The Prime Minister of England had sat at a round table with Gandhi. Nkrumah after all represented something: anyone with ordinary eyes in his head could have strolled past the Ghana Representative Assembly and seen what Nkrumah represented. The government refused to take any notice of him. Positive action was on the order of the day.

By this time everyone was well acquainted with what positive action meant. Even before the Ghana Representative Assembly, a council of colony chiefs, the Ga State Council, had summoned Nkrumah before it to ask him what he meant by "positive action." Nkrumah had explained fully. Members of the United Gold Coast Convention were present and attempted to hound down Nkrumah and even to suggest that the party be banned and he should be deported.

But the paramount chief who was presiding overruled them and proposed that Nkrumah should call a meeting of his followers and explain to them what he had just told the Council. Nkrumah went further. Using the suggestion of the paramount chief as a lever, he not only called the meeting for two days later, but was ready with a five thousand word pamphlet explaining what he meant by "positive action." The Ghana Representative Assembly therefore met and took its decisions in full cognisance of what lay beyond. Nkrumah toured the countryside to explain. On 15 December 1949 in Accra, the executive committee of the CPP took the plunge. In its name Nkrumah wrote a letter to the Governor stating that if the government continued to ignore the legitimate aspirations of the people as embodied in the demands of the Ghana Representative Assembly, the party would embark upon a campaign of positive action *and that they would continue with this until such time as the government gave consideration to the right of the people of Ghana to commence their own constituent assembly.* This constituent assembly would consider and amend the Coussey constitution or write one of its own. Nkrumah writes: "In short, we were prepared for a showdown." And a showdown it would be, for if the British government had not yielded to entreaty (the round table conference) it would most certainly not yield to threats, and public threats. And if it didn't, then what?

I spent what may have seemed an inordinate amount of space in chapter 3 discussing the implications of a programme of militant non-violence and non-co-operation, and I was quite emphatic in stating that the analysis, limited as it was, could not possibly have been written at the time. The situation now reached shows what takes place in every revolution worthy of the name. Every revolution must attempt what by all logic and reason and previous experience is impossible. Like anything creative it extends the boundaries of the known. At that moment the reasoning of the leadership cannot be understood by the ordinary intelligent man. In fact the more intelligent he is, the less fitted he is to understand. What seems to be happening is this. The revolutionary leader has usually grown with the growth of his own forces. He understands where they have come from to where they are, and he has some instinct not as to where they can go in general, but as to how far. The developing situation being what it is, he can dare to lead them. He has also been in constant conflict with the counter-revolution from the start. They can have their advances and retreats, their skirmishes and head-on clashes. The revolutionary leader, therefore, has a good working idea of the forces opposed to him and what they are able and likely to do. Finally, he is in the heat of an action, long-meditated and in this particular case, scientifically foreseen. Somewhere out of this cauldron now at boiling point comes the decision to declare economic boycott and non-co-operation *until the government grants self-government.* You can declare non-co-operation and economic boycott for twenty-four hours, or for three days, as a demonstration to the government and to the world. It is a means of mobilising your own followers. You can even bring down the government by it. But all that is only as a rule preliminary to a final advance or a definite retreat. You can call for an indefinite economic boycott for a specific grievance, such as the lowering of prices, or the end of segregation in buses as in Montgomery, Alabama. But you cannot call for a total boycott of all activity in a country until a total demand is granted, and self-government is the most total of all demands. The request is unreasonable and even madness, but that is what revolution is, reasonable madness.

What Nkrumah and the others did can be made more clear by what others in a similar situation did not do. In Britain in 1921, the leaders of the miners, the transport workers, and the railwaymen (the triple alliance) called a strike and paralysed the country. Mr Lloyd George summoned them and told them what amounted to this: "You have the power. I cannot stop you, for the army is affected. But if you bring the life of the country to a standstill, you will have to assume responsibility." It is not surprising that the three labour leaders shrank from this prospect and retreated before the threat or the bluff, whichever it was.

In cold blood, writing from documents and information, I find it hard to believe that Nkrumah expected the government to capitulate before the general strike. At best it could be the beginning of a new series of negotiations. At worst, the people might, without or with provocation, lose their control. There would be a horrible massacre. There was another by no means remote possibility. The people might, by the usual combination of force and persuasion, win over the local government forces and repossess themselves of their country and of themselves by force. They were perfectly able to do it.

There were other possibilities. There is no need to go into them. It is enough if we understand that we are here in the presence of imponderables. With this objective before them and the people behind them, these young men, now at the climax of a long preparation, did not flinch. They threw down the challenge.

The party had taken no chances. The people were well prepared and all understood what they were doing. During December they had been warned, sometimes from the public platform by Nkrumah himself, that they were to save their money and not spend it in Christmas festivities so as to be ready to endure the privations of the coming strike. The cooks of the Europeans found it difficult to buy food in the markets because the market-women were reserving the food for the strike days.

It may seem strange to the Western reader that the party seemed to be able to call a monster meeting at such short notice. The party propaganda vans would tour the city calling the people to the Arena. The market-women could get out thousands of people at the shortest possible notice, and Nkrumah's often-repeated statement, "the market-women made the party," conveys one of the great truths of the revolution. Here (and in many other places), we get curious reminders and indications of politics in that most political of social formations, the Greek city-state. In his speech on the crown, Demosthenes in an enigmatic passage describes how, at the news that Elatea had been taken, the high officials of the assembly went into the market, drove out the people and set fire to the wicker stalls while trumpeters summoned the population to the assembly. This was done from above and it was the last days of the democracy. The market-women in the first days of Gold Coast democracy did it from below.

The CPP vans and propagandists covered the country for days carrying the slogan "Positive Action without Violence for Full Self-Government Now" to the remotest parts of the country. But all their preparation, though indispensable to success, did not ensure it. Trotsky has made quite clear that though the Kerensky government in October 1917 was worm-eaten and, as events were to show, needed only a push to collapse, that push had to be made and those who had to make it approached the final step with resolution, but nervous enough; in such situations so great are the unknowns that no one can possibly tell how things are going to turn out.

And now for the enemy. While the whole country was talking about positive action without violence and openly preparing for the general strike on a national scale, the government obstinately refused to believe that Africans could carry out any such project. It is believed that the lawyer-merchant supporters had assured them that any such large-scale action by the people of the Gold Coast was impossible, and some of the UGCC went around the country denouncing Nkrumah as a communist.

However, some observers and travellers were more serious than these. Members of the police intelligence service told the government that the action was being prepared and that the whole country appeared willing to respond. It is remarkable how often in similar situations police officers, their minds unclouded by political passion, give an accurate and comprehensive view of the facts and the perspectives. The officials, therefore, prepared to take counter-measures but to the end they stuck to their fundamental premise, the organic incapability of Africans. Mr Saloway, the Colonial Secretary, summoned Nkrumah before him. Nkrumah told him exactly what he proposed to do. Mr Saloway in turn warned him that if any violence or disorder took place as a result of positive action, Nkrumah would be held personally responsible. Mr Saloway then quite openly, in fact sympathetically, told Nkrumah why he was bound to fail, that is to say, why the government was sure to win. Why was this? The backwardness, primitiveness, instability, call it what you will, of the Africans. Mr Saloway had served in India. Indians, he told Nkrumah, can suffer pain and deprivations, but Africans cannot:

> Mark my words, my good man: within three days the people here will let you down—they'll never stick it. Now, had this been India. . . .

Boiled down to the ultimate, the issue posed here is but the issue I have treated in the first chapter and entitled "the myth." The colonial administration had learnt nothing from its mis-judgement of the Africans at the time of the economic boycott. Its premise, blurted out here at a moment of crisis, is always the backwardness, the primitiveness, the illiteracy of Africans as a mass. Nkrumah, on the other hand, believed that the people could do whatever was required in their efforts to realise themselves and win self-government.

This revelation of the state of mind of the rulers would have been of no particular value to Nkrumah except to confirm his sense of the fanatics he was dealing with (but these fanatics had guns, cruisers and planes). However, not what was said, but the mere fact of a meeting played a role. Hitherto the CPP had been denounced as communist-inspired hooligans, an irresponsible minority. Now Saloway had asked for the meeting, and after the meeting for the first time the name of the party was heard on the Gold Coast radio. Truly the ways of colonial officials are their own ways, known only to themselves, explicable in terms of reason only by the mythology which encloses them. The CPP could bring together in Accra ninety thousand people and every African organisation in the country, except two of chiefs and one that was on its last legs. No mention on the radio. Conversation with the Colonial Secretary. Immediate promotion to the radio. The people were moving fast but feeling their way at the same time. The youth, in particular, saw this conference as evidence of the political skill of the party and the tenacity of Nkrumah. They hailed it as the first moral victory of the party.

On 8 January 1950, at 5 o'clock, Nkrumah held a meeting at the Arena and called for the general strike throughout the whole country, with the exception of those on public utilities and the police, to begin at midnight. As far as it is possible to trust evidence, written and spoken, in such an action spread over so large an area, the response was complete. Certainly in the more easily accessible areas it was not only complete but instantaneous. The people saw in the party a government of their own. They were listening to it, and not to the one with the power and the police and the laws. If there was any doubt of this, an unimpeachable proof was soon to come. Nkrumah had left

Accra to go in person to the provinces to declare positive action. During his absence the government, having control of the radio, used an ancient trick to disrupt the strike: in each area it broadcast appeals to go back to work, claiming that the people in other areas were doing so. An attempt was being made to resume normal business even in Accra. Nkrumah called a meeting in the Arena and after this the shutdown was absolute. The economic life of the whole country came to a standstill. All employed workers stayed at home and employers, including the government, the biggest employer of all, closed down.

That this revolution was blood and bone of the twentieth century is shown not only by its planned character, but also by the role of the Trades Union Congress. Ten thousand workers organised in a union are ten times more effective than a hundred thousand individual citizens. The trade-union movement co-operated with the CPP but preserved its independence. After the vain attempt to get the chiefs or the Aborigines' Society to sponsor the Ghana Representative Assembly, it had been held under the chairmanship of Pobee Biney, an ex-engine driver and the leader of the TUC. Now a dispute arose between the workers of the Meteorological Employees' Union and their employer, the government. The workers went on strike and the government dismissed them all from the service. The TUC supported them and threatened a general strike of all the unions in the country unless they were reinstated. Anxious not to get the imminent general strike for self-government confused with an issue so limited as an industrial strike, Nkrumah sought to intervene and offered his services to the government as mediator. The government refused, with the result that the country finally embarked on positive action under two demands:

1. Full self-government within the British commonwealth of nations;
2. reinstatement of the meteorological workers.

The workers, few as they were, had set their own proletarian mark upon the national revolution. But dominant over all was the will of the people symbolised in the person of Nkrumah. At the time when through government propaganda on the radio Accra was uncertain as to what exactly was happening to the general strike, he appeared on the streets of Accra to walk to the headquarters of the paper to call a meeting for that day. He never reached the office and the meeting organised itself. By the time he had walked a few hundred yards he was so surrounded by people that all traffic was brought to a standstill. Sending them on to the Arena, he escaped with difficulty in a taxi to a suburb whence an hour later he returned to see what seemed to be the whole of Accra assembled for the meeting.

At this stage, I hope, those who have been sceptical about the very word revolution, and the way in which I have treated it, may be jerked into sitting up and taking notice. There are not many times in the history of any nation when its whole economic life comes to a dead stop. Still more rarely does this happen in pursuit of so abstract an aim as "self-government now." Still more rarely does this take place under the planned leadership of a man and a party who twenty-four months before were almost unknown in the country. If there is anything similar or comparable in the history of revolutionary struggles on a national scale, or for that matter on any scale, I have never heard of it, and I have spent many years in the study of similar matters. Judged by any standard this is one of the most remarkable of historical events and an indication of the future of political action during the rest of our century.

The government, having declared a state of emergency, moved in on the party. One by one, it arrested the party leaders, leaving Nkrumah for the last. The party headquarters were raided, the premises wrecked, the files taken away, the party members beaten up and gaoled. Nkrumah believes, or rather is convinced, that only accident saved him from being torn to pieces after a clash between the ex-servicemen and the police in which two policemen were killed. The people held firm. On 19 January the strike was called off, and the people resumed their ordinary life in good order. Nkrumah and his associates were tried and sentenced to prison terms. Nkrumah defended himself but his own view of the matter is contained in a single sentence which should be compulsory reading for every schoolboy in England:

> The idea of defending my case . . . had never entered my head, for whatever defence was put up, I felt that the authorities would not allow me and my colleagues to escape conviction, for the judiciary and the executive under a colonial régime are one and the same thing.

I want to repeat the last dozen words or so: the judiciary and the executive under a colonial régime are one and the same thing. There is not a politically-minded colonial who does not know this, and all things considered it is to be expected. What is unbearable is the constant repetition of the myths: the independence of the judiciary, the impartiality of the civil service, and so on and so forth.

The calculated indignities to which Nkrumah and his fellow prisoners were subjected have been related by him. To recapitulate them will hinder rather than help. This much must be said, however: if the government of Nkrumah had subjected any political opponent, Englishman or African, to such deliberately bestial conditions of imprisonment, the headlines of a hundred papers from London to Paris, Washington and Rome, would have proclaimed the inherent barbarism and unfitness for self-government of an African people.

The administration had not only taken the expected offensive to smash the movement by terror. It also had a long-term plan. It pinned its faith in the Africans of ability and ambition and the chiefs, and the opportunities that the Coussey constitution would offer them. It dangled before them the sweets of office and built a number of elegant houses set apart for the African ministers-to-be. These gentlemen themselves and their ladies prepared for their initiation into the mysteries of government by ordering new clothes of a ministerial dignity, wives went abroad to become acquainted at first hand with the fundamentals and most up-to-date nuances of ministerial entertaining. I am reliably informed, and I think it is in print somewhere, that members of the Labour Party, in anticipation of the first or the second Labour government, were also put through their social paces. The Labour members had at least won the election. Their African brothers had not got that far. But they and the colonial administration had every reason to expect success. The Coussey constitution had given universal suffrage only to the five municipalities. They could depend on the secondary electors in the colony and the chiefs in Ashanti and the Northern Territories to give them a majority. Many CPP leaders were put away safely in gaol for a long time, including the chief agitator, organiser and inspirer of these disruptive activities. The knowledge of the degradation and humiliation to which they were being subjected in prison should be enough to tame the more intractable spirits, especially as they knew that the government could send any of them up whenever it wanted. That was taken care of by a sedition ordinance so wide open that a magistrate could read into it whatever he liked. To complete the terror the government dismissed right and left from government service those who had taken a prominent part in the strike. It prosecuted a number for meeting to strike or being responsible for incidents connected with the strike.

In the projected constitution the government would have in its hands defence, external affairs, justice and police. The leader of government business in the House was to be the Attorney-General, a colonial official. With ordinary luck the administration could count on ten years at the very least during which time it would initiate into the mysteries of government its African ministers. In official phrasing the policy was, in the words of the Watson Commission, "to give every African of ability an opportunity to help govern the country, so as not only to gain political experience, but also to experience political power." Quite so, quite so. The Colonial Office and colonial administrations have a long experience in the corrupting and taming of colonial politicians. When Nkrumah, on first coming into power, publicly told his new ministers, "no fraternisation", and warned them that "what imperialists failed to achieve by strong-arm methods, they might hope to bring off with cocktail parties," he was merely taking cognisance of what is common knowledge, with diverse fat and greasy examples among nationalist politicians. I wrote some pages on it at the beginning of the thirties,[1] and this deliberate attempt to corrupt nationalist leaders has not lessened, it has grown.

There was only one thing wrong with all this, but it was a very big thing indeed, in fact the very biggest thing in the Gold Coast, beside which everything else was pygmy-size. The people. They had won the greatest of all victories— the victory over themselves. In the general strike they had acted as a whole in this national undertaking, they had learnt their own power, their own incredible solidarity, had seen themselves mobilised under a leadership of their own choosing against the alien government and seen that, despite all appearances, they were masters in their own country. These paradoxes constantly appear and reappear in revolution. The government was certain that it had defeated the general strike. The truth was that the general strike had defeated the government. The people were far stronger now than they had ever been. The party, apparently shattered, was now in reality an integral part of the people. The government had acted swiftly, and this shows how carefully it had planned. Positive action had been declared on 7 January. A state of emergency was declared on 11 January. Positive action was called off on 19 January. Nkrumah and his committee were safely in gaol on 22 February.

The state of emergency continued. CPP meetings could not be held in the towns, and whereas in any national political movement the actions of towns like Paris or Petrograd can make or break the movement at a particular stage, in a country like Ghana the towns are like beacons to the villagers. The government thought the movement was dead, and in this it was grievously misled by its all-African allies who, thinking like the government, also believed that the movement was dead and openly rejoiced at the imprisonment of their opponents. "We told you so" was their leitmotiv.

Romantics and those whose second line of defence is to emphasise the ability of the leader (usually in order to discredit the people) make great play with the leadership of the movement from gaol by Nkrumah and the directives written by the light of the street-lamps on toilet paper. For a movement to be led it must exist, and what Nkrumah had taught in the brief two years was far more important than what he taught on the toilet paper.

The gates had barely closed on him before the second line of leaders began to rebuild a national headquarters, the moving spirit being A. Y. K. Djin, a local merchant with no international experience at all. The city branches began to meet again, though without holding public meetings. The villagers did not know what was going on and many believed that the CPP was dead. Revolutionary history is full of accidents which, as Karl Marx says, sometimes help a movement forward, sometimes retard it, and it would be foolish to discount them. But if the movement is flowing in channels deep enough, it uses the favourable accidents and takes the unfavourable ones in its stride. If we hold tight to the fact that the general strike had consolidated and clarified, given a new dimension to the struggle of the past two years, we can then savour the exquisite appositeness of the series of accidents which now followed.

It had so happened that the government, imprisoning people at the slightest opportunity, had sentenced K. A. Gbedemah, the vice-chairman of the party, to six months on 17 October 1949. He thus escaped the round-up which concluded the general strike and came out of gaol in the early part of March 1950. He was thirty-seven years old, locally educated, and had tried his hand both at teaching and in business before he became one of the founders of the CPP, bringing great ability, energy and determination to whatever the movement required of him, journalism, oratory or organisation. He seems to be a man who does not see too far into the distance but he has an exceptionally clear and comprehensive view of what is before him. He saw that what was now required was the building of the party as an effective force both for the people themselves and against the enemy. It is hard not to think of Lenin in hiding and Trotsky leading the revolution between July and October 1917 under his guidance.

Gbedemah came out of gaol a few days before the end of his six months' sentence on 17 March. The party burst into activity like a river that had been chafing behind a dam. A rally was called in Accra. Thirty thousand people turned up and Gbedemah produced a master stroke. Intimidation, loss of jobs and the threat of gaol were the government's chief weapons. Nkrumah had written his article, "Gbedemah Marches to Calvary," where he made a virtue of being prosecuted and persecuted. At the rally Gbedemah introduced the cap worn by the prisoners in gaol, naming it the sign of the Prison Graduate, or P.G. The gesture delighted the populace, awakened a readiness for anything in the youth.

Two weeks later, on 1 April, a municipal election was due in Accra. The government therefore had to declare the emergency at an end. You cannot have an election under emergency powers. On the solid foundation of the principles laid by Nkrumah, Gbedemah performed a task of reorganisation and extension which is still talked about as one of the highlights of the revolution. The government had intended to cripple the movement for good. Instead the blows had strengthened it. The régime of training for self-government was severe but effective.

The successes of the people fell like a never-ending hail of stones on the head of the bewildered administration. One distinguished African declared that the people of the Gold Coast seemed to have gone mad. The remark is valuable. Baron Budberg, returning to Russia from abroad after the March revolution, found this same widespread insanity among the Russian people. Another nobleman who returned to France after 14 July found the people suffering from the same strange epidemic: he had left behind an absolute monarchy, now he found all Paris deep in argument as to whether the king should or should not have a veto over bills passed in a legislative assembly.

On 1 April the CPP won the seven seats of the Accra municipality. The party campaigned on the slogan of the general strike, "Self-government now." It did not merely win seats. Its vigour, its sense of tactics, its propaganda vans touring the town, won the admiration of the people of Accra. The all-African merchants and lawyers, and their friends who had been "fully representative" of the African people in the eyes of the colonial administration and His Majesty's Government, were resoundingly defeated. The whole country celebrated the victory and the villagers who had been wondering if the CPP was finished, came to life again.

On 1 June 1950, the party won two by-elections for the municipality in conservative Cape Coast where, if anywhere, the lawyer-merchants were well-established. On 14 June, one of the locally-educated young men of the party, Kwesi Plange, already a municipal councillor, defeated his own uncle in a by-election. In this period the party vans penetrated to the remotest corners of the country and the party grew until it was believed that by 1951 it had between a million and a million and a half members. Full-time officers were appointed in the national and regional headquarters. Even certain provincial branches employed full-time officers and from end to end of the Gold Coast the Red, White and Green flag of the party flew in every town and village.

The people have their own doubts, their own secret needs, things they are confident of, others on which they need reassurance. They discover themselves day by day in all sorts of ways that, as usual in such circumstances, are entirely unpredictable. If the political skill and organisational discipline of the party had been hailed, in Accra, the reason was not far to seek. It was a demonstration, an assurance that their party, the people who were claiming self-government, knew how to organise, would know how to govern. Now they had a member in the legislature, a young man in his early twenties, one of their own.

On the opening day of the legislative session in which Kwesi Plange was to take his seat, thousands of people came to see and to hear at close hand (for all most certainly could not see) how this young man would conduct himself on the Council. Not only friends but enemies came. It is stated that a delegation of conservative elements came from Cape Coast to see Kwesi Plange disgrace himself, for in the words of the CPP chronicler, "to them he had not been to the United Kingdom and therefore was not intellectual." Kwesi Plange rose to the occasion. On the first day, 4 July 1950, when his turn came, he said:

> Mr President, honourable members, today is a great day in my life. The Fourth of July has a significance all its own. If you go back into history, you will find that the American Day of Independence is on the Fourth of July. The Fourth of July is the day of the assault on the Bastille in French history. The Fourth of July in my history is the day on which, according to the words of the President, a very young man has been admitted to the portals of the highest governmental machinery of the Gold Coast—the Legislative Council. I have come to join your ranks with youthful blood. . . . I have entered this Council definitely conscious of the great work that is being done. I shall at a more opportune time declare my policy, but, for the present, this much I have to say. I am slightly inconvenienced by the fact that I never received the papers relative to the session in good time, nevertheless I hope that there will be a time they will reach me at a moment when I shall have the opportunity to consult my electorate. . . . I am also grateful for the welcome address given me by Mr President and the very many good things he said about me, and I shall do my best to prove myself worthy of the esteem and confidence placed in me as the representative of the suffering masses in this august assembly.

The hungry who had come to be fed were not sent away empty. From the first word to the last the speech was the CPP as they knew it, and being toned down to show that the CPP could be as legislative as the best, would not make it lose, on the contrary, would help the general cause in the minds of the people.

Kwesi Plange himself was only twenty-four years old and the Coussey constitution had limited the vote to adults of twenty-five years of age. This at one stroke would disenfranchise the core of the movement. When the legislature was discussing this recommendation of the commission, Kwesi Plange opposed it, and the House turned him down. Many members of the commission were members of the House and the imperialist-merchant-lawyer-chief combination had every reason to keep the turbulent and rebellious youth out of politics. Kwesi Plange returned to the attack. He declared himself to be representative of the people, the common man in the street, and he announced that if the age limit was not reduced, these people would not pay taxes, would not cooperate in the running of the country and would not join the forces in the event of war. Positive action had shown that this was no empty threat. It was also an immediate one. The numerous chiefs in the House drew a substantial part of their revenue from the tax paid by the young men in the villages. If they voted for this clause in the constitution, the young men of the villages might refuse to pay and there would be created an impasse from which they could expect no benefits and only trouble. One after another, the legislators felt compelled to reverse themselves, spoke in favour of the reduction, and the reduction of the voting age was carried by an overwhelming majority. The debate had attracted national attention and there was immense jubilation all over the country at this further convincing demonstration that the CPP represented the people, and, despite the odds against them, knew how to make that representation effective. Kwesi Plange took up the cause of the aged and brought about an increase in the pensions and gratuities of retired civil servants. His very isolation in the Legislature brought home to the people the aims and capacity of the CPP.

In November the elections of the Kumasi Town Council took place, the CPP concentrated all its forces and won every seat. "Self-government now." The words reverberated around the country and in all minds except the well-insulated instruments of the governmental officials.

By this time the attention of the political world had been drawn to what was taking place in the Gold Coast. In February 1948 a telegram sent by Nkrumah to the Secretary of State about the disturbances had also been sent to the following addresses:

Secretary-General, UNO, New York.
Reginald Sorenson, House of Commons, London.
Willie Gallacher, MP, House of Commons, London.

The New African, 94 Gray's Inn Road, London, WC1.

Pan African News Agency, 22 Cranleigh House, Cranleigh Street. London, W1.

Pan Africa, 58 Oxford Street, Manchester.

Editor, *WASU Magazine*, 1 South Villas, London, NW1.

Editor, *Daily Worker*, London.

Associated Negro Press, Chicago.

New York Times, New York.

New Times, Moscow.

Gbedemah had followed suit by sending telegrams all over the world announcing the long unbroken succession of electoral victories of the CPP. The colonial administration had abused the party leaders as an "irresponsible minority" and similar names. But in election after election the irresponsible minority was winning majorities, irresponsible if you wish, but remarkably large and convincing, and all shouting in chorus, "Self-government now." By the time of the Kumasi municipal election journalists sent especially from the United Kingdom covered the elections and reported to the British public the irresistible success of the CPP. Henceforth both the Colonial Office and the colonial administration knew that they were under scrutiny by the British public at home. And that was not the least of the victories of the CPP.

The next and biggest station on the road was the first general election to be held under the new constitution in February 1951. By 11 December, when a vacancy had to be filled on the Cape Coast Town Council (owing to the death of a lawyer) the CPP candidate was returned unopposed. Riding the tide the CPP leadership now brought off a daring and long-premeditated manoeuvre wherein political skill, as usual, took advantage of the change good fortune had thrown in their way.

The election law stated that anyone who had been given a sentence of over twelve months in prison thereby lost his electoral rights. The judge who tried Nkrumah had put him away for three years in all, but he had sentenced him for only one year each on the separate counts. Nkrumah, therefore, although in gaol, demanded that his name be put on the electoral roll as a voter, and after some insistence was successful. The wise men who ran the government never for a moment suspected what the party had in store for them. After much arguing for and against, for nothing is as simple and straightforward as it seems after the event, Nkrumah had convinced the party leadership that he should run for Accra from prison. The secret had to be kept, for (and there is no doubt that in one sense the backward colonials do receive valuable training in certain aspects of politics) the CPP leaders had no doubt whatever that if the government got any hint of what was being prepared, the law would be altered so as to exclude Nkrumah. The information was therefore bruited around that Gbedemah would be the candidate for Accra and he campaigned as such. Late on the afternoon of the last day on which candidates would be named, Gbedemah went to the European official in charge and submitted as candidate for Accra the name of Kwame Nkrumah. The official was taken completely by surprise. Nkrumah? Impossible. No, it was not: Nkrumah was a registered voter, and therefore entitled to run as candidate. That was the law. Just as expected the official asked for time and ran to higher authority. But, as the CPP had foreseen, it was too late to do anything; the name had to be accepted. Having managed this, the indefatigable Gbedemah had now to take care of his own candidacy. It had been decided that he should run for Keta, but to lull any suspicions the party there had been allowed to put up a prospective candidate who had campaigned. Now at this late minute Gbedemah had to rush off to Keta and inform the party leadership and the candidate there that his campaigning for Accra had only been a ruse. Candidate and members accepted it in good part, and once more the CPP had matched its wits with its masters and exposed them before the country as politically club-footed.

The general election of 1951 was the climax of the Ghana revolution. It translated into political terms set by the government what the people had already said in their own way in the general strike. The CPP won thirty-four of the thirty-eight municipal and rural seats in spite of the indirect method of election everywhere except in the municipalities. Nkrumah polled 22,780 out of a total of 23,122 votes cast, a total defiance and contempt of the law and the government which had imprisoned him. The Coussey constitution had made no provision for these excesses of the insane people of the Gold Coast. The constitution fell apart, and Nkrumah, coming out of gaol, dictated his terms, among them his own selection of ministers, to the colonial administration now rudely awakened out of its day-dreamings and illusions. The merchant-lawyer caste on whom it had depended had not been defeated in the election. Except in odd places it had not dared to come out into the streets and campaign. Two of them got in by narrow squeaks, and at the next election one of them, Dr Danquah, was retired.

This was the end of the long, utterly shameful, unbelievably brazen assertion and reassertion by the British government in and out of the colony, in and out of Parliament, that its all-African commission was the greatest "step forward" yet in colonial government and truly representative of all shades of opinion in the colony except for an irresponsible communist-inspired minority. Others will have to record in detail the numbers of occasions up to the very end on which they continued to repeat this and to act upon it. It is not malice nor gloating nor respect for history which dictates the repetition here of one statement made just two years before by Mr Justice Coussey at the opening session of the constitutional commission. The voice is the voice of an African, but the ideas, the sentiments, the perspectives, are the perennial platitudes of the myth:

> It should be unnecessary for me to state that this committee does not meet to form a ministry composed entirely of Africans to assume, immediately, power and responsibility for the government of this country.
>
> That is not within the recommendations of the Watson report, nor of the proposals of His Majesty's Government, nor of our terms of reference. Although it is the cry of some, who have not considered fully its implications, that self-rule should be granted at once, it must be obvious to those who place foremost the true welfare of the masses, that a system must be created, flexible and progressive enough to permit the orderly evolution to responsible government within the shortest practicable time.

How?

> The objective is to be achieved by constitutional means, by fostering public spirit, promoting national unity, developing the intellectual and moral gifts, organising the economic resources of the country, educating the people in the grammar of democracy and studying urgently the complex machinery of government.

The reader will read and hear the same coming from the Colonial Office, the two Houses of Parliament, and from all parts of colonial Africa. It is to be hoped that henceforward when he hears or reads these sentiments, he will recollect how disastrously they fared in the Ghana revolution. No reflection is intended on Mr Justice Coussey, a distinguished gentleman who has served his country well. He owes his place here, in fact, to the dignity of tone and the beauty of the phrasing. As Lord Rennell said in the House of Lords: he wished that he had been able to state the position with such grace and style. It was no crime to think that way in January 1949. The crime was to continue along that road after the general election of 1951. For Nkrumah to decide to work the constitution was to put the revolution into the mouth of the lion. It emerged in the end safe but not sound, bruised and scarred with wounds which it will have to carry for many a day.

The general election of 1951 completely changed the course of the struggle. Previously the decisive events had taken place in the open. To repeat. It did not so much matter what was said at the Ghana Representative Assembly. It had taken place. Anyone who wanted to see could see ninety thousand people. The total general strike of a nation cannot be easily misunderstood, though some managed to do so, but these were colonial officials. Equally, few normal people can misunderstand the Saltpond Conference or the sending of the Executive Committee of the CPP to gaol. Only a statistician dealing in the most rarefied atmosphere could have misunderstood the results of the elections.

Now the whole process is altered. First, the masses are removed from the centre of the stage where they always are in a revolution. The colonial administration and the British government have challenged these, have been hopelessly beaten in the street and in the ballot-box, they seek to remove the struggle to places where these tempestuous Africans can no longer intervene. Nkrumah knows that without them he is lost, doomed to destruction either in gaol or in a ministerial office. He never lets anybody, least of all the government, forget that the last word rests with these people, that in any negotiation they are his actual last word. But the struggle is now internal, embedded in official and semi-official statements, parliamentary speeches and bills, full of doubletalk, to much of which Nkrumah himself is forced to contribute. This was, and remains, of profound political importance to the revolution. It also creates problems for the historian and the reader. You have to read between the lines. Many of the most crucial moves are unrecorded and those which are recorded remain hidden in secret despatches. If the Ashanti crisis had not brought the underground struggle right out into the open, even more would have remained obscure. Nevertheless, it had not been too difficult to put together the evidence that the British government gave nothing, handed over nothing, fought to the last second to retain everything that it could, and when finally it was forced to retire, left the Gold Coast tied up in knots which Ghana will have to spend a long time untying. This phase of the struggle needs the most careful analysis of the new positions and perspectives.

First of all, the British government, with whom lay the final word on all plans for training the people. We do not and we cannot document the course of its discussions. But this much I have every reason to believe was the deciding consideration in its support of the measures that were envisaged in 1951. The government had the power to suppress the people by sheer force of arms, or it believed that it had. But the international situation in 1951 was loaded with perils and difficulties and much of Britain's weight in the diplomatic tug-of-war depended upon her position as centre of the world-wide commonwealth. The struggle in the Gold Coast could not be settled quietly as if the Gold Coast were hidden away in the centre of Africa like French Equatorial Africa or the Belgian Congo. The Gold Coast was on the coast, and thanks to Nkrumah's strategy from the beginning, the struggle was now on the political map of the world. Furthermore the people were up in arms. The blood and brutality needed to suppress them would be no slight matter and would have worldwide repercussions. This was the heart of Nkrumah's: organise, organise, organise. And those who will attempt to follow his example would do well to meditate upon this, that you have to organise the people so completely that the government trembles at the prospect of violence. Without this, non-violent non-co-operation opens the way to bloody retribution. After the general strike in 1950 and the election, any such retribution was dangerous. Russia would take the injustice to the United Nations or to St Peter himself. Under its direction the communist parties of the world would make the welkin ring with it, and the subterranean movements and petty trading by which governments arrange the problems which can be arranged, the Kremlin, as it had before, would demand a heavy price for turning off the heat. In the climate of 1949 and 1950 there would be hell to pay at home, which would add to the complications abroad. Decisive, however, was this consideration to which all the others would contribute. The destruction of the movement in the Gold Coast by fire and sword would in all probability split the Commonwealth wide open, and that no government could afford. All this is not written in the light of the events which followed Eden's attempt to play the role of the 1856 Palmerston in 1956. These are the realities of colonial politics, particularly before the Ghana revolution reached its climax in 1951. I am not reconstructing in imagination when I say that these possibilities were soberly and realistically discussed by those who had to take the decisions. There are people around, not members of the government, who know this.

Nkrumah, on his side, had no alternative but to go into the government. The reasons that he gave and gives—the necessity of keeping out the merchant-lawyer stooges, the need to demonstrate the capacity of Africans to govern, etc.—are no doubt true. But at critical turning-points in history the writings and speeches of politicians rarely comprehend the fundamental motives of their actions. The situations are too new and too complicated for adequate expression. A wiser course is always to look at the alternatives objectively offered. If Nkrumah had not gone into the government, the only course open to him ultimately was a repetition of positive action, and positive action this time would be taken against a government which would be safely hidden behind African politicians. The question was not one of getting arms. The people were able, in a few minutes to take all the arms that were in the Gold Coast away from the police and the soldiers. But there remained looming over everything the immense military power of the British government which it would use if it were pushed to desperation. Nkrumah did not exclude the possibility of a final resort to positive action and said so loudly and clearly more than once. There were close friends and advisers who believed that in this attempt at infighting with the British government he was sure to lose. But after all circumstances had been taken into consideration, a territory in tropical Africa (not Morocco, Tunisia or Algeria) should allow itself to be driven to the resort of arms only as a last and unavoidable extremity just so long as the metropolitan power remains stable and in full control of its own government.

But here some resentful Englishman will say: "Surely you are carrying this too far. We are willing to accept the basis from which you begin, and though not necessarily to accept your conclusions, at least to understand how things look from over there. Agreed that our government failed entirely to see and understand what the people of the Gold Coast were doing between 1948 and 1951; yet you yourself admit that all this was new. After the general election they accepted the obvious and thenceforward worked out with Nkrumah the procedure of independence. Some of the old colonial officials no doubt found it hard to adjust to the new conditions, but they were new and sudden. Politics is not mathematics. Everybody cannot change to such new conditions overnight. That sort of thing was inevitable. In any case it was worked out. Nkrumah himself had not only made official speeches. He has written an autobiography and there he seems to take a view of this more sane, more balanced, and looking to the future rather than to the past. I have gone along with you so far even with a certain sympathy, but what you are saying now is impossible to accept, and in fact it is not only mischievous but manifestly untrue."

Very well, then. Let us see.

On 11 May Sir Charles Arden-Clarke, Governor of the Gold Coast from 1949 to March 1957, was leaving Ghana. The Ghana government presented him with gifts and a ceremonial banquet. After paying the usual tribute to Sir Charles, this is how Nkrumah continued:

> Much credit has quite properly been accorded to him in the press and elsewhere for the attainment of our independence. I am happy that this is so for without him our struggle would have been a far more bitter one, a more violent one, and one calling for even greater sacrifices on the part of us all.
>
> But I know that Sir Charles as an honest man himself will agree wholeheartedly with me when I say that when honours are handed out, those who should rank first and foremost are the members of the Convention People's Party, the pioneers and the footsloggers of the National Independence Movement. And I say with all emphasis that without the Convention People's Party there could not have been any independence for this country.
>
> For let it never be imagined for a moment that our independence was given to us for the mere asking. Every hour, every precious minute of this our glorious freedom was fought for relentlessly and untiringly by them. We have won independence and founded a modern state.
>
> The end we have reached has been attained at the price of suffering self-denial and patient work.

Nkrumah is a man of great generosity of spirit, and it is common talk in Ghana that even in internal party relations, except where political principle is involved, he is a soft rather than a hard man. Yet he found it necessary to say to a man whom he has genuinely liked exactly what I said at the beginning of this chapter: " . . . let it never be imagined for a moment. . . . Every hour, every precious minute . . . was fought for relentlessly and untiringly." Nkrumah continues:

> There were times, of course, when stumbling blocks came hurtling out of the Colonial Office diplomatic bag and caused each of us to have doubts

about the sincerity of the other, but because of his genuine sympathy and understanding of the demands and aspirations of the people it was not difficult for us to patch up our differences and get back on an even keel.

I am quite sure that nobody can even appreciate the amount of patience and sacrifice that the underground work of independence demanded. Perhaps I will one day write my memoirs of that period, if I am lucky enough to find a publisher courageous enough to publish them.

For Nkrumah to use here the phrase "underground work" in reality says everything. The word is used usually for work done secretly away from the police and spies of the state. The work up to the election of 1951 was open to the sky. Nkrumah did not let the cat out of the bag but opened the bag sufficiently to let people know that there was a very strange animal inside:

As a tiresome and meddlesome pest tormenting and challenging the strength of the British lion, I expected that I should be anxiously watched as I gradually closed in for the final attack. But the day came when I began to wonder seriously whether I was the sole object of interest in the game and whether in fact Sir Charles was not himself being eyed suspiciously by those above him.

Nkrumah also chose this conspicuous occasion to give a warning to the civil servants who remained behind now that Sir Charles was going. This was, please to remember, six years after the general election. I give this part of the speech as it was reported in the *Daily Graphic* of Accra:

As a free and independent people, we want to make it understood that we will warmly welcome those of our British friends who wish to continue to work for us. But we expect them to go the whole way with us and to give of their utmost in the best interests of Ghana.

The people of Ghana, the British public and the world had been deluged with speeches and writings and gestures (quite a number of them by Nkrumah himself) about the joint collaboration and the Nkrumah government and the British government which had led to independence. Now Nkrumah had blown this fiction sky-high. Sir Charles took up the challenge. Here is the report from the *Daily Graphic*:

He said the Prime Minister, as the leader of a great party, had singled out one particular section of that team which won independence for a special commendation.

Sir Charles then paid tribute and expressed his high sense of gratitude to members of the country's public service for their loyalty, skill, energy, encouragement and whole-hearted devotion during his tenure of office both in the Gold Coast and the new state of Ghana.

Ghana, Sir Charles maintained, had inherited a splendid public service. He described it as a service "deeply imbued with the tradition of devotedly serving the government" and "a service where the personal political sympathies of its members are kept in proper restraint."

The Governor-General observed that Ghana public service had gained its skill the hard way, not by studying in schools in public administration but by wrestling daily with the practical problems of government.

Sir Charles recalled the independence celebrations two months ago, and said that it was unlikely that they could have celebrated them without the support, loyalty, efficiency and steadfast devotion to duty of public servants.

Continuing, he warned that the tasks that awaited the government of independent Ghana were formidable.

He told his audience that there needed be no ground for anxiety if the Ghana public service could, as he knew it would, maintain and even improve the qualities which had earned it so excellent a reputation.

Sir Charles spoke in vain. Within a few days of this dialogue, some dozens of British civil servants had resigned.

I have spent some time on this last public appearance together of two men who had worked together for six years, and on whom the success of the venture, such as it was, depended. Later I shall have to try to give some political estimate of this last representative of the settled policy of Her Majesty's Government in the Gold Coast. As soon as one is rid of the unspeakable foolishness that the British government in 1951 began to "hand over" the colony to the people, it will be understood in what a cruel position he was placed. It is the cant and hypocrisy of the myth, here at its thickest, which obscures the true significance of the role he played and the exceptional powers and character which it demanded. He deserves well and very well of the British people for preserving the British government from the risk of adventures in which the character of the British people would have been indelibly besmirched.

Of Sir Charles, Nkrumah said at the dinner, "Another man in his position during these critical moments might well have created a national crisis and have bred a hatred and contempt in this country for the British people."

That is true. And this strange crossing of swords in the open at the very end of the association (and it has its pathetic sides) is the evidence bursting irresistibly to the surface of the long gruelling catch-as-catch-can which lasted for six years in the underground depths below. I hope that by this time my hypothetical English reader, the man of liberal views, is ready to go on, even if still a little suspicious and somewhat disgruntled.

The British government and Europeans, in Ghana and at home, were fighting. They did not know in 1951 even the little that they had learnt by 1957.

Their methods can be subdivided under three heads, though no single one excluded another. They were:

a. To fight for the maintenance of power inside the ministries against the ministers and the cabinet. This was of necessity guerrilla warfare, every man fighting his own particular battle in the circumstances in which he found himself. There were some who have since resigned, others who stayed to fight and yet others who adapted themselves to the new situation and worked with enthusiasm. But on the whole they were fighting a losing battle.

b. The second method was far more dangerous. It was to stir up and encourage opposition and disorder so as to prepare the justification for an authoritarian intervention by the British government. Nkrumah says categorically: "And I could at one time almost guarantee that if there was any movement afoot against the government, every attempt was made on the part of the Civil Service to enhance the opposition against the government."

c. This was the worst of all, because it was carried out by all including even those who would peremptorily have rejected any participation in (a) or (b). It took the form of imposing upon the people and government of Ghana the forms, legalities, shapes, safeguards, committees, and above all, the objectives, procedures, morals and moralisms of British parliamentary democracy, not excluding prayers in the Assembly, the mace and a Loyal Opposition. The plain and simple diehards among the officials, the disrupters and intriguers could be dealt with. But this was an opponent as intangible as the myth. Nkrumah and the people could not fight it on equal terms because they had nothing to fight it with. The British people, the people of the United States, the people of France had at various critical stages of their evolution worked out their own constitutions and amended or repealed them in accordance with their own internal relations, historical past and perspectives of the future. The people of the Gold Coast were well on the way towards doing just that as late as February 1951. But as soon as the struggle became internal, the revolutionary impetus was lost, and constitutions are created by revolutions, not by jurists. Nkrumah tried to bring the people in by requesting organisations to send in their constitutional proposals and even holding a constitutional conference. That could be no substitute for a revolutionary constituent assembly that would begin from the premise that the old government was finished and that its first task was to make a new one to suit itself. Nkrumah knew this very well. His autobiography, for the most part an easy and genial book, is prefaced by a harsh statement which contains within it the problem which a constituent assembly would have had before it from the very beginning:

The economic independence that should follow and maintain political independence demands every effort from the people, a total mobilisation of brain and manpower resources. What other countries have taken three hundred years or more to achieve, a once dependent territory must try to accomplish in a generation if it is to survive. Unless it is, as it were, "jet-propelled," it will lag behind and thus risk everything for which it has fought.

Capitalism is too complicated a system for a newly independent nation. Hence the need for a socialist society. But even a system based on social justice and a democratic constitution may need backing up, during the period following independence, by emergency measures of a totalitarian kind.

The word "total" would have done better than totalitarian, without its evil implications. But this new people with its peculiar social system, its immense tasks, the dangers which face it from its internal contradictions alone, has been strait-jacketed in a British constitution before it could take a single hesitant step. Justification for it there was none because by 1951 it should have been clear that if the people of the Gold Coast had one national gift, it was for politics. In the organisation of the Convention People's Party, a creative adaptation of the most advanced political ideas of Western civilisation to their own environment and needs, they had created by far the most important political instrument that has yet resulted from the European contact with tropical Africa.

PART II

| | | | |

Comrade Van der Pol, Ladies and Gentlemen:

We have here this evening Mr C. L. R. James, Secretary of the West Indian Federal Labour Party which is the governing party of the Federation. Mr James is also editor of *The Nation*, the official organ of the People's National Movement. Now he is an author and we're very fortunate to have him here this evening to give us a talk on a subject which I think is very thought-provoking indeed. The topic is "Imperialism and Underdeveloped Countries: Who are the Backward Ones?" Now, ladies and gentlemen, I give you Mr James.[1]

Comrade Chairman and friends:

For many years now I have been a supporter of the revolution that has been taking place in Ghana and of the policies which have flowed from that revolution. I have defended it and advocated its policies in many countries of the world but I always looked forward to the time when I should stand before an audience in Ghana and tell them what I think of the political course their country and their leaders have been following. This therefore for me today is a memorable occasion, and it is memorable for one particular reason. All who look with a certain contempt and believe what was being done in Ghana was being exaggerated today at this very moment will learn for the first time that with the independence of Ghana and with the establishment of the All-African People's Conference a new force has entered into world politics, and is now making its weight felt in that terrible disturbance in the Belgian Congo in which soldiers of Africa's Ghana will be able to. [Loud applause] And if my topic is "Imperialism and Underdeveloped Countries: Who are the Backward Ones?" that is the first example I want to give you. Who are the backward ones in the Belgian Congo today? Those who, having misgoverned that country for over sixty years, leave it in a state of disorder and not only leave it but leave behind elements who are trying to destroy the unity which they themselves built up in their own interests; or Roy Welensky over in the Federation of Rhodesia who is intriguing and corrupting in order to win over Katanga to call itself an independent state which he will control? Who are the advanced and who are the backward ones, they, or those elements in the Belgian Congo who are striving for the unity and independence of the Congo and those elements outside, the members of the African states, who are striving to establish some kind of order and progress in that territory? Who are the advanced and who are the backward ones? Between imperialism on the one hand and the underdeveloped countries on the other?

Now the first point I would like to make is that the policies which have been associated with Ghana and your great political leader are already established as policies for the emancipation of Africa. That is undoubtedly true, and that is something we all have to be proud of. What I want to establish this evening is that these policies if followed by the great labour and socialist movements of the world are the policies which could lead not only to the emancipation of Africa but to the emancipation of the whole of modern society from the terrible evils from which they are suffering at the present time. [Applause]

Nkrumaism it is called, and I am quite ready to call it Nkrumaism because he is the originator. Nkrumaism claims that every vestige of colonialism must be wiped away from every corner of Africa. [Loud applause] That is a policy for Africa. What I want to say is that if that policy were adopted by the labour and socialist elements of the most advanced countries of the world it will not roll over Africa alone but it will lead to the emancipation of all oppressed peoples and classes in every section of the globe. [Applause]

Nkrumah claims, Nkrumaism claims that there must be a union of all the independent states of Africa and he goes further to state in the constitution of Ghana that the constitution of Ghana is so organised that if need be the sovereignty, the national sovereignty which has been fought for and for which so many have suffered will be given up in the interest of a United States of Africa. [Applause] My friends, I am an international socialist and I have studied as was necessary the history of the world socialist movement. Never before to my knowledge, never before in the most advanced political circles has any state ever declared that it is ready to abandon national sovereignty in the interests of a continent. [Loud applause and shouts] They talk about the United States of Europe. They form a Common Market. They have an Iron and Steel Community. They cry about the need for unity. They are prepared to make all sorts of advances, but at one point they stop. Each one is prepared to fight to the death to preserve their own national sovereignty, and in this respect the policy of Ghana which also I gather has been followed by the policy of Guinea stands as a beacon light in the political development of the modern world. [Loud applause]

Nkrumaism states further that it will not in one single iota join or submit itself to or support the two monstrous blocs of imperialism which today hang over the world like a monster threat which threatens to destroy us. In other words it will have nothing whatever to do with either the East bloc or the West bloc. Such a policy carried out in London, in Moscow, in Washington, in Paris, in other parts of the world, could lead to the emancipation of the world from the terrible threat which is hanging over it. In that respect the policy that is being proposed by Nkrumaism is not the policy of a backward country. It is the political policy of one of the most politically advanced countries in the world at large. [Applause] Nkrumaism states that it will repudiate nuclear warfare of any kind as a modern barbarism. Nkrumaism states that it will oppose the establishment of bases of any kind of military organisations on the continent of Africa. Nkrumaism states that it proposes to form a nonnuclear club of governments and that they will resist and oppose in every possible way the terrible threat of nuclear warfare which is being held over the world at the present time and which may lead to the destruction of humanity. Nkrumaism goes further. It calls upon all the states of Africa to train people who will take direct action against any state which attempts to establish or to test any kind of nuclear fission on the African continent. And it goes still further. I don't want to say that the Ghana government does this, but the CPP, the Convention People's Party, this political party has taken steps to give in Ghana aid and comfort to all the freedom fighters from Africa and other parts of Africa, one of the greatest revolutionary steps that has been taken for many years. My friends, I want to tell you: I have written, and there are people here who know it, a history of the Communist International. It began with the study of Marx. It went on to the study of the Second International which originated and was inspired by Engels, and it went on to make a close study of the Third International which was established by Lenin. I want to say here and I want to say it most emphatically that when the time comes and the history of international socialism and the revolution to overthrow capitalism is written at the head of course will be names like Marx, there will be names like Engels, there will be the name of Lenin. But a place will have to be found for Kwame Nkrumah . . . [drowned by applause and shouts]. I state, as one who has studied the history of the revolutionary movement, that at the present time those policies that I have enunciated for you, those policies that you know spring from here, are fundamental policies for the emancipation of all classes and all oppressed peoples in the world. And that today—I don't say yesterday, I don't say tomorrow, but I say today, the centre of the world revolutionary struggle is here in Accra, Ghana. [Loud applause]

Advanced and backward countries. I know how backward we are in certain things and I'm going to speak about that later. But I want to speak now and to establish the things in which we are advanced. I want to say a word about South Africa. There are many people who will subscribe money in court cases in South Africa, who will write and speak about the oppression of the African people in South Africa, and who will denounce the South African government. That is good and that is helpful. But there is one thing that they cannot do. They are unable to say plainly and clearly that the present troubles in South Africa can only be solved when there is a nationalist African government in South Africa. Now why is it they cannot say that, despite all the sympathy that they have for the African people and their sufferings? They say this: in South Africa it is the white people who have the most widespread education, who have great knowledge of science, who are very skilful in the organisation of industry, who possess to a substantial degree all the elements of civilisation and culture and to the extent that the Africans have it, it is only a few of them, it is not their fault, but nevertheless we have to face the fact that these elements of civilisation, knowledge and scientific knowledge are in the hands of the white people. And therefore they state whatever happens we must struggle in order to prevent the oppression and to help the education of the Africans but we have to accept the fact that they the whites are the ones who must continue to rule. My friends, I repudiate that conception utterly and this is my reason. If you look at South Africa today undoubtedly this great amount of knowledge, science, etcetera, is in the hands of the white people. But the black people of South Africa have already shown two things. One, their capacity to learn, and number two their readiness and anxiety and willingness to take the road of modern civilisation. [Applause]

Now let us look at what will happen in the next fifteen to twenty years. If a South African government is established, a nationalist native government, we can be certain that in fifteen or twenty years great progress will have been made in education, they will have learnt the processes of industry, they will have mastered many of the aspects of modern science, and they will show that they can carry on the tradition that has been established by the South

African whites without the tyranny and oppression and the constant disorders which are characteristic of the government of South Africa today. That is the perspective in twenty years' time. Furthermore there is a substantial white population in South Africa and I have never heard any reputable African nationalist say that if he or his party or his people came to power they would destroy and utterly ruin whatever whites were there. Ghana is an example that they can live here and have their lives as they are accustomed to be. In other words, the whites in South Africa will have their place in an African state. That is the perspective of a South African native government whatever may be the deficiencies of the South African people today. But what is the perspective if the South African white government continues? It means continuous oppression, it means continuous and cruel efforts to suppress the African people who it is clear will no longer be suppressed. It means that that disorder that is going on there will be doubled and trebled and intensified as the years go on. A national scandal in South Africa, a continental scandal in Africa and an international scandal which makes ashamed all decent people in every part of the world, that is what is going to go on if that white South African government continues and as sure as day there will come a time when the South Africans will revolt; then the states of Africa and other states will have to come to their rescue, the continent will go up in flames, there will be, to the great regret of all of us, great massacres of white people. Isn't it clear that the future of progress, of democracy, of harmony lies with a black South African government and with those who are there now despite all the civilisation and culture and science and knowledge that they have? [Applause]

That is what I mean by asking the question. "Imperialism and the Underdeveloped Countries: Who are the Backward Ones?" You know, I have lived in Europe a long time and I have lived in the United States. At the present time I am doing some work in the West Indies for the local party there, and that's why I am wearing what would otherwise be this fantastic shirt. This emblem is the balizier, a local plant, and the People's National Movement with a very powerful leader, Dr Eric Williams is the head of it. I work for them and edit their newspaper, and I'm sure that you feel happy that in coming here to speak to you this afternoon I wear the emblem of the party that I am serving at the present time. [Applause]

Now, in Europe and the United States I have frequently been in very close contact with people who are sympathetic to Africa and African aspirations. You see, I don't bother with the enemies of Africa. They are enemies, they are over there, that is no problem; we just have to fight them to the end, that is all.

But it is those who are friendly and who are genuinely friendly that we have to concern ourselves with. And I notice their attitude is something like this. You must have read it in the papers. You must have heard it: "Well, we have to see how the newly independent countries, the underdeveloped countries that have just come into nationalist power, emancipation, how they will be able to develop themselves as modern civilised states." They are always looking upon us, although with sympathy, with a certain critical eye and their whole attitude is, "Well, we have shown what we are able to do so let us examine if these whom we have had to train and develop, if they are able to establish anything corresponding to what we have been able to do." That is their attitude. And I want to deal with it because it is their folly, their superficial view of society which leads them to take what is essentially an absurd attitude to the problems of the underdeveloped countries.

My friends, France, England, Holland and Belgium are undoubtedly today, at least yesterday they were great nations. They have made marvellous industrial progress, they have added to culture and civilisation. How did they begin? They began more or less about four hundred years ago, 1560 or thereabouts. And when they began they had about three or four hundred years of steady progress in industry, in the towns of those territories, they had built up accumulation of capital. Nobody had taken it away from them, they had it themselves and some of their merchants had learnt and studied business, so that they were capable businessmen. That is what they started with. But there was more to come. Soon they began to discover how to exploit America. And gold and other products came from America to help to develop them and came also from the Far East. And then a little later they discovered the greatest gold mine of all, the slave trade from Africa. And it is established today that for Britain and France in particular the greatest contributing force to the industrial empires that they have built up have been the profits that they made from the slave trade and slavery. What are we starting with? We have no accumulation. They took it all while they were here. We have nobody to exploit. We have no people whom we can raid and sell them for profit and make them work to accumulate wealth. I have to tell some of them often, please, when you look at us in this way, please remember all the advantages that you had and all the advantages that you took in order to establish what you have today. Your attitude should be a little more sympathetic and a little more humble. Look at that industrial power the United States today. It is a wonderful industrial structure. But how was it built? First of all they had a magnificent continent. And I don't wish to say a word here which would imply that the

American people are not a very vital and energetic and able people. Not at all. Nevertheless, when the great days of their industrial development began after the Civil War, capital poured from Great Britain into the United States by the million in order to help them develop what they have today. And something more important than capital. From every single country in Europe, the ablest, the most energetic, the most skilful, those who loved democracy, those who felt that they wanted to go to a new country where they could get better opportunities, they poured into America by the million. And it is their energy and vitality and their skill aided by the capital from Europe and what was already there that helped to build up that big industrial power that we see today.

When we get some technical skill from abroad we have to pay for it through the nose. You know that, don't you? Any capital that comes from abroad, we get it in little scraps and bits, nobody comes here in order to make a place for themselves, in order to develop their talents and help the country along. I have often told friends of mine, if you all had started where the underdeveloped countries are starting today, I wonder where you would be today. One things is certain. You would not be casting snide remarks, as we say in the United States, upon the difficulties and problems faced by the underdeveloped countries.

My friends, you may have seen in the paper yesterday that I told a reporter that there are some elements of colonialism still lurking in the minds even of independent countries. And as long as our speakers and our writers and our people are not able to speak to the members of the advanced countries and show them the advantages that they have had and the difficulties of the underdeveloped countries, and make them understand that we, in the struggles that we are undoubtedly having, do not by any means admit that what they have done we are unable to do: as long as we are not doing that and throwing it back in their faces, we are still being guilty, however great revolutionaries we may be, of keeping a little bit of colonialism in our minds. We have to throw it back at them and make them to understand that we understand our difficulties but we understand too the advantages that enabled them to develop as they have done. [Applause]

That is what I mean by saying, who are the advanced and who are the backward ones? They speak of aid, of capital loans, of technical aid and various things of the kind. And some of the people are undoubtedly very sincere. But an economist two years ago made a calculation, and I want to give it to you to remember. These advanced countries control the prices of commodities produced by the underdeveloped countries. And they control the prices of the manufactured goods that they sell to the underdeveloped countries too. Over the last few years, as you know, prices have gone down for the kind of stuff that we produce. This economist has calculated, and if anybody doubts it I can give him the reference, that the underdeveloped countries have lost nearly $600,000 million in solid values owing to the depression of the prices of the goods that they produce. And he went on to say that against this $600 billions, as they would say in the United States, that have been lost by these communities, all the technical aid and all the loans and all the gifts when you add them up together, they amount to not even a shadow of the vast amounts that have been lost by the depression of prices. In fact it would be comparatively true to say that if they had given no aid, if they had given no technical assistance, if they had given no loans but they had kept the prices up so that the people would get what they were getting for it, we would have been better off today than we are at the present time. That is the kind of problem that we face. I want to say with that magnificent marxist and ally of your president, Sekou Touré, we are aware of the slenderness of our resources, but our will to conquer is boundless as the sea. That is the attitude that we have to take, to recognise the difficulties that we face but not to be demoralised by them. Not to be afraid of them. And above all not to let other people stand aside and look upon us critically as if we were some experiment and they were watching if we were going to be successful or not. That we will not stand.

Now I want to deal with the internal problem of the underdeveloped country. On the external field not only do we have nothing to be ashamed of but in political insight and in moral superiority of the attitudes that we adopt we are an example to the rest of the world and not in any way backward.

But when we come to the internal situation there is no doubt about it that we face severe difficulties. I want to go into them this afternoon because I have spent about two years in the West Indies, watching this, working with them and editing a paper. I am fairly familiar with what is taking place in India and other parts of the world and some of the conclusions that I will give you are of a general nature. You will be able to decide whether what I am saying applies to Ghana or not.

There are two points, two ways in which the difficulties of the internal situation of the underdeveloped countries can be resolved. I want you to get the distinction that I am going to make very clearly. The first is and most of them accept it, that they wish to establish a socialist pattern of society. In that respect they are absolutely right, they mean to get socialism if they can and they take care however to say, "to establish a socialist pattern of society." But the second point is no question of pattern at all. The salvation of the economy, the salvation of the society, all aspects of the life of an underdeveloped community in my opinion depend upon the establishment of a completely socialist party. There must be no misunderstanding between the difference between the two. One can only be for the time being a socialist pattern. But the party, the leading party in every country, must be completely, a hundred per cent north, east, south and west, a socialist party. These are the two fundamental requirements for the development of the economy in a harmonious manner.

Now why is it we say "a socialist pattern of society" and not say, point-blank, "socialism"? We should be careful in dealing with these matters to call things by their correct names, and classic socialism, and it is always good to begin with the classic definition, demands a very highly developed technological and industrial society. It demands people who for some years have been familiar with the latest developments of modern science and technology. It demands a population which is in its majority industrial workers or if they are far more developed in co-operative and in the farming community must use mechanics, must be mechanised almost as much as the economy of the industrial sector. Now none of the underdeveloped countries have got that. And in fact that is why they are underdeveloped. And that is why we are careful and I notice this Convention People's Party is careful to say, a socialist pattern of society. [Applause] But not because we cannot have complete socialism immediately it means that we must have capitalism. I do not know a single underdeveloped country which does not look at capitalism with suspicion and in most of them they look at it with hostility and are determined to use it only to the extent that they cannot avoid it. What is the picture of classic capitalism? Capitalism produces for profit. It produces where it likes, when it likes, how it likes, governed always by the necessity for profit. If a community wants a hundred thousand workers' houses but capitalism finds that it can make profit by building five thousand houses for rich merchants and bureaucrats, capitalism builds five thousand houses for rich merchants and bureaucrats. It does not concern itself about houses for a hundred thousand workers. Furthermore capitalism always has and always will seek either to bend the government of the country in which it is functioning to its will or it seeks to corrupt it to make it pliable so that government measures can help capitalism. I am glad to say that, following the policy of Ghana, I have been glad to note that the policy in Ghana is a model to many other countries and is being followed out with infinitely greater difficulty of course like India and Burma. The policy of the government of Ghana as I understand it, and I have read as much as I can and discussed it very closely, is to say quite frankly to capitalism, particularly foreign capitalism: we need you; we need the advanced technology and capital that you have; we wouldn't rub it in that you need us as much as we need you; let that stay for the time being. But we need you. We are prepared to let you come in. We invite you in. We know you want your profits; you can make your profits. But you are not going to produce what you like, why you like and when you like as long as you are functioning in this country. [Loud applause] We are going to tell you what we want, we are going to tell you how we want it and we are going to tell you what we don't want.

Number one, you will have to teach our young people, our sons and daughters, the techniques that you are bringing in here, because we don't want you in here indefinitely. We want you to teach us so that as rapidly as possible our own people will be able to take control over what you brought. If you don't like that, don't come. [Loud applause]

The second point is this. The government of Ghana is the greatest employer of workers in the country. It is so in most if not all of the underdeveloped countries. The workers are either directly employed by government or in industries which are supervised or controlled by government. The underdeveloped country says to the capitalist coming in: we have a standard to set for the treatment of our workers. It is not only a question of wages, it is a question of the human conditions and human relations of the labour movement in this new country of ours. We are going to set a pattern and you capitalists, you have to follow this pattern. You are not going to be able to treat workers as you all treated them when they were defenceless in the early days of your nationhood. Our workers today, poor as they are, have established unions. Our workers' leaders go to the International Labour Organisation at Geneva and they work out standards and they bring them back. It is very hard for us to maintain them but we are going to try. And you, Mr Capitalist, you will have to treat your workers in this country in the way that we are treating our workers. [Applause]

And finally the government of the underdeveloped country tells the capitalist this: we are seeking to build socialism. We know all the difficulties; you need not tell us. But we are going to as far as it is possible to plan our economy. We are going to decide what is the public sector and what is the private sector. Those spheres in which we allow capitalism to operate and those spheres in which the government is going to develop the industry or hand it over to the corporations which are being supervised by the government, and all capital that enters here has to submit itself to the terms of the government to the building of a socialist pattern of society. To put it crudely, the underdeveloped countries are inviting capital in, and capital will come as it is certain of a certain amount of profit, but it is telling capital quite plainly that it is using capital in order to destroy all the capital in a country like Ghana and the other underdeveloped countries. That is the policy which is being followed. And that is the policy, I am glad to state, that is in the minds of those who are ruling in Ghana. It is a policy which corresponds in intention to the magnificent political policies which you have developed in regard to the independence of Africa and world politics as a whole. But my friends, I have to tell you that this policy is not easy to carry out. This policy is beset with terrible dangers. It is a policy which can even be defeated. And that is why I say that you need a completely socialist party, a socialist party, in order to help the people and the government to carry out the plans for a socialist pattern of society. This is the last point I'm going to make and I want to make it as carefully as possible so that you will understand it. When I was here in 1957, I got certain impressions of what was taking place. Since I have come back here in 1960 there has been great progress. The situation however has changed and I notice now what was not noticeable then, a tremendous concern with bribery and corruption in government. I have seen it in the newspapers and people are talking to me about it and people who are patriotic citizens are talking about it because they want their country in that respect also to be as advanced as any other country in the world. And that is why I want to go into it in some detail. So that you will be able to check it with your experience, and perhaps at another time let me know if what I have said has been of some value to you.

The underdeveloped countries today are not suffering from dishonest men, men who like to grab and men who are weak in character and are unable to resist temptation. If it was that alone it would be very simple to deal with. The police would see after them and that would be very easy. This question of bribery and corruption which in one way or another affects every underdeveloped country in the world today (and some developed ones too, but that is their problem, we needn't go into that), this question is a social and economic question. You know, we have to study very carefully the history of those developed nations, because they will teach us a lot about ourselves. What has happened for instance in Ghana, and in the West Indies and these other places, is that a society was being sat upon by people who restricted men of ability and energy and capacity. The monarch and the aristocracy used to oppress the ordinary people in much the same way as the imperalists and racialists oppress the colonial peoples. A great revolution took place; that oppression, those restrictions were broken and the nation started afresh, so to speak. But the energy, the power, the desire to improve, the desire to establish yourself, went then into private capitalism, free enterprise. Follow me closely. Once the chips were down and the nation moved forward, most of its force and the energies of its most dynamic men went into free enterprise and into industry, to finance and to banking. When the French revolution took place in the eighteenth century, the same thing happened. Once the privileges of the aristocracy and the monarchy and the clergy were broken down, again you have this tremendous development of free enterprise, capitalism, industry, men making money, establishing themselves. The same thing happened in the United States. But when in the underdeveloped country today the privileges of an aristocracy are broken down and everything is thrown open to men who have been bursting for generations for the opportunity to develop themselves, they don't go into free enterprise. Where do they go? They go into politics and go into the government, because the government today is the most powerful determining economic factor in the country. So that all that disorder and struggle and crisis and pressure which took place in free industry, free enterprise, capitalism in these countries, now are transferred into the governments. That is why political struggles in underdeveloped countries are so fierce. Because whoever wins the political battle wins the economic battle as well, because it's the economy that is directed by the government that is the most powerful force in the country. So that we must look upon a whole social group of men just out of restriction, difficulty, prevention from being able to act as they want: as soon as they get the opportunity they are thrown into the government, and the government is the economic director of the life of the nation. What should take place outside now takes place inside the government, and that is the reason why bribery and corruption affects all underdeveloped countries to the degree that they do.

Now that is not all. International capital knows that you are trying to establish a socialist pattern of society. International capital has dealings with the heads of government missions and the heads of the economic life of the country. And they systematically try to bring these people under their control. So that you not only have to be an honest man in that you do not seek to get bribes and to be corrupted. You have to be doubly and trebly an honest man because these fellows are seeking to bribe you and corrupt you all the time, because that is the only way they can control or affect the economic life of the country. And every little capitalist, every little moneylender in the place, he also is sympathetic to this sort of business and therefore you have the tremendous difficulties from which we are suffering. The point that I want to make clear is that it is not in the nature of the African to be subject to bribery and corruption. It is not in the nature of the West Indian to be subject to bribery and corruption. It is not in the nature of the Indian. It is the particular economic and social conditions at the stage of development in the underdeveloped countries that produces these conditions as they produced them in every single advanced country today when this particular historical situation was being gone through.

That is the essential point. And how to cure it? Nothing else but the socialist party. A party based upon the workers and the advanced farmers, the youth, NASSO, intellectuals who are honest and are determined to do all that they can for their country. That is the political party which must see to it that the government runs the way that the government says that it intends to go. Your great president, and he is a very great political leader indeed, at the tenth congress of the party, he stated you remember that the government did not give any power to the party. It was the party that gave the power to the government, that henceforth the party was supreme. You remember that at that conference. I want to go a little further. History has shown that at times like these when the government is going in one direction and all sorts of pressure are being placed upon it, it isn't only that the party is supreme. It is that the party has to fight for that supremacy. And you have a constant tension between the party and the government, and in that battle it is necessary that at all critical moments the party, having worked out its programme, should prevail on the government if it sees the government going in any direction that it should not go.

Every great revolution has faced this problem. And sometimes the party has been defeated. The party has to study the foundations of scientific socialism. It must set a high standard of morality for itself. It must study the experience of past countries. It must study what is taking place in the underdeveloped countries. It must scrutinise with the utmost vigilance and severity not only the actions of the government but the actions of itself, because that is the only way it will have the moral authority to bring the government back if it shifts from the line. Because the government is in the middle of the battle. And therefore it must make compromises and have difficulties. But the party is able to stand aside and observe and say, you are going a little too far here, we have made a retreat there, let us accept it and so keep the country along the lines of socialism at home and the success of the international socialist movement abroad.

My friends, I began by saying in what way you all stood way in advance of the advanced countries today in the way of political ideas and political policies. We have to admit the fact that as far as economic development is concerned, we are behind. We have a long way to go. But I want to add this, that in regard to the strength and the morality and the intelligence and the power of the socialist party, there is no reason why, despite the backward economy, you cannot here build a socialist party which will be as much of an inspiration and a beacon light to people abroad as I know your political policies are and as time goes on will be.

Long live the Convention People's Party of Ghana.

Long live Nkrumaism.

And long live the African revolution.

[Standing ovation]

1 Ward Street,
Tunapuna,
Trinidad,
West Indies.

21 July 1962.

Osagyefo the President
Dr Kwame Nkrumah
Christiansborg Castle
Accra
Ghana.

Dear President Nkrumah,

Allow me, for old acquaintance sake, to begin by informing you of one of those strange dramatic confrontations which I have always found indicate new and urgent historical reorientations.

Only a few days ago I drew the attention of the people of the West Indies to the fact that Dr Price Mars of Haiti, M. Aimé Césaire of Martinique, Marcus Garvey of Jamaica and George Padmore of Trinidad had been leading pioneers in the great movement for the redemption of Africa which had been imperishably established by the people of Ghana and yourself not fifteen years ago. These West Indians had found in Africa a field for the exercise of their powers which the West Indies did not afford. You will find it on page 171 of my book, *Party Politics in the West Indies.*

Now barely a week afterwards I find that an African repays the West Indies for the services rendered. Your letter to West Indian premiers and your interest and concern about the West Indian situation as expressed in your report to the National Conference of Freedom Fighters represent the very first intervention of non–West Indians into our sad situation which gives the West Indian people a view of their opportunities and responsibilities, which makes them aware of themselves as a political force in the great crises which today are shaking mankind. I well remember how in the days when Ghana was still the Gold Coast and you were an unknown African agitator you never once deviated from your view that the people of the Gold Coast could only succeed in their national emancipation if they became and felt themselves part of the worldwide movement towards human emancipation. That feeling the West Indians badly need today. I do not know that it could come from anyone with more national achievement, worldwide authority and personal force than yourself. I want to assure you that after four years residence and work in the West Indies I am convinced as I have said in my lecture in Jamaica in November 1959 that there are tens of thousands of young people in the West Indies who are of the same stamp as our late beloved collaborator and friend George Padmore.

Those are the reasons which have prompted me to publish the letter to the West Indian premiers and relevant material. For that I take full responsibility and if the publication is not exactly according to the highest principles of protocol, I am certain that you will understand fully if you do not officially approve.

In conclusion I want to make public in this letter that despite the constantly unexpected demands and requirements of contemporary politics on a national and international scale, you are one of the few of whom I can say that from the time I have known you, you have always had as your undeviating aim the emancipation from a subordinate position of the people of Africa and of African descent and your struggle for that emancipation in the context of worldwide events and the emancipation of the whole of humanity. I consider it not only an honour to us West Indians that you have made our troubles an integral part of your worldwide view. I believe that this intervention of yours will be the mark of our release from the mental shackles and limited outlook of colonialism and that the day is not too far distant when to the names of Marcus Garvey and George Padmore, the West Indian nation will be proud to add the name of Kwame Nkrumah.

To one of your habitually realistic scrutiny of the essentials of politics, I would like to add that it is my firm conviction that, contrary to the general belief, the West Indian people more than most people from underdeveloped countries have within their own hands assets and circumstances fully equal to their establishing themselves as a modern progressive people. I can think of little that would so assist us in making the break with colonialism as your continued interest in our welfare and the expression of that interest.

Believe me, Osagyefo, more than ever in the crowded past, I am thankful and happy to know that Africa has produced so distinguished a master of the general strategy and details of the politics of humanity in the inhuman world in which we live.

Yours as always,

[signed] C. L. R. JAMES.

The following two articles were first published in the Trinidad Evening News *in February 1964.*

My dear Francis,[1]

> This is a terrible business, bound to have effects far outside Ghana and in Ghana itself. I shall have to speak and write about it; people, not enemies, already are asking me along these lines—"Well, James, what have *you* to say?" But I will not say anything until I know what you have to say. I am not particularly concerned about the Chief Justice as I was not particularly concerned about Busia. What I am concerned about is the impact that Ghana and you are making on the world and on Africa. If even you are very occupied could you see that a secretary or Dorothy sends to me any relevant documents or particulars? I hope, my dear Francis, you have people around you able to tell you quite plainly what is now required from you. *It is quite possible that this unfortunate happening can be turned into a positive stage in the evolution of Ghana,* all Africa and in fact governments everywhere. If there is anything you think I can do, you know that I am at your service.

> Believe me, as always, your sincere supporter and friend,

> (signed) James

That letter is dated 14 December 1963. Today is 18 January. I have had no reply and therefore I make the letter public. I suppose it brings to an end an association of twenty years that I have valued more than most. I signed myself a sincere supporter of Nkrumah: a bad phrase. Nkrumah did not and does not need my support. I needed his. I have been and am concerned with and active in a lot of politics, one part of which was and is the expulsion of imperialism from Africa and the development of underdeveloped countries. In the expulsion of imperialism from Africa, a small group of us have been remarkably successful. It is by no chance that our fellow countryman George Padmore is called the father of African emancipation. In all this Nkrumah played a great role; he is one of the greatest of living politicians. I always appreciated the splendid work he was doing amid immense difficulties. When people pointed out what they considered negative aspects of his régime I held my peace because I knew the positive aspects, the immense positive aspects.

But when he was shot at the second time, I wrote to him hinting more than broadly that something was wrong with his régime which demanded serious attention, otherwise people don't shoot. I knew, I was certain I knew what was wrong, but it is not my business to go lecturing prime ministers. He did not seem to understand what I was telling him. I started to prepare a document, but events have overtaken me.

Whenever you deal with a grave political problem, you have to do two things. You have to analyse it, get to the roots and above all you have to say what to do. Otherwise you are just a cheap politician or worse still expressing yourself. In that letter the key sentence is this: "I hope, my dear Francis, you have people around you able to tell you quite plainly what is now required from you." That was as far as I could go in a first letter and at so great a distance. If I were nearer or if he or anyone else had replied I would have been unhesitating. All his closest supporters, the people he could trust and who trusted him, should have got together to tell him quite plainly, "Mr President, you cannot dismiss your Chief Justice after he has made a judgement from the Bench. Publicly declare that you made a mistake. You personally go to his house, make a public apology. We will try to get him to go on a long vacation and you go to the country and tell the people what has happened and why and what you think ought to be done now. That is it, Mr President. You continue with this dismissal and you dismiss us, all of us."

A prime minister who has not got people around him who can tell him that is living on borrowed time. If he hasn't got such people around him it is his misfortune and his fault. Worse still it is the misfortune of the people over whom he rules.

That is what concerned me from the start—the people of Ghana. They, under the leadership of Nkrumah, started and set the example for the more or less peaceful expulsion of imperialism from Africa—today Mr Macmillan talks of it as one of the achievements of his premiership that he is proudest of. OK with me. Credit is one of those rare commodities which grows greater the more that people claim it.

But the people of Ghana have made great history. I spoke to them in 1960. They applauded mightily when I reviewed what they had done, they listened intently and somewhat uncertainly as I began with what they had to do. I was quite confident, however, for I had submitted what I wanted to say, and got his OK, to Nkrumah beforehand. And when I was finished they stood to tell me what they thought. I will never forget it—I have a recording of the speech and the tremendous sustained applause of people who had heard things that they wanted to hear. That afternoon I knew they were uncertain of the future and needed someone to reassure them. I know that more than ever today. What did I tell them? What would I tell them today?

How has all this catastrophe overtaken the people of Ghana? First Nkrumah, like all the other African leaders, and Asian leaders too, has been fooling himself and a lot of other people with a dangerous fiction—its name is democratic socialism. As long as you don't take it too seriously, as Mr Manley, Sir Grantley Adams, Dr Jagan, Mr Nehru do not take it too seriously, it does no particular harm except to confuse a majority of voters on your behalf. But if like Nkrumah you do, and Nkrumah is a very serious, determined person, you end up with the totalitarian state—no democracy and no socialism.

Let us for the time being put socialism, democratic or one-party state socialism, way up on a shelf and get down to serious business trying to find out why this has happened to Ghana. We can learn something of great value to ourselves.

These African countries are backward countries. I know one which is offering any typist, passage, holidays and £3,000 a year, and you contract only for two years. The great body of the population is illiterate or semi-illiterate. Their native language is not English or French. That is the language of the government and the educated. The people for hundreds of years know, have in their bones, the tribal way of life, where the man and his family are responsible for the tribe and the tribe is responsible for the man and his family. They have developed not only a way of life, but a philosophy of life, a way of looking at the world.

Recently the statement has been made that there are no savage people any more: Western people once assumed that because the material life of primitive people was backward, their mental capacities were inferior and that they lacked social instinct for working out a view of themselves in relation to nature and to society. All such assumptions have been proved hopelessly wrong. We are daily astonished at the profundity and comprehensiveness of the philosophy of life worked out by so-called savages in relation to their specific national circumstances. Africans are not a primitive and not a Western people. Their whole historical experience makes them see and feel their world differently.

Now ruling these people are Africans but Africans dominated by the Western way of life and Western ways of thought. The best of them, and Nkrumah is one of the best, aim to westernise their country as fast as possible, bringing it up to date. Every step forward creates more and more Westernised Africans, who not only speak Western but live Western, the individual job, the bungalow, the television, the fridge, the trip abroad. In these new countries the government controls a substantial part of the economy. The Western world has not grown up that way. After a revolution like the French you had the career open to talents, that is to say, all sorts of careers, particularly business careers, were thrown open to and developed by new sections of society. But today in an underdeveloped country opportunity and power are concentrated in government, which means a Western way of life.

The worker in the factory follows his superiors and aims at as much of the same as he can get.

Thus the main social aim is to place yourself in a position away from the native mass and into the Westernised élite. The result is a ferocious political struggle, the breakdown of parliamentary government, an almost irresistible movement to the one-party state, the whole economic and social movement pushing in that direction. In such a society corruption of all kinds is inevitable.

The harder you drive for westernisation, modernisation, the more you create these conflicting forces. And Nkrumah has been driving hard, none harder anywhere. The statistics of economic development in Ghana are the most advanced in Africa. But, given the original conditions, every economic advance means social disruption. To a man in his position it would seem that the only thing to do is to drive on and if to go on means ruthless suppression of opposition, well, history and progress demand it.

I was in Ghana in 1957, and when I spoke to them in 1960 I hinted, merely hinted, at these problems. But they understood me. I knew that they felt I knew what was troubling them. But Nkrumah did not respond to my opening, in fact he asked me for my speech to publish it, I sent it to him and he never did.

Now the mess has overflowed. The question is: what to do? Luckily, an African, a man named Chisiza (he is dead) has written one of the finest documents in African society and politics ever written. During the last forty years I have not seen a finer political analysis and programme anywhere. Next time.

————

THEY NEVER SHOULD HAVE LET THIS YOUNG MAN DIE

This horrible mess in East Africa—a coup d'état in Zanzibar, followed by military revolts and British military intervention by request in Kenya, Tanganyika and Uganda—makes it more than ever urgent that you should know about Chisiza, the young African about whom I promised to write last week.

In the life and death of Chisiza is concentrated the past, present and future of Africa. Chisiza was a young African from Nyasaland who was killed in a motor accident when he was driving his own car, and there has never been any hint of foul play. He was a high functionary in the government of Dr Hastings Banda who was recognised by all who knew him as the most brilliant African they knew. Still, I do not look upon his death as purely an accident.

This is what I have heard. Chisiza, the week before he died, had headed a majority against Dr Banda in council. But Chisiza understood politics. He understood what it meant to be up against the Prime Minister—and the Prime Minister of an underdeveloped country. He was heard to say: "When we become independent I either go to jail or go into exile." He used to work from early morning until late at night and then drive home in an obviously reckless and dangerous manner.

I asked: "But didn't his party or his leaders give him a chauffeur and command him not to drive at night?" "No," was the reply. "Nobody bothered." I am not able to prove this, but the political-psychological situation is not a new one and is a well-known historical occurrence.

This young man could see what he was up against in Africa and I have no doubt in Nyasaland in particular. He did not commit suicide, but just worked around the clock, and drove home like mad in the early mornings.

I have a deep sympathy for Chisiza. What I do not forgive is the people who saw this going on and did not put an end to it. The cabinet should have told him: "You are risking your life in that car. Stop it. You listen or we will transfer you, make you a High Commissioner somewhere." I am so confident about what Chisiza thought (and about the mess Africa is in today) because he wrote it all down. As you read what he said, think of Nigeria, Ghana, Zanzibar and Tanganyika, Kenya and Uganda.

The British two-party system (so wrote Chisiza) is unsuited to Africa. It is useful as a democratic medium of expression. Don't abolish it, but for next ten years let the party that wins invite members of the opposition to form a national government. Chisiza understood politics in terms of people, not people in terms of politics. For example, Africans, he said, have grown up in a tribe where the whole family is responsible for an individual. When he gets an individual job in a city he and his wife and children are quite bewildered and need special care.

I here intervene to say that with this fact in mind the statistics proving that so many more Africans are working in factories leave out much that no statistics can tell us. Political leaders (wrote Chisiza) are not usually intelligent; although they think they are, they are often very mediocre personalities. They should learn humility. There are citizens in an African state far more intelligent and better educated than the politicians. They must take part and be made to take part in public affairs. Only Africans can lead Africa. But they should periodically get together with the best thinkers in Europe and seek to work out some adaptation of the African way of life and Western civilisation.

Africans had to work out a way that was neither the way of the West nor the way of the East. Furthermore, African leaders had to meet periodically and exchange ideas, experiences and economic prospects. Every African state should take as many young Africans as possible and systematically educate them in Western and African problems.

Finally, he wrote, Africans had to have something to believe in. He did not know what it was. It might be built up from Christianity, Islam, Communism, from everywhere—but Africa had to find some common belief.

This profound thinker and analyst produced and convinced the members of his country of the validity of what has been called the most brilliant plan of economic development ever put forward for an African state. That was his department—economic planning. But Africa (and other countries as well, but Africa in particular) will go crashing from precipice to precipice unless the plans for economic development are part of a deep philosophical concept of what the mass of the African people need.

That is where Nkrumah failed.

The countries known as underdeveloped have produced the greatest states-men of the twentieth century, men who have substantially altered the shape and direction of world civilisation in the last fifty years.[1] They are four in number: Lenin, Gandhi, Mao Tse-tung and Nkrumah. They are not merely gifted individuals and effective politicians. They of the underdeveloped must be seen against the background of the developed civilisation of their times. The very words underdeveloped and advanced need some definition. It is a commonplace of contemporary life to be horrified at the fact that the Hit-ler régime murdered six million Jews. That is only part of the gruesome his-tory. By 1941 Hitlerism ruled and tortured and massacred its enemies from the Bay of Biscay to Eastern Poland. Since the twentieth congress of the Rus-sian Communist Party, it is possible to say without dispute that stalinism was doing the same from Eastern Poland to Vladivostok. Thus a vast area of civilisation had degenerated into elementary barbarism, primitive cruelty and disregard of human life, of ordinary common decency. The rest of the advanced countries of Western civilisation need to be seen within the con-text of this frightful reality. For a century, the United States had perpetrated against millions of its citizens a civil and psychological brutality of which it itself is only now becoming fully aware. James Baldwin, popularly regarded at home as well as abroad as the effective spokesman against the century-old persecution of Negro Americans, has unequivocally stated that the problem is not a problem of the black skin—it is a sickness in American civilisation itself which has expressed and expresses itself in the persecution of the Negro population.

France killed eighty thousand in Madagascar and fought to the end to pre-serve its domination of Indochina, Morocco, Tunis and Algeria. Just a few miles across the Mediterranean, France killed a million Algerians, a million of a total population of ten million people, equivalent in terms of the United States to the extermination of the Negro population. Obviously the need of French civilisation at all costs to continue its domination was very great. The great mass of the British people have been the sanest in Europe for many years. But they have need to be on guard against what remains in Britain which formerly made hewers of wood, drawers of water and subordinate helots of hundreds of millions of Indians and over a hundred million Africans. What remains hidden in contemporary Britain we do not know, only that Britain is a part of Western civilisation, more obviously so every day. That civilisation now contemplates itself frantically seeking to detonate the powers of what self-destruction it so assiduously cultivates. On the whole we can say with confidence that the powers and creativeness which the political leaders of the underdeveloped countries have so signally shown, spring from the fact that they represent something new in the world, the rejection of the role on which a dominant civilisation for centuries had built itself, and without which it sinks deeper and deeper into moral and political decay.

Whatever the faults and blunders of the underdeveloped countries, they represent something new in a decaying world, and the importance (not necessarily the judgement) of Lenin is that he first raised the banner and organised the revolt against what we have seen and experienced from 1914 to 1964. It is therefore a historic need to examine as scrupulously and objectively as possible what the leader of the first underdeveloped country seeking to make the transition thought; what he hoped to do, what he believed he had done, and the directions for the future he left behind him. There are many values in such a procedure when scrupulously carried out. One of them is that it does not imperatively demand an estimate of the success or relevance of his achievements. That debate began before Lenin became a world figure, continues to the present day and will continue. The reader will maintain, develop or even change his own opinion. Yet the facts, the facts within the terms prescribed, are as clear as it is possible for the statements of the head of a revolutionary state to be. They are worth examination first because the internal problems posed and tackled are still the problems faced by all underdeveloped countries. In Africa no less than elsewhere.

Secondly, his view of the problems as he saw them, and the solutions he proposed, have disappeared from history as completely as if they were Etruscan hieroglyphics carved on stone. Lenin's recommendations to his party for the consolidation of the Soviet state were two: (1) The reconstruction of the governmental apparatus which, he said, despite the name soviet, was no more than an inheritance from tsarism; and (2) The education of the almost illiterate peasantry.

There is no but or maybe. He says there are two essential points and then names these two. They cannot be said to be forgotten, because they have never been noticed.

The reason for this I can indicate with confidence and certainty born of a fully documented experience—my own. Twenty-five years ago, I wrote a history of the period.[2] I am certain that in preparation for the work, I read the relevant passages. But today I can find no concern with them on the numerous sympathetic pages I devoted to Lenin's ideas. I must simply have read them and passed them by. And my experience is that all other students of the period and writers on it have done the same. I was for years active among the leading trotskyists: no trotskyist that I knew ever even spoke, far less wrote of them. I translated from the French nearly a thousand pages of the life of Stalin by Boris Souvarine, a book based on personal acquaintance with the Russian leaders and the Russian scene of Lenin's day, and mastery of all available material. These ideas of Lenin's are barely mentioned. In a wide acquaintance with Trotsky's voluminous writings on Lenin and revolutionary Russia, I have found no treatment of them. In authoritative and extensive examinations of the whole Russian revolution by Isaac Deutscher and E. H. Carr, you find the same blank incomprehension. None of us says that Lenin was wrong, that these ideas marked a decline in his mental powers due to the illness which killed him. Simply the modern world is so constituted that it cannot take seriously such political recommendations as the construction of an honest and efficient government, and the education of an illiterate peasant population. These were not accidental or psychological utopias. They were, in Lenin's view at least, the summation of his life's experience and studies, and his six years' experience as leader of the Russian revolution. A decent, honest government and the education of an illiterate peasantry. Those were the last words of leninism.

The last period begins with the victory of the Russian revolution over the invasion by Britain, France, the United States, Japan, etc. At its tenth congress in 1921, the Bolshevik Party posed the question: we have made a proletarian revolution aiming at socialism; we have for the moment defeated invasion, what shall we do now with this state of which we find ourselves the masters? The leninist Bolshevik Party was the most highly politically educated and self-conscious party in history, and this debate is the greatest political debate that I know. The only thing to compare with it is the debate at Putney between Cromwell and Ireton on the one side, and the revolutionary soldiers of the army on the other. The problem of the Puritan revolutionaries was of the same scope as the problems that faced the Bolsheviks—now that they had defeated the former rulers, what political and social form were they to give, what were they to do with the country of which they were now the masters? We are concerned here only with tracing the growth of Lenin's ideas to their incredible climax.

The first thing to be noticed in this marxist is his empiricism and his frank admission of it. For years before the revolution and immediately after October, Lenin had insisted that Russia, an underdeveloped peasant country, was not ready for socialism. Socialism he always saw as the organisation of an advanced economy by the state—the economy of advanced countries or some substantial part of them.

Now, after three years of civil war, the Bolsheviks found themselves with a national economy originally backward and now almost destroyed but organised on communist lines. War communism was the name it bore, and to the end of his days Lenin could not say definitely whether the Civil War had pushed them into it or whether in a rush of enthusiasm (initiated by the necessities of war) they had plunged into a communist experiment for which the country was unsuited:

> The peasantry demands a practical demonstration of the ability of the workers who own the factories, the works, industry, to organise exchange with it. On the other hand, an immense agrarian country with bad means of communication, boundless spaces, different climates, different agricultural conditions, etc., inevitably presupposes a certain freedom of turnover for local agriculture and local industry, on a local scale. In this respect we made many mistakes; we went too far; we went too far along the road of nationalising trade and industry, of stopping local turnover. Was this is a mistake? Undoubtedly.
>
> In this connection we did much that was simply wrong, and it would be a great crime not to see and realise that we did not keep within proper limits. Some of the things, however, we were compelled to do by necessity; up to now we have been living under such conditions of furious and incredibly severe war that we had no other alternative but to act in a wartime manner in the sphere of economics. The miracle was that a ruined country was able to hold out in such a war. The miracle did not come from heaven, it arose out of the economic interests of the working class and the peasantry, who performed this miracle by their mass enthusiasm; this miracle

repulsed the landlords and the capitalists. At the same time, it is an undoubted fact, and we must reveal it in our agitation and propaganda, that we went further than was necessary theoretically and politically.[3]

An examination of a country in the throes of revolution, any examination which is not aware that much that happens is unforeseen, unexpected, and cannot be logically explained even by the participants themselves, is sure, in Milton's phrase, to make confusion worse confounded. How they had got themselves into that hopeless confusion Lenin never worked out. The most urgent task was to get out of it, and when revolt broke out in Russia, with a startling abruptness, Lenin abandoned government regulation of peasant production and trade and introduced the New Economic Policy. Contrary to what is now popularly (and even learnedly) believed, to Lenin this economic policy was not in any sense of the word new. As far back as May 1918,[4] he had urged on the party and the population the necessity and validity of what he called state capitalism.[5] In April 1921, speaking after the Tenth Party Congress, he quoted, literally, the 1918 speech to the extent of ten pages.[6] He was always making references to this 1918 speech, and in the last months of his life, he referred to it again: "Whenever I wrote about the New Economic Policy I always quoted the article on state capitalism which I wrote in 1918."

More indication of the way he thought, of the totally unprecedented problem which his government faced—unprecedented then—were some of the personal expressions, *obiter dicta* (and rebukes) which he introduced into the great debate of 1921. As is familiar, Trotsky, acutely aware of the magnitude of the magnitude of the economic crisis, wanted to make the trade unions a part of the state. That, he argued, was not only imperative for Russia of 1921, in a workers' state it was legitimate marxism.

Equally well-known is Lenin's refusal to accept this drastic regimentation of the Russian working class. Russia, he said, was not *quite* a workers' state. The debate is, or ought to be, familiar. What is not so well-known is how, in a mass of confused action and conflicting proposals on all sides, Lenin arrived at his view of the root cause of the crisis in which the party found itself. We babble sometimes with great profundity of analysis and learning (sometimes with less) of the learned considerations by which politicians arrive at crucial decisions. Here is Lenin himself telling us what enlightened him, what gave him his insight into this historic moment in a great historical conjunction.

That is why, when the "scrap started" at the Fifth All-Russian Conference of Trade Unions, November 2–6, 1920 (and that is exactly where it started), when immediately after that conference—no, I am mistaken, *during* that conference—Comrade Tomsky appeared before the Political Bureau in a high state of extraordinary excitement and, fully supported by Comrade Rudzutak, who is the calmest of men, began to relate that Comrade Trotsky at that conference had talked about "shaking up" the trade unions, and that he, Tomsky, had opposed this—when this happened, I immediately and irrevocably made up my mind that the essence of the controversy was one of policy (i.e. the trade union policy of the party), and that Comrade Trotsky was entirely wrong in his dispute with Comrade Tomsky over his policy of "shaking up" the trade unions; for, *even if it were partly justified* by the "new tasks and methods" (Trotsky's thesis 12), the policy of "shaking up" the unions at the present time and in the present situation cannot be tolerated because it threatens a split.

This was the profoundly human and personal origin of the profundities of political and philosophical analyses which Lenin developed before the debate was ended.

Other observations are equally relevant to any consideration of politics at any time. This is about Trotsky's proposals:

Take this controversy as you like, either as it arose at the Fifth All-Russian Conference of Trade Unions, or as it was presented and *directed* by Trotsky himself in his pamphlet-platform of 25 December; you will see that Trotsky's *whole* approach, his whole trend, is wrong. He has failed to understand that it is necessary and possible to approach the trade unions as a school even when one raises the subject of "Soviet trade unionism," even when one speaks of production propaganda in general, and even when one puts the question of "coalescence," of the trade unions participating in the management of industry, *in the way* Trotsky does. And as regards the latter question, in the manner in which it is presented throughout Trotsky's pamphlet-platform, the mistake lies in the failure to understand that the trade unions are a *school of administrative-technical management of production*. Not "on the one hand a school and on the other hand something different" but *from all aspects*, in the present controversy, with the question as now presented by Trotsky, *trade unions are a school*, a school of unity, a school of solidarity, a school for learning how to protect one's interests, a school of management, a school of administration. Instead of understanding and rectifying this fundamental error of Comrade Trotsky's, Comrade Bukharin made a ridiculous little amendment: "On the one hand . . . on the other hand."

Let us approach the question still more concretely. Let us see what the present trade unions are as an "apparatus" for the management of production. We have seen from incomplete returns that about nine hundred workers—members and delegates of trade unions—are engaged in the management of production. Increase this figure tenfold if you will, or even a hundredfold: as a concession to you and in order to explain your fundamental mistake, let us even assume such an incredibly rapid "advance"in the near future—even then we get an insignificant number of those directly engaged in *management* compared with the general mass of six million members of trade unions. And from this it is still more clearly evident that to concentrate all attention on the "leading stratum" as Trotsky does, to talk about the role of the trade unions in production and about managing production, without taking into account the fact that 98½% *are learning* (6,000,000 − 90,000 = 5,910,000 = 98½% of the total) *and will have to learn, for a long time,* means committing a fundamental mistake. Not school *and* management, but *school of management.*

This is Lenin's thesis all through. The backwardness of Russia imposed on the party the necessity of teaching and above all teaching themselves. We have to administer. But the main business is to teach:

Even in ten years' time we shall probably have to say that not all our party and trade-union workers have sufficient industrial training, just as in ten years' time not all the party, trade-union and War Department workers will have sufficient military training. But we have made a *beginning* with industrial training by the fact that about a thousand workers, members and delegates of trade unions, participate in the work of management boards, and manage factories, head offices and higher bodies. The fundamental principle of "industrial training" of the training of *ourselves,* of the old underground workers and professional journalists, is that we ourselves set to work, to study our own practical experience in the most careful and detailed manner in accordance with the rule: "Measure your cloth seven times before you cut." Persistent, slow, careful, practical, and business-like testing of what this thousand has done; still more careful and practical correcting of their work and advancing only after the usefulness of the given method, the given system of management, the given proportion, the given selection of persons, etc. has been fully proved—such is the basic, fundamental, absolute rule of "industrial training"; and it is precisely this rule that Comrade Trotsky breaks with all his theses, the whole of his pamphlet-platform, are such that by their mistakes they have distracted the attention and forces of the party from practical "production work'" to empty and vapid word-spinning.

For Lenin the backwardness of an underdeveloped country imposed on the party the necessity of teaching and above all teaching themselves.

It is not my business here to go into any detail about Russian economic development, and more particularly the development of agriculture. That would involve controversy of which there is enough already and material abounding. I shall stick to the continuous development and progression of Lenin's political ideas. On 17 October 1921, he delivered a report to the Second All-Russian Congress of Political Education Departments. Now of all political organisations, the Russian Bolshevik government believed in the necessity of the political education of the Russian people, especially in the new doctrines of marxism, of socialism. The operative word here is *not* socialism. It is education.

Lenin was coldly if not brutally realistic:

Raising the level of culture is one of our most immediate tasks. And this is the task of the Political Education Departments, if they can serve the cause of "political education," which is the title they have adopted for themselves. It is not difficult to adopt a title, but how about acting up to it? Let us hope that after this Congress we shall have precise information about this. A commission for the liquidation of illiteracy was set up on 19 July 1920. Before coming to this congress, I deliberately read the decree establishing this commission. It says: All-Russian Commission for the Liquidation of Illiteracy. Let us hope that after this congress we shall receive information about what has been done in this sphere, and in how many gubernias, that we shall receive a precise report. But the very fact that it was found necessary to set up an Extraordinary Commission for the Liquidation of Illiteracy shows that we are (what is the wildest term I can use for it?), well, something like semi-savages, because in a country that was not semi-savage it would be considered a disgrace to have set up an Extraordinary Commission for the Liquidation of Illiteracy. In such countries illiteracy is liquidated in schools. There they have tolerable schools, where people are taught. What are they taught? First of all they are taught to read and write. But if this elementary problem has not yet been solved, it is ridiculous to talk about a New Economic Policy.

The reader will I hope allow me to interject here a solitary observation. The day that I hear of one political leader of an underdeveloped country speaking in these terms to a political gathering of his own people (and publishing it), my confidence in the future of underdeveloped countries would take a great bound forward.

Russia, you must remember, was a country of many universities, publishing houses, a wide variety of established journals. Beginning with Pushkin, born in 1801, right up to Chekhov, who died in 1904, Russia had produced men who even outside of Russia were acknowledged as the greatest artists of the nineteenth century. All this Lenin ignored. His concern was the people, the common people: "First of all they are taught to read and write. But if this elementary problem has not been solved, it is ridiculous to talk about a New Economic Policy."

This was no chance remark, no individual aside. Lenin then proceeded to make his first summation of the three principal enemies now confronting Soviet Russia "irrespective of one's departmental functions."

The three enemies were: "the first—communist vanity; the second enemy—illiteracy; and the third enemy—bribery." The thing to note is that none of these are psychological appraisals about the weakness of men, nor the vices of the instincts (according to the depth psychologists), nor the lack of experience in democracy (beloved by the Western liberal), nor the lack of character (beloved by the European reactionary). These are strictly social defects of a historical origin. The vanity Lenin speaks about is the political conceit of a member of the governing party, employed in a government institution, who believes that he can solve the urgent problems affecting millions of people, by issuing government decrees.

Next illiteracy. "An illiterate person," Lenin decrees, "is outside politics, he must first of all be taught the alphabet. Without that there can be no politics. Without that, there are only rumours, gossip, fables and prejudices, but not politics."

Finally, there is bribery, or to use the more modern and comprehensive term—corruption. Corruption, in Lenin's view, rises on the soil of illiteracy.

Some time after his speech, Lenin grew physically much worse, but before he took to his bed, never to leave it again, he was able to address the Party Congress once more, and in the course of this address, he referred to the mess the government was in, and the responsibility for it. *Nobody was responsible!*

It would be unfair to say that the responsible communists do not approach their tasks in a conscientious manner. The overwhelming majority of them, ninety-nine per cent, are not only conscientious: they proved their loyalty to the revolution under the most difficult conditions before the fall of tsarism and after the revolution; they literally risked their lives. Therefore it would be radically wrong to seek for the cause in this. We need a cultured approach to the simplest affairs of state. It must be understood that is a matter of state, of commerce, and if obstacles arise one must be able to overcome them and take proceedings against those who are guilty of red tape. I think the proletarian courts will be able to punish, but in order to punish, the culprits must be found. I assure you that in this case no culprits will be found. Look into this business, all of you; no one is guilty, all we see is a lot of fuss and bustle and nonsense. . . . Nobody has the ability to approach the business properly; nobody understands that affairs of state must be approached not this way, but that way.

What Lenin was looking at were the defects of a system, a society, a backward society which corrupted good men.

Before we come to the last words, the summary of a lifetime, we have to know what he was seeing—only then shall we be able to understand what he said and why. At the Eleventh Party Congress, Lenin told Russia (and the world) his reflections on where Soviet Russia had reached and where it was going:

Well, we have lived through a year, the state is in our hands; but has it operated the New Economic Policy in our way during the past year? No. But we refuse to admit this. It did not operate in our way. How did it operate? The machine refused to obey the hand that guided it. It was like an automobile that is going, not in the direction of the man who is driving it, but in the direction desired by someone else, as if it were being driven by some secret, illegal hand, God knows whose, perhaps that of a profiteer, or of a private capitalist, or both. Be that as it may, the car is not going in the direction the man at the wheel imagines.

We now approach his last writings—three articles.

The three articles are the climax of Lenin's reflections on what the underdeveloped country was to do with its unprecedented control of the economy. These are reflections on what we must remember was an entirely new and entirely unprecedented phenomenon. It began in 1921; in 1922 illness drove

Lenin from his desk. By the early months of 1923, he had lost the power of speech, and his last three articles represent his last will and testament. We do not assume any loss of intellectual power. The very last article of the three, "Better Fewer, but Better," is perhaps as fine a production (and as famous) as ever came from his pen. The articles contain much that is new, either never said before or giving entirely new emphasis to objectives stated before but not made fundamental. He had no opportunity to translate these ideas into political action. (We have therefore to watch the articles, not only in themselves, but in the light of what has happened since.)

The first article, dated 4–6 January 1923, is entitled, "On Co-operation." Lenin states at once that precisely because of the New Economic Policy, the co-operative movement "acquires absolutely exceptional significance"—such words he did not use lightly. His new point is that since state power is in the hands of the working class—and he at once concretises this claim "since this state power owns all the means of production"—the only task that remains to be done is to organise the population in co-operative societies. It is no wonder that from that day to this the words and the new ideas contained in them seem to elude, to baffle all commentators. Lenin is very serious, for he goes on to say:

> When the population is organised in co-operative societies to the utmost, the socialism which formerly was legitimately ridiculed, scorned and treated with contempt by those who were justly convinced of the need for the class struggle, for the struggle for political power, etc. automatically achieves its aims. But not all comrades appreciate the enormous, boundless significance that the organisation of Russia in co-operative societies now acquires.

Enormous, boundless. He had not spoken about the co-operatives like that before. In fact, speaking on the Food Tax on 14 April 1921, he had given a distinctly different appreciation of the co-operatives.[7] Co-operatives have now become all that is necessary for the building of socialism, first from the aspect of principle, and secondly, underlining the words, Lenin makes clear what he is getting at and the reason for this new orientation: from the aspect of the transition to the new order (socialism) he has found "the means that will be *simplest, easiest, and most intelligible for* the peasantry."

This for Lenin is not only important. Everything else, economic planning, the organisation of the state, is subordinate to the response of the small peasants, whom Lenin will later remind us constitute nine-tenths of the population of Russia. They are what matters. "It is one thing to draw up fantastic plans for building socialism by means of all sorts of workers' associations; but it is quite another thing to learn to build it practically, in such a way that every small peasant may take part in the work of construction." Lenin now makes a criticism of the NEP which he has mentioned at various times but which he now states was the central mistake in that perpetually discussed new orientation. The mistake was that they forgot to think about the co-operatives, they are underestimated, their "enormous significance" is forgotten. No directive on the Russian economy was ever raised by Lenin with greater force and greater emphasis. None has been so signally ignored. Before we are finished we shall see why.

As was his way, especially when introducing something new, Lenin now proceeds to deepen the argument. Every new social system arises with the assistance of a new class. The new class he has in mind for the new Russia is the peasantry. The state must give the co-operative peasants a bonus but not for any kind of co-operative trade. The assistance, Lenin says, he underlines the words, must be for co-operative trade in which *real masses of the population really take part.* The whole point is to "verify the intelligence behind it, to verify its quality."

Lenin knows that the kind of participation he has in mind is today beyond the peasant population. It will take one or two decades. It will require universal literacy, the population must acquire the habit of reading books. (Here we see why, in his address to the Political Education Departments, he laid such heavy stress on illiteracy.) The Russian peasant trades in an Asiatic manner. He has to learn to trade in a European manner. This task of instructing them he recommends should be undertaken with new enthusiasm. The emphasis now must be on educational work. There is some highly original and highly significant phrasing: if we confine ourselves "entirely to economic internal relations," the weight of emphasis is certainly shifted to educational work. The literacy Lenin is now talking about is not primarily concerned with politics or what in the English-speaking world is known as culture. It is the precondition of economic progress.

How unambiguous Lenin is can be seen in the final paragraph in this brief article. Two main tasks constitute the epoch. The first we shall come to in a moment. But the second drives home what Lenin believes he has now securely established: "The second is to conduct educational work among the peasants. And the economic object of this educational work among the peasants is to organise them in co-operative societies. If the whole of the peasantry were organised in co-operatives, we should be standing firmly with both feet on the soil of socialism."

There are immense difficulties in the way of this cultural revolution but the difficulties are "of a purely educational (for we are illiterate) and material character (for in order to be cultured we must have reached a certain level of development of the material means of production, we must have a certain material base)."

Let us carefully avoid what may be viewed sceptically as a biased interpretation. There is no need to interpret, we can only presume that Lenin means what he says.

How deadly serious (and systematic) he was is proved by the next article which is dated three weeks later, 23 January. We remember that he defined the number of tasks which constituted the epoch as two. Educational work among the peasants had been the second. The first had been in its way quite as uncompromising and quite as new.

"The two main tasks which confront us constitute the epoch: the first is to reconstruct our apparatus, which is utterly useless, and which we took over in its entirety from the preceding epoch; during the five years of struggle we did not, and could not, make any serious alterations in it." It is to this reconstruction of the governmental apparatus that Lenin now addresses himself. The form it takes is a series of proposals addressed directly to the Twelfth Party Congress. As we grasp the precision of the proposals we see that if Lenin had been well enough to attend the Congress, these proposals would have dominated its energies and attention in the same way that in 1921 the Trade Union question had dominated the Tenth Congress. The first thing Lenin does is to condemn the whole Soviet government as nothing more than a survival of the old tsarist government (notoriously, by the way, the most backward government in Western Europe): "With the exception of the People's Commissariat for Foreign Affairs, our state apparatus is very largely a survival of the old one, and has least of all undergone serious change. It has only been slightly repainted on the surface, but in all other things it is a typical relic of our old state apparatus."

That is where we begin; there should be no minimising of what Lenin means to say. These are soviets, and the government departments are headed by Bolsheviks and Communists. But the whole thing is rotten. It is not that the new Soviet government is unworkable. It is that under the thin covering of new forms the old tsarist apparatus still remains. Thus in the view of Lenin (a view entirely unique) it was not the new Bolshevism but the old tsarism from which Russia, after six years, was bleeding. The régime faces a crisis comparable to the most dangerous moments in the Civil War. We have to bear in mind the article on co-operation. The tremendous task posed there will have to be carried out by the new government that Lenin proposes. Lenin proposes that the Congress attempt the reorganisation of one government department, just one, and this one, the Workers' and Peasants' Inspection. And here we run right up against one of the great historical perversions of our times. The Stalin and Trotsky conflict and the debate which has followed it has confused and even obscured what Lenin tried to do at this Congress. His proposals and the article that followed particularised Stalin as the most offending bureaucrat, and his department, the Workers' and Peasants' Inspection, as the most offensive department in the government. But Stalin is not and never was the main issue, though it was in those terms that Trotsky and Stalin represented the conflict to Russia and the whole world. Lenin was not concerned with Stalin but with the whole Russian apparatus of government. And we must know what the Workers' and Peasants' Inspection was intended to be and why it is the whole apparatus of government Lenin has in mind and not primarily Stalin.

In January 1920, long before the Civil War was over, Lenin had addressed a memorandum to Stalin on his Commissariat, copies of which had been sent to other members of the government. Instructions on the reorganisation of the Workers' and Peasants' Inspection had been issued by the Central Committee. Lenin wanted Stalin to add the following points. The whole Workers' and Peasants' Inspection should aim at abolishing itself. Its function should be to introduce a section of the Workers' and Peasants' Inspection in all departments of state control and then cease to exist as a separate department.

Lenin's additions read suspiciously like a totally new reconstruction of whatever the Central Executive may have had in mind. The object of the department is to enlist all the toilers, men "and particularly women" in the work of the Workers' and Peasants' Inspection.

Local authorities should compile lists of all (except office employees) who should take part in the work of the inspection in rotation. The department should exercise "wider" control over the accounting of products, goods, stores, materials, fuel etc. Lenin obviously had in mind a continuously spreading inspection and checking of every sphere of government by workers, especially women, "all women."

Gradually peasants were to be invited from the local districts to take part in the work of state control at the centre. Peasants were to be invited to take part "unfailingly," "non-party peasants."

Lenin may have been a utopian dreamer. That question is not being debated here. What is certain is that he did not have utopian ideas before and while he aimed at power, only to be transformed by power into a one-party totalitarian dictator. If his ideas were utopian then it is clear that after six years of power, he turned to them as the sole solution of the mess into which the Soviet government was sinking, had already sunk. That he saw the problem as Trotsky v. Stalin is a totally false view of this which seemed to him the greatest crisis the Soviet state had hitherto faced. The Central Control Commission was a purely party body which was responsible for the discipline and control of party members all over the country. Lenin proposed to amalgamate this party body with the government departments of the Workers' and Peasants' Inspection.

The Congress was to elect from seventy-five to a hundred workers and peasants as new members of the Central Control Commission. These elected persons were to be selected on the same principles, subjected to the same tests, as the members of the Central Committee. This severe selection was due to the fact that those chosen were to enjoy the same rights as the members of the Central Committee.

Let us see where we are now. For this is Lenin's organisational counterpart to a political policy such as the education of tens of millions of illiterate peasants. We have now organised in one body what was originally two distinct bodies, to which is added a new one. The bodies are:

1. The Central Committee of the Bolshevik Party which in reality politically controls all aspects of life in Russia. Its most important subcommittee is the Political Bureau, the actual rulers of Russia. There is also an organisation committee, a secretariat, etc.

2. The Central Control Commission of the Party so far has had nothing to do with government. It will have seventy-five to a hundred new members, workers and peasants. Lenin proposes that the staff of the Workers' and Peasants' Commissariat should be reduced in number to three or four hundred. This reduced personnel should be put to the strictest tests in regard to (a) conscientiousness, (b) knowledge of the state apparatus. They should also undergo a special test in regard to their knowledge of the principles of the scientific organisation

of labour in general and of administrative and office work in particular. Then comes a revealing admonition. These highly trained, carefully chosen and specially paid members of the staff should "perform
purely secretarial work" for the members (workers and peasants) of
the Workers' and Peasants' Inspection and the new members of the
Central Control Commission. The workers and peasants are to do the
inspection. The staff is to do what they are told.

If Lenin's ideas were utopian, he was completely and whole-heartedly utopian. What does Lenin expect to gain by this organisational reconstruction?
Two things.

First, the prestige of the Workers' and Peasants' Inspection will be enor-
mously increased as these workers and peasants go round inspecting and
checking the activities of all government functionaries. They will have the
authority and meet with the respect that will come to them from being full
members of the ruling organisation of Russia.

Secondly, the Central Committee and the Central Control Commission
in their two-monthly meetings will more and more assume the character and
function of a superior party conference. This will increase the "methodical,
expedient and systematic" organisation of its work and it will help to add to
its contacts with really broad masses.

This is Lenin all over, the broad comprehensive democratic aims and the
tight but tentative organisational structure by which the work will be begun.
How will it work out? That would be seen. His whole method was summed
up in his quotation from Napoleon on War: *"On s'engage et puis on voit."* Napoleon was the most meticulous planner of military campaigns who ever
lived. But after the plan was made: you engage, and then you see.

If we want to understand the stage at which Lenin's ideas had reached (and
also the past and the future development of an undeveloped country), one
must now pay special attention to the violent, absolutely unbridled condemnation and abuse which Lenin continues to shower on the Russian apparatus
of government after six years of Bolshevik rule. It is not Stalin who is responsible for this. The whole party is responsible. The enemy consists of those
who advocate "the preservation of our apparatus in the impossible and pre-
revolutionary form in which it exists to the present day."

Lenin makes other technical recommendations, but the main point of his
proposals is the reorganisation proposed. It seems that the proposal was not
eagerly received and by 2 March Lenin unloosed his consuming detestation

and repudiation of the Russian form of government, a repudiation which had been disciplined but ill-concealed in the original proposals. The first five years of the Bolshevik Russian revolution have "crammed their heads with disbelief and skepticism." For a socialist republic the culture of Western European bourgeois states would be too modest an aim. But as a start they should be satisfied with getting rid of "the particularly crude types of pre-bourgeois, bureaucratic or serf-culture" which they have. The present form of government in Russia is "so deplorable, not to say outrageous" that "we must come to our senses in time." The Russian apparatus does not deserve the name of socialist, Soviet, etc. Such elements of decent government that they have are ridiculously small and to build a decent apparatus will take "many, many years."

To continue with this drastic criticism of the Soviet government, the most drastic ever made, Lenin tells his party members that "we must set ourselves the task first of learning, second of learning, and third of learning. . . . We have been bustling for five years trying to improve the state apparatus, but it was mere bustle, which during the five years, only proved that it was useless, or even futile, or even harmful. This bustle created the impression that we were working; as a matter of fact, it only clogged up our institutions and our brains."

This is the road that they must follow.

"It is better to get good human material in two years, or even in three years, than to work in haste without hope of getting any at all." Lenin reaches lengths of advocacy and desperation hitherto untouched by him. Nothing that might happen in Russia would have surprised the man who wrote:

> I know that it will be hard to follow this rule and apply it to our condi-
> tions. I know that the opposite rule will force its way through a thousand
> loopholes. I know that enormous resistance will have to be offered, that
> devilish persistence will have to be displayed, that in the first year at least,
> the work in this connection will be hellishly hard. Nevertheless, I am con-
> vinced that only by such work shall we be able to achieve our aim, and only
> by achieving this aim shall we create a republic that is really worthy of the
> name Soviet, Socialist, etc.

The extremity of what might legitimately be called desperation is reached in the following sentence: "If we cannot arm ourselves with patience, if we are not prepared to spend several years on this task, we had better not start on it."

This is not an ill-considered angry remark. It follows directly upon this sober evaluation:

Either it is not worthwhile undertaking another of the numerous reorganisations that we have had, and therefore we must give up the Workers' and Peasants' Inspection as hopeless, or we really set to work, by slow, difficult and unusual methods, and testing these methods over and over again, to create something exemplary, which will win the respect of all and sundry for its merits, and only because rank and calling demand it.

If the party is not ready to throw itself into this gigantic task, with the necessary energy and patience, then it had better leave it alone. The government apparatus of a country was not something to play with.

We will not go into Lenin's exceptionally severe requirements for the training of the functionaries needed for this gigantic and, even in the eyes of its founder, almost impossible operation. One thing we can say. It was a task which he saw as big as the October revolution. It was possible that it could be carried through, at least initiated, projected on lines which would have inspired the nation with a new national purpose. But only Lenin could have done it. Today, after forty years, I have never read or heard anyone who seems to have understood even what Lenin had in mind. What we have to understand is the tremendous break with all his previous conceptions—a break in its way as gigantic as the break in March 1917 when with the perspective of the bourgeois-democratic revolution, and the new conception of power to the soviets, on the way to the proletarian socialist revolution. Before we conclude with the unmistakable evidence, both positive and negative, of what he said and what he did not say, of this dynamic new perspective, we think it would be well to establish once and for all the unparalleled gravity of the situation as he saw it: "In essence, the question stands as follows: either we prove now that we have learnt something about state construction (we ought to have learnt something in five years) or we prove that we have not matured for that sufficiently. If the latter is the case, it is not worth while starting on the task."

What then were the changes in the basic and guiding ideas within which Lenin had worked certainly from 1905 and particularly since 1917? He always believed and often said that any serious and notable change in the social and political constitution of Russia came from the proletariat or from the masses, only when the masses take part does real politics begin. This was his creed.

Now in the face of the threatening catastrophe of all he had worked for, he faced the fact that what was required the proletariat could not do. What elements, he asked, do they have for building this new apparatus instead of the pre-bourgeois, bureaucratic serf-culture which they had? "Only two." What were these?

> First the workers who are absorbed in the struggle for Socialism. These elements are not sufficiently educated. They would like to build a better apparatus for us, but they do not know how to do it. They cannot do it. They have not yet developed the culture that is required for this; and it is precisely culture that is required for this.

That was for Lenin the end of a road. The workers on whom he depended for everything creative, everything new, were incapable of initiating this mighty reorganisation. He had indicated in what way the energies of peasants could be channelled into the social reconstruction of Russia. But neither peasant nor proletariat could reconstruct, reorganise the pre-bourgeois, bureaucratic, serf-culture with which Soviet Russia was still saddled.

"Secondly, we have the element of knowledge, education and training, but to a degree that is ridiculously small compared with all other countries." Lenin recognised very clearly what he was saying and what he was leaving unsaid. What he was saying was this:

> For this purpose the very best of what there is in our social system must be utilised with the greatest caution, thoughtfulness and knowledge in building up the new Commissariat.
>
> For this purpose the best elements in our social system, such as firstly the advanced workers, and secondly the real enlightened elements, for whom we can vouch that they will not take the word for the deed, and will not utter a single word that goes against their conscience, must not shrink before any difficulties, must not shrink from any struggle, in order to achieve the object they have seriously set themselves.

This utter dependence on the subjective element, on the personal qualities of individuals, for so gigantic a social task, that was something new and this perhaps explains Lenin's desperation: if you are not going to tackle it with a full consciousness of the magnitude of the efforts required, it would be better not to tackle it at all.

But what you will look for in vain in these three articles is any reference to the Soviet structure of government. This had been Lenin's constant indication of what Russia had brought new into the world, of what was the strength of the Russian revolution. Now that was gone. For the new peasantry, he was looking to the co-operatives, for the new apparatus of government he was looking not even to the party as a whole but to the best elements in both government and party. Perhaps the illusionary character of these ideas, the last explosion so far of what had begun in 1789, is proved by the fact that not only did they make no impact on the Russia of Lenin's time. They have completely disappeared from the Russia of Lenin's time. They have completely disappeared from the estimates and details about what was Lenin's real contribution to modern politics and modern thought. And yet the article, "Better Fewer but Better," is to this day one of his famous articles. It was in this article that he wrote the famous words: "the outcome of the struggle will be determined by the fact that Russia, India, China etc. constitute the overwhelming majority of the population that, during the past few years, has been drawn into the struggle for its emancipation with extraordinary rapidity, so that in this respect there cannot be the slightest shadow of doubt what the final outcome of the world struggle will be. In this sense the final victory of socialism is fully and absolutely assured."

Russia, he ended, had to build an economic and efficient government and hold on:

> That is how I link up in my mind the general plan of our work, of our policy, of our tactics, of our strategy, with the task of the reorganised Workers' and Peasants' Inspection. This is what, in my opinion, justifies the exceptional attention which we must devote to the Workers' and Peasants' Inspection in order to raise it to an exceptionally high level, to give it a head with the rights of the Central Committee, etc. etc.
>
> And this justification is that, only by purging our apparatus to the utmost, by cutting out everything that is not absolutely necessary, shall we be certain of holding on. If we do that we shall be able to hold on, not on the level of a small-peasant country, not on the level of this universal narrowness, but on the ever-rising level of large-scale machine industry.
>
> These are the lofty tasks that I dream of for our Workers' and Peasants' Inspection. That is why I am planning for it the amalgamation of the most authoritative party body with an "ordinary People's Commissariat."

Lenin always did his best to guard against being misunderstood. We especially, of the underdeveloped countries, should not misunderstand his views. We may claim that they are utopian, visionary, unrealistic, unworkable, a fantasy. We should bear in mind that these were exactly the charges that the majority of his colleagues made against him in March 1917, when he arrived in Russia, and, almost alone, hurled the masses of Russia at the bourgeois régime and initiated a new epoch in world history, with the slogan, "All power to the Soviets."

[To overthrow a discredited régime is a great political achievement. However, what is now needed is the creation of a new régime. The decline of the African régimes which followed Nkrumah's success continued until Dr Julius Nyerere came forward with Tanzania's Arusha Declaration in 1967. The following essay from my History of Pan-African Revolt (1969) states what Nyerere advocates as the basis for an African civilisation in the modern world. Today, the forward movement in Africa is headed along the lines of Dr Nyerere's policies.]

For many hundreds of years, in fact almost (though not quite) from the beginning of the contact between Western civilisation and Africa, it has been the almost universal practice to treat African achievement, discoveries and creations as if Western civilisation was the norm and the African people spent their years in imitating, trying to reach or, worse still, if necessary going through the primitive early stages of the Western world. We therefore will, before we place it historically, state as straightforwardly as possible the historical achievements that are taking place today in an African state.

First the Tanzanian government has nationalised the chief centres of economic life in the territory. That, though important of economic life in the territory. That, though important and necessary, is not sufficient to create a new society. Less and less is nationalisation becoming a landmark of a new society—today right-wing military dictators (Peru) and the Catholic hierarchy (with the blessing of the Pope) are ready to nationalise and even confiscate. The government of Tanzania has gone further. In the Arusha Declaration of 29 January 1967 it aims at creating a new type of government official:

PART FIVE

THE ARUSHA RESOLUTION

Therefore, the National Executive Committee, meeting in the Community Centre of Arusha from 26.1.67 to 29.1.67, resolves:

A. *The Leadership*

1. Every TANU and Government leader must be either a Peasant or a Worker, and should in no way be associated with the practices of Capitalism or Feudalism.
2. No TANU or Government leader should hold shares in any company.
3. No TANU or Government leader should hold Directorship in any privately-owned enterprises.
4. No TANU or Government leader should receive two or more salaries.
5. No TANU or Government leader should own houses which he rents to others.
6. For the purposes of this Resolution the term "leader" should comprise the following: Members of the TANU National Executive Committee; Ministers, Members of Parliament, Senior Officials of Organisations affiliated to TANU, Senior Officials of Para-Statal Organisations, all those appointed or elected under any clause of the TANU Constitution, Councillors, and Civil Servants in high and middle cadres. (In this context "leader" means a man, or a man and his wife; a woman, or a woman and her husband.)

Such a resolution would probably exclude ninety per cent of those who govern and administer in other parts of the world, developed or underdeveloped. The government aims at creating a new type of society, based not on Western theories but on the concrete circumstances of African life and its historic past.

Perhaps the most revolutionary change of all, it will reconstruct the very system of education in order to fit the children and the youth, *in particular the youth in secondary education,* for the new society which the government of Tanzania seeks to build. The simplicity with which Dr Nyerere states what his government proposes to do disguises the fact that not in Plato or Aristotle, Rousseau or Karl Marx will you find such radical, such revolutionary departures from the established educational order:

Alongside this change in the approach to the curriculum there must be a parallel and integrated change in the way our schools are run, so as to make them and their inhabitants a real part of our society and our economy. Schools must, in fact, become communities—and communities which practise the precept of self-reliance. The teachers, workers, and pupils together must be the members of a social unit in the same way as parents, relatives, and children are the family social unit. There must be the same kind of relationship between pupils and teachers within the school community as there is between children and parents in the village. And the former community must realise, just as the latter do, that their life and well-being depend upon the production of wealth—by farming or other activities.

This means that all schools, but especially secondary schools and other forms of higher education, must contribute to their own upkeep; they must be economic communities as well as social and educational communities. Each school should have, as an integral part of it, a farm or workshop which provides the food eaten by the community, and makes some contribution to the total national income.

This is not a suggestion that a school farm or workshop should be attached to every school for training purposes. It is a suggestion that every school should also be a farm; that the school community should consist of people who are both teachers and farmers, and pupils and farmers. Obviously, if there is a school farm, the pupils working on it should be learning the techniques and tasks of farming. But the farm would be an integral part of the school—and the welfare of the pupils would depend on its output, just as the welfare of a farmer depends on the output of his land. Thus, when this scheme is in operation, the revenue side of school accounts would not just read as at present—"Grant from government . . . ; Grant from voluntary agency or other charity. . . ." They would read—"Income from the sale of cotton (or whatever other cash crop was appropriate for the area) . . . ; value of the food grown and consumed . . . ; value of labour done by pupils on new building, repairs, equipment, etc. . . . ; government subvention . . . ; grant from . . ."

Perhaps nothing shows more clearly the radical, the revolutionary, the complete break with Western habits and Western thought than the new attitude to the Tanzanian farmer. Some of them have followed the advice given to the African farmer officially and unofficially by Westerners: wishing him and his country well, they have encouraged him to individual effort, essentially capitalistic. Following this advice farmers in certain districts of Tanzania (mainly the slopes of the Kavirondo mountain) have followed this Western type of agriculture with success. Note now the economic, in fact the political attitude of the Tanzanian government to this type of farmer. Reviewing Tanzania in "After the Arusha Declaration," Dr Nyerere outlines the co-operative socialist community Tanzania aims at. He continues:

This is the objective. It is stated clearly, and at greater length, in the policy paper. We must understand it so that we know what we are working towards. But it is not something we shall achieve overnight. We have a long way to go.

For what has been happening over recent years is quite different. We have not been enlarging and modernising our traditional family unit as much as abandoning it in favour of small-scale capitalist farming. Many of our most dynamic and energetic farmers, especially those with the most initiative and willingness to learn new techniques, have been branching out on their own as individuals. They have not been enlarging their farms by joining with others in a spirit of equality, but by employing labour. So we are getting the beginnings of the development of an agricultural labouring class on the one hand, and a wealthier employing class on the other. Fortunately, this development has not gone very far; we can arrest the trend without difficulty.

But we must not make this change by persecuting the progressive farmers; after all, we have been encouraging them in the direction they have been going! Instead we must seek their co-operation, and integrate them into the new socialist agriculture by showing them that their best interests will be served by this development. For energy and initiative such as these farmers have displayed will be very important to our progress. We need these people.

This is something new in the history of political thought. The co-operative villages aimed at are called *Ujamaa* and Dr Nyerere has called the whole new attempt to create a new society Socialism. In our view he is entitled to do so, and a proper respect for what the Tanzanian government is doing demands that it be related to traditional and contemporary concepts of socialism.

First of all, no one today believes that what exists in Russia and Eastern Europe is, in any sense of the word, socialist; that is to say, a society having achieved and aiming at even more comprehensive stages of liberty, equality and fraternity, social relations higher than those achieved by the most advanced parliamentary democracy. That is socialism or it is worse even than capitalist decay, being then a deliberate and conscious fraud. Worse still, most unfortunately, certain of the new African states, anxious to rid themselves of the capitalist stigma, have invented a new category labelled African socialism. Worthy of repetition is the exposition of this African socialism by one newly independent state:

Adaptability

15. African socialism must be flexible because the problems it will confront and the incomes and desires of the people will change over time, often quickly and substantially. A rigid, doctrinaire system will have little chance for survival. The system must—

(i) make progress towards ultimate objectives; and

(ii) solve more immediate problems with efficiency.

16. No matter how pressing immediate problems may be, progress toward ultimate objectives will be the major consideration. In particular, political equality, social justice and human dignity will not be sacrificed to achieve more material ends more quickly. Nor will these objectives be comprised today in the faint hope that by so doing they can be reinstated more fully in some unknown and far distant future.

Whenever was there a state, beginning with the state of Adam and Eve, that did not, could not, proclaim that it had in mind ultimate objectives while paying attention to immediate needs? That is not socialism. It is nonsense. It is not African. It is bureaucratic balderdash, to which we are by now well accustomed in advanced as well as in under-developed fakers—a bold attempt by newcomers to dress the old reality in new clothes.

Far more important than this fakery is the recognition by President Kuanda of Zambia that the attempt merely to ape European ways, which has brought such wide fields of disaster to Africa, must not only be rejected but that there are new African paths to be explored. In his significantly named *Humanism in Zambia* President Kaunda says:

This is a key point, for if the distribution of wealth is not done properly, it might lead to the creation of classes in society and the much-valued humanist approach that is traditional and inherent in our African society would have suffered a final blow. If this happened the world as a whole, and African in particular, would be all the poorer for it. For you would then have the "haves" and the "have-nots." Politically you would be creating room for opposing parties based on "the oppressed" and "the oppressor" concept which again would not be in keeping with the society described above; a society in which the chief as an elected or appointed leader of the people held national property like land in trust for the people, and he was fully aware that he was responsible to them. He knew, too, that his continuing to be their head depended on his people's will.

President Kaunda wants to show how important it is for Africans to break cleanly with the ideas of European well-wishers, that African progress depends on educating first a small number of Africans and then an increasing number who will gradually (without undue haste) educate more and more African natives to capitalist energies and the moderate mastery of parliamentary democracy. His rejection of this concept is total.

Now we must ask again what effects will persistently increasing levels of specialisation have on our much valued traditional society in our country. This field of specialisation drives people to resort to new groups in society. In other words, people with common interests group together, partly because of the community of their interests and partly as the means of promoting and protecting the welfare of their group. For example, a carpenter will find his own interests are not the same as those of the commercial farmer. The teacher finds that his interests differ from those of the mineworker. And so the whole list of different interests can be outlined. The point is, all this gives birth to a new disintegrative tendency. This, as can be seen, cuts right across the traditional society which has been described above as a mutual aid society which was an accepting and inclusive community.

Despite the low level of economic development in African states, this new African conception of the future of Africa lays claim not only to a future, but also to deep roots in the past.

President Kaunda insists on this:

The traditional community was a mutual aid society. It was organised to satisfy the basic human needs of all its members and, therefore, individualism was discouraged. Most resources, such as land, might be communally owned and administered by chiefs, and village headmen for the benefit of everyone. If, for example, a villager required a new hut, all the men would turn to forests and fetch poles to erect the frame and bring grass for thatching. The women might be responsible for making the mud-plaster for the walls and two or three of them would undoubtedly brew some beer so that all the workers would be refreshed after a hot but satisfying day's work. In the same spirit, the able-bodied would accept responsibility for tending and harvesting the gardens of the sick and infirm.

This new recognition so characteristic first of Tanzania and now of Zambia does not turn its back on the modernisation necessary in the modern world. Once more let the African President speak:

From what has been said above, it is clear that we cannot ourselves expect to achieve once again the Man-centred society without very careful planning. And in this direction nothing is more important than institutions of learning . . .

Here the model is or will have to be that so clearly delineated by Dr Nyerere.

That is the essence of the matter. And the newly independent African states are in such crises that success in Tanzania and real strides forward in hard-pressed Zambia can initiate a new road for Africa—the mobilisation of the African people to build an African society in an African way.

It would be a great mistake not to make clear how closely this profoundly creative response to the African reality corresponds with and indeed carries further the highest stages so far reached by Western political thought. Lenin had no illusions about the Russian revolution. He knew that socialism in the marxist sense was impossible in the Russia he knew, and in 1923 was leaving behind. In the last days he increasingly drew attention to two important aspects and needs of the Russia which he insisted on calling Socialist Russia, despite the fact that the great majority of the Russian population consisted of illiterate peasants. The Soviet state, he insisted in those last days, was not new. Behind the marxist terminology and proletarian window dressing was the same old tsarist state, not even a bourgeois state but a "bureaucratic serf state." His proposals to alter these we need not go into. It is sufficient to know that Dr Nyerere has seen through the reactionary, bureaucratic colonialist state which he inherited, and has gone further than anyone in the determination to break it up and make a new type of state.

Lenin also knew, none better, that the Soviet official had to leave high-flown theorising and personally go to work among the backward Russian peasants. In perhaps the most moving of his many statements of what the people needed from the marxist officials of the government, he says:

> Less argument about words! We still have too much of this sort of thing. More variety in practical experience and more study of this experience! Under certain conditions the exemplary organisation of local work, even on a small scale, is of far greater national importance than many branches of the central state work. And these are precisely the conditions we are in at the present moment in regard to peasant farming in general, and in regard to the exchange of the surplus products of agriculture for the manufactures of industry in particular. Exemplary organisation in this respect, even in a single *volost*, is of far greater national importance than the "exemplary" improvement of the central apparatus of any People's Commissariat; for three and a half years to such an extent that it has managed to acquire a certain amount of harmful inertness; we cannot improve it quickly to any extent, we do not know how to do it. Assistance in the more radical improvement of it, a new flow of fresh forces, assistance in the successful struggle against bureaucracy, in the struggle to overcome this harmful inertness, must come from the localities, from the lower ranks, with the exemplary organisation of a small "whole," precisely a "whole," i.e., not one farm, not one branch of economy, not one enterprise, but the *sum total* of economic exchange, even if only in a small locality.
>
> Those of us who are doomed to remain on work at the centre will continue the task of improving the apparatus and purging it of bureaucracy, even if in modest and immediately achievable dimensions. But the greatest assistance in this task is coming, and will come, from the localities . . .

Note in particular one of his last sentences: "We who are doomed. . . ." Lenin wanted to go and work among the peasants. The great marxist would have understood the profoundly socialist and human conception which has moved Dr Nyerere to break to pieces the old system of education and substitute a genuinely socialist and humanist procedure for the youth of Tanzania. In a conversation with Dr Nyerere, the present writer (having previously read his writings) drew his attention to this particular passage from Lenin and what Lenin was striving to teach as far back as 1923. The African leader said that he did not know it—he had arrived at his conclusion by himself and with his people.

It is sufficient to say that socialist thought has seen nothing like this since the death of Lenin in 1924, and its depth, range and the repercussions which flow from it, go far beyond the Africa which gave it birth. It can fertilise and reawaken the mortuary that is socialist theory and practice in the advanced countries. "Marxism is a humanism" is the exact reverse of the truth. The African builders of a humanist society show that today all humanism finds itself in close harmony with the original conceptions and aims of marxism.

Notes on Appendix 1 LESLIE JAMES

These letters from C. L. R. James to his comrades in the Correspondence Publishing Committee, researched and selected by Robert Hill, offer some insight into James's thinking during the period when he first drafted his book on Nkrumah. The first begins with a transcription by James of the letter of invitation he received from Kwame Nkrumah to attend Ghana's independence ceremony.

The next two letters, written after James's return from Ghana, set out some of his impressions of his two-week visit and detail his plans for the book. James's visit lit a fire that influenced him so much that he proposed to put aside the committee's current work on a pamphlet on the Hungarian Revolution. His enthusiasm appears to have been due in large part to James's interpretation of Ghana as forging new trajectories in revolutionary history. James tracked historical developments of revolution first in *The Black Jacobins* (1938), in which he situated enslaved Haitians as an early form of mass proletarian rebellion that forged a new republic, as well as in *World Revolution* (1937), a history of the Communist International. These, James states, had converged and each been surpassed by what was occurring in Ghana. What this meant for world history, to James's mind, was immense. As he writes in the March 20 letter, "The African revolution (as a process) is no longer to be seen as supplementary to or subordinate to the revolution in Western Europe."

James's main interlocutors on the Correspondence Publishing Committee at this time included Martin Glaberman, Grace Lee Boggs, Jimmy Boggs, Lyman Paine, Frances Drake "Freddie" Paine, Constance Pearlstein, and Ed Pearlstein. From their base in the United States, James appeals to them for their analysis of how Ghana's independence was received by African Americans in the United States. His point in the March 21 letter that what Martin Luther King Jr. had done in Montgomery, Alabama, was revolutionary is particularly interesting given the letter's timing. Although both James and King attended the independence celebrations in Accra, they did not interact until they both arrived in London. On the evening of March 22, James attended a dinner with the Kings and invited them to lunch at his home on March 24, where James heard about the Montgomery Bus Boycott in detail.

What these letters do not detail is the fact that tackling three books was too ambitious. James's wife, Selma, quit her job to assist with the manuscript, and Grace Lee Boggs traveled from Detroit in late April 1957 to assist. Grace Lee Boggs became coauthor, with James, on the "Hungarian pamphlet," which came out under the title *Facing Reality* in 1958.[1]

Extract of Letter from C. L. R. James to the Correspondence Publishing Committee, Addressed to Martin Glaberman

This extract includes a copy of an invitation from Kwame Nkrumah for C. L. R. James to attend the celebration of the Gold Coast's independence and the new nation formed in its place, Ghana.

February 8th, 1957

Strictly confidential. I have received the following letter from Nkrumah, the Prime Minister of the Gold Coast. Some of you will remember him in the U.S. and the time he spent with us.

PRIME MINISTER

23rd January, 1957

Dear James,

I am enclosing, herewith, a formal invitation to the ceremonies which will be held in Accra between the 2nd and the 10th March to mark the attainment of independence by the Gold Coast under the name of Ghana. It would give me great personal pleasure if you should be able to attend.

The Government of the Gold Coast will be pleased to bear the cost of your passage to Accra and return and you would, of course, be a guest of the Government while you are in the country during and immediately before the period of the celebrations.

I attach a provisional outline programme and some notes on the country in particular relation to the celebrations. Apart from the central events covered by the programme, there will be a number of subsidiary functions which should be of interest.

Yours sincerely,

(signed) Kwame Nkrumah
Prime Minister

I presume first that the government of Ghana is anxious to get as many people of color with some reputation to the celebrations. And secondly I know that the early work that a group of us in London did has always been remembered by the Gold Coast nationalists. At any rate, there it is. It makes a tremendous mess in many respects but I am sure I ought to go, I shall try to go and I certainly will enjoy it, learn a great deal, do my best to pass on what I have seen. How big the occasion is in the minds of the political world is shown by the fact that Nixon is going. The next thing is to see whom the Russians will send. More of that later.

Letters from C. L. R. James to the Correspondence Publishing Committee

London, March 20, 1957

Dear Everybody,

The general perspective and the particular tasks are such as to require complete understanding by *everyone*. . . .

1. The *year* 1956 was decisive. That is now as clear as day. The ferment here is like a bubbling volcano. Everywhere the same. That I shall treat in detail over the coming period. You do not need to publish old articles in the Newsletter. I shall write new ones. It should not be Letter From London, but Letters From Abroad.

2. You have to prepare all your affairs, with scrupulous attention to detail and a *fixed programme*. We here have to do our share. The most important thing is to realise *concretely* a political line.

3. *I propose to postpone the Hungarian [Revolution] pamphlet for 46-weeks and do instead a 70,000 word book on Ghana. Why? The structure of the book will tell you why.*

   i. My own observations and impressions of the trip. I met *people*. The university student who served as my ADC: the man who drove my car. I met their parents, families. The attendants in the hotel. Civil servants. Ministers. A mass of *people*, seen through the dialectic. Strict observation of human individuals in their social and historical setting. I saw and understood more in 14 days than people who have been studying the subject for 14 years. It sounds wild, but I am sure it is because of that that the politician spent so many hours with me in that busy time, and is looking forward to the book as the first satisfactory exposition of what has happened there. They will give all possible assistance.

   ii. I propose to review past writings particularly *Black Jacobins*. I shall quote and show how clearly the future was foreseen there, when practically everybody thought we were crazy. Read in particular p. 314–16; p. 11; p. 222. I shall draw the argument to a head.

   iii. I shall review Nkrumah's book and break completely with, or rather develop qualitatively the theoretical premises of the *Black Jacobins* and the Leninist theory of the colonial revolution. . . . The African revolution (as a process) is no longer to be seen as supplementary to or subordinate to the revolution in Western Europe. I shall examine it in relation to the French Revolution; the Russian, the Chinese and the Hungarian.

The chief point is *The Party* (now draw a deep breath). At the height of the movement [in Ghana] the Party consisted of about a million people in a population of 5 million. Now it is about 500,000 which is astonishing enough. It would mean in the U.S. a party of 15 million people by arithmetical calculation. Socially calculated it would mean 30 or 40 millions.

I hope you realise what that means in terms of our theory. The way power was achieved was beyond all praise. *I shall deal with it in detail.* Now for Part iv.

   iv. The party is in mortal danger. The danger is that it will succumb to the fact that it is now a government party, a ruling party subject to the corruption that has overtaken all revolutionary parties that rule. (The kind of "corruption" that critics are talking about, financial, etc., I shall treat with the utmost contempt. In twenty-four years Ghana will not achieve the corruption that takes place in the U.S.A. in twenty-four hours.)

This is the kind of thing and there are plenty of them, that has to be driven home and so place the Ghana question in an entirely new framework.

No, the danger is more deeply rooted. It can be overcome in only one way: the revolution must be permanent. This can manifest itself in the following ways.

1. Ghana must become the centre of the struggle for African liberation. That Nkrumah has made absolutely clear. So far, so good. But

2. The very backwardness of Ghana makes it able to start its social and political life in accordance with the most advanced conceptions of the Twentieth Century. I shall detail them. Farming co-operatives in Denmark and Belgium; collectives in Israel; shop stewards movement in England (I shall need help here) but you see the idea. The *state must take the initiative.*

In colonial countries even more than in advanced countries, the weakness of the economy compels the state to initiate new projects. All the colonial countries now must follow India in what they call a socialist pattern of society.

What we have to say is that the party being what it is in Ghana, the new state must take the lead not only in organising the economy from above but in initiating new social relations from below.

It must be repeated that if it does not work along these lines, nothing can prevent it from becoming a government party divorced from the population.

There are also the democratic instincts and practices of the African tribes, not those damned chiefs with their feathers and umbrellas and stools, made into petty tyrants by the British Government, but the old tribal method of appointing them by election and throwing them out if they were unsatisfactory.

To sum up. The Ghana Government must break at once with the idea that its task is to show the imperialists that they have learnt to govern in the British tradition. Instead they must break right out of that tradition and to aim at being a modern socialist society, or rather to build in that direction. *They cannot succeed by themselves.* But they must start, or they will be overwhelmed by their own backwardness. That is the issue. To achieve that, to grapple with it continuously is much harder than to achieve power.

3. How concretely? The decisive question is the future of the party. It is a government, it must rule, the country is appallingly backward. Yet it must aim high and far, or succumb. The great antagonism is between the party as party and the party as government. The party must maintain its ideological domination over the party as government.

A continuing struggle. What we can do is to make them and the public aware of it. To pose it this way, lift it out of the colonial status both for themselves and for people in Britain and the U.S., for the first gives them the opportunity to see this question in international and social and not in provincial terms.

4. We can be more concrete—

a. The party must lead the proletariat and the unions. Otherwise the proletariat as sure as day will in time split the party and take away the leadership of all the masses, pushing the Government into the arms of the big companies and the conservative professional classes who hate it now. I went to Takoradi, a modern part, with a proletariat 10,000. You could have picked up any one of them and dropped him in Detroit. My conversations with them will have to wait.

b. They will have to let the British and American *public* know what they are doing. The British public wishes them well and feels a sort of paternal interest in them which it does not feel for example towards India. If they can show that they are not content with "independence" but are, despite their poverty and backwardness, aiming at the most advanced conceptions of a modern society, they will create a vast reservoir of good will, concrete desire to help and for the first time educate the British public in particular as to what was involved in the colonial relationship and what must now be the relationship between a contemporary society of an advanced character and the backward countries. For they are backward. Let no one have any doubt about that. You only have to look at the strides Britain for example is making in atomic energy for industrial purposes and a powerful industrial structure like the Ruhr in Germany and then compare cocoa farmers in Ghana to realise the gap.

One sure sign will be when young people here begin to emigrate to Ghana. We must work for this. I shall here.

The same with the U.S. and the U.S. Negroes. I shall expect from you all and from Heinz in particular a statement as to what is the attitude of the American Negroes in particular to Ghana. Particularly I want to know the attitude of the proletariat in general and in particular towards emigration later.

The old conception and the new face each other. Formerly three types of people went to Africa: i) imperialists to conquer and rule; ii) officials at high salaries; iii) missionaries to work hard, teachers, etc. But these last were dominated by the imperialists. The "missionary spirit" is still very strong in Puritan Britain. Now they can go without the taint and corruption of imperialism.

c. The most important. Nkrumah (who is a splendid fellow) has formed a Socialist Youth Society in the party, to study socialism, etc., and help educate the party and the people. We shall point out that *they* have to be the most advanced section of the population *intellectually*. In this sense. They have to study dialectic, Stalinism, Greek Democracy, *everything*. They must be able to hold their own in any international conference. The Government must protect them even against itself. They must make the University above all a battleground. The party youth must continually be a challenge to the Government, the union leadership and the University. They must be a totality, intellectuals, worker youths, farmer youth. Their function is to maintain and develop the flow of ideas, so that the party leadership can never be overwhelmed by the routine tasks of government which embrace you so much on all sides that they kill all political initiative unless they are consciously fought.

I also intend to bring in a section on the Negro struggle in the U.S.

Now it is should be clear what this book can be. We shall put forward our *whole program* in a most concrete context, for Ghana and for everybody else. . . .

I expect that the Ghana book will make some money . At any rate it will pay for its expenses and will be a flying start for the general publicising of the ideas *both here and in the U.S.* and in colonial Africa. The days when we were content with a few hundred copies of either the *Black Jacobins* or a few hundred copies of SC&WR [*State Capitalism and World Revolution*], those days we must consider as over. Unless we think so and plan in those terms, we shall never, not merely meet the reception that is waiting for us. We shall not be able to do what every historical movement can do, create by its own actions receptivity when none existed before or it existed at a very low level.

You never can tell when the break will come. The thing is to see it and sieze [*sic*] it, in fact sometimes to push out into the dark confident that events are shaping and will come to meet you . . . This work is of a killing character. And only the inner conviction that is now or never enables me to fac[e] it at all . . . I only wish I could help you to see what I am seeing, so that you could lay a foundation big enough for anything that turns up.

Remember good old William S.

"There is a tide in the affairs of men. . . ."

London, March 21, 1957

Dear Friends . . .

By now, or soon, most all of you have a draft of the political line as expressed most concretely in the proposed book on Ghana. Tomorrow night I am going to meet the Rev. Luther King at a dinner arranged by our friend . . . and I expect to see him afterwards. He was in Ghana but I missed him there. I have already started on the book and the more I do of it and think of it, the more I see that this is the first big statement on a public scale of our position. There is no doubt that it will be read in Britain and in the U.S. . . .

In reading the book you will see that Nkrumah has worked on much the same ideas as Luther King. A section on the struggle in Montgomery should make both sides of the Atlantic aware of what is involved. . . .

I am working also on the "Black Jacobins." You will note that at last the two strands which I have worked on for the last twenty years, beginning with "The Black Jacobins" and "World Revolution," have at last merged quite naturally into one. Please remember that the last part of the book is going to pose very sharply the enormous difficulties which face Nkrumah and the CPP [Convention People's Party]. He expects me to do so because I have told him that in no uncertain terms.

I would like to hear from all of you on this, so that I could feel you understand what is involved and the great effort that it is going to take. This is no hole and corner business. It aims to put everything before everybody.

The central question is Nkrumah's rejection of armed revolution. He says, and he tells me that I can quote him on this, that looking over the experience taking over the government and between 1957 he is not certain that the method he adopted was correct. I am fairly certain that it is. But the real danger comes now, and originates with the lack of momentum with which he was compelled to approach the problems of government. Revolutionary it was, profoundly so, as Luther King in Montgomery, Alabama was revolutionary. The fundamental principles of Leninism as we know them are not affected....

The strike of the Hungarian workers after the defeat by the Soviet tanks is something of the same kind, and AC [Alan Christianson] has been telling me for many a day that he now is opposed to old-fashioned strikes particularly in advanced industries. He says that the workers themselves feel there is no need for them. All you have to do is cut down production by 25% and the situation worse than a strike is created. This is merely to show you all that is involved here.

"Africa: The Threatening Catastrophe—
A Necessary Introduction," 1964

Notes on Appendix 2 LESLIE JAMES

This "Necessary Introduction" appeared in a 1964 typed manuscript, which James titled "Nkrumah Then and Now." Most of this manuscript, as you will see from the contents page, was published as Nkrumah and the Ghana Revolution. *However, although substantive portions of this version of the Introduction remain in the published 1977 version, notable points also were excised. The manuscript contains a stamp for "University Place Book Shop, 69 University Place, New York," which was run by Walter Goldwater, a friend of James.*

References to multiple events in the summer of 1964—including the accession of Moïse Tshombé to prime minister of a coalition Congolese government in July, as well as a general strike in Nigeria in June 1964—suggest that the draft was written near the end of the year. The fact that in 1973 James handed another typescript of the same text to a student in Washington, DC, with a note that it was "written around 1964–65," suggests that either James was fuzzy on the date by then or that the text was written on the cusp of the new year.

The year 1964 would be the last James spent in Britain for some time. According to the American historian George P. Rawick, who lived with C. L. R. and Selma James in London in 1964, James spent his daily routine following cricket, giving lectures on Shakespeare, and bantering with West Indian market vendors on his shopping route.[1] Given the range of African political events he references in this manuscript, he also clearly paid close attention to events on the African continent. His praise for Malawian leader Dunduzu Chisiza, who lived in Birmingham from 1957 to 1958, indicates James's own concern, in this introduction, over identifying the growing peril of authoritarian leadership in several African liberation movements. Chisiza served as parliamentary secretary to the Nyasaland Ministry of

Finance from 1961 to 1962 but was killed in a car crash on September 2, 1962, in circumstances that many, including James, have questioned. Before his death Chisiza hosted an economic development symposium, sponsored by the Ford Foundation, in which he warned of the dangers of dictatorship in African states.[2]

James's interpretation of a general strike in Nigeria is also notable as an indication of James's abandonment of Bolshevik-style organization in favor of the peasantry as the crucial component of Third World revolutionary movements in the 1960s. In this draft, James argues that the success of organized labor in influencing the Nigerian government would actually spell its own disaster. The numbers were on the side of the peasantry in Nigeria, not on that of the smaller industrial proletariat, James argues, and the workers were no longer the vanguard. This point would be realized more fully in James's own politics in 1965, when he returned to Trinidad and founded the Workers and Peasants Party.

Excerpt from "Nkrumah Then and Now"

Dedication

> *To Francis*
> In never-to-be-forgotten memory of the things you have done
> In the hope springing eternal of the things you yet can do.

Contents

Introduction. Africa: The Threatening Catastrophe

I. Africa: The Threatening Catastrophe—A Necessary Introduction

The British public is periodically inoculated with an African serum. From the pronouncements of British statesmen and the British press, it would appear that the future of Africa (and the Commonwealth) now hangs upon the statesmanship of Mr. Jomo Kenyatta of Kenya. Mr. Kenyatta's competence in his own language or the language of the tribes of Kenya is beyond the scope of this writer and, it seems, of most writers about him. Mr. Kenyatta, however, never uses an interpreter. And the widespread suspicion that he is unable to express himself intelligibly in the language of his government—the English language—has now been popularly confirmed. To that I can add a further political fact. It is quite clear to me that Mr. Kenyatta today, after twenty-five years, is still to a substantial degree unable to understand the English language when spoken with competence and ordinary fluency: I have very vivid memories of George Padmore, founder and Chairman of the African Bureau, with inexhaustible patience and sympathy translating quite commonplace political expressions into a particular kind of basic English (illustrated with elemental dramatisations) to gain the approving nod of Mr. Kenyatta and his "O.K. George. *I take it from you.*" Mr. Kenyatta is the latest of a series of African comets which the British public finds it hard to keep track of. First there was the impressive Nkrumah who is now sadly shrivelled from his high estate. The public has now equally seen through the leaden inadequacies of Kenyatta the sociologist and the paper-thin veneer of Dr. Nyerere, the product of Edinburgh and Paris. It is now digesting the threats of being secretly murdered and the incitement to public murder of the former Presbyterian elder, Dr. Hastings Banda. It is beginning to wonder if the gangster Tshombe is not the perfect exemplar of the type destined to emerge as the saviour of Africa from the rapid disintegration from independence into catastrophe. That is the grim, remorselessly enclosing reality. Before any analysis of historical record is made, can be at all understood, some introductory preparation is imperative. I offer my own. Its validity will lie in itself.

In 1957 in Accra, Ghana, I had long conversations with Nkrumah about the Gold Coast Revolution. It was the Gold Coast Revolution ending in the state of Ghana which had struck imperialism in Africa the blow from which it would never recover. I told Nkrumah that I thought it was one of the most significant revolutions of the century and there was still much of great importance to past and future history to be said about it. He said he had been thinking the same and ultimately I willingly undertook to write a history of the Gold Coast Revolution. I felt myself particularly qualified to do so. At that time I had already written *World Revolution: The Rise and Fall of the Communist International, The Black Jacobins*, the history of Toussaint Louverture and the San Domingo Revolution, and *The History of Negro Revolt* which Raymond Postgate who published it advertised as the "first ever." I had also translated from the French Souvarine's *Life of Stalin*, a massive study of the Russian Revolution. I had further exceptional advantages. I had known Nkrumah in New York before he came to London to join George Padmore; Padmore was from 1935 the founder and guiding spirit of the African Bureau and today is universally known as the Father of African Emancipation. It was under the auspices of the Bureau that Nkrumah went from London to the Gold Coast in 1947 to begin his preparations for the revolution which was to initiate a new Africa.

I went to work at once and completed the history by 1958. What I then wrote is Part I of this book.

On reading this part of the book an experienced literary agent expressed the view that it was "dated." To which there are two relevant observations. First I should hope that this history is dated. I had been the editor of the journal, *International African Opinion*, published by the African Bureau, and between 1953 and 1957 had seen a great deal of Padmore, not only a close political associate in the struggle for colonial emancipation but a friend from boyhood in the West Indies. During the struggle for independence Padmore had been Nkrumah's personal representative in London. Padmore stage by stage in articles and in books had publicly recorded the development of the African struggle for independence. He and I had been in Ghana together in 1957 when I was discussing with Nkrumah. We examined the African revolution in Ghana itself in 1957 and what I wrote in the history expressed, I believed, more or less what our circle, which had lived with the African question for over twenty years, thought of the future of the struggle for African independence at the time of its first success. By 1957 we had acquired great confidence in our own approach to these questions, for in the years before World War II we had been the sole political grouping which not only foresaw the coming independence of Africa but under the guidance of Padmore worked unceasingly for it. We were not wrong in 1935 and events since 1958 give me no reason to modify and bring up to date (i.e. to 1964) what I wrote in 1958. The record needs to be kept clear. To listen to Mr. Harold Macmillan and Mr. Ian Macleod today you would believe that they had spent hard years plotting and planning to free Africa. Today they show as little comprehension of what is taking place in Africa as they did twenty-five years ago. They react to events. In 1958 I outlined the events to which people would have to react.

I did not publish the book in 1958 because in that year I went to the West Indies. There as Secretary of the West Indian Federal Labour Party which governed the now defunct Federation, I had a practical and illuminating experience of a colonial territory on its way to independence. I am now in a position to say that the political officials and pundits, especially the ones sympathetic to colonial freedom, illuminated their far less complicated bankruptcy over Africa by their miscomprehension of the West Indies. In 1960, on political business connected with the West Indies, I again visited Nkrumah in Ghana. We talked, not as much as in 1957, but this time I knew more about these matters and renewed acquaintances and friendships in Ghana. Ghana, from being the finest jewel in the crown of Africa, was obviously in a state of impending crisis. After getting Nkrumah's agreement as to what topics I should deal with, I addressed a meeting of his party in Accra. The speech was recorded and I have reprinted it without annotation or omission. Nkrumah learnt about the speech and its reception, expressed his approval and told me that he would get the text printed. I sent the script to him and it was never acknowledged far less printed: Nkrumah is very acute and, knowing my general political ideas well, he must have recognised far more than anyone else what I was saying: without fanfare I had not modified the perils that I saw ahead. As I had occasion to say later, I was quite certain that my audience understood what I was talking about. As I moved into their problems and the future, the frequent bursts of applause ceased altogether and I was listened to in a dead silence which continued for a period after I was finished to be followed by a burst of understanding and approval (I have a tape-recording of the meeting).

After the stir this meeting created a newspaperman in Ghana asked me for an article on Ghanaian problems of government, to be published in a government-sponsored journal. I sent the article to him—receipt was never acknowledged. The Establishment in Ghana did not approve of what I was saying.

I nevertheless continued to consider Nkrumah one of the forward looking politicians of the day and the most important political leader in Africa.

Against all criticism of the unquestioned anomalies of his regime, I stood firmly by the fact more important than all others added together that in a situation of enormous difficulty, on the whole he was not only doing his best but was, as politicians go, one of the most enlightened. As late as 1962 I had occasion to say so. Deeply disturbed at the impending collapse of the West Indian Federation and the effect of this defeat on his struggle for a United Africa, Nkrumah addressed a carefully phrased but no less powerful political letter to every head of government in the West Indies, pointing out what the collapse would signify for the public image of black men, and with firmness and sobriety asking them to reconsider. He also sent me a copy of the letter saying rather formally that he knew my interest in the subject. I was a little surprised but not for long. No West Indian political leader allowed it even to be known that he had received such a letter. I therefore published it, and Nkrumah's regime then being under fire for its anti-democratic tendencies (putting the Opposition in jail)[3] I took the opportunity to add to the publication a personal letter to him stating that then, 1962, as over the previous twenty years, I had always found him a great African statesman and one who stood in general on what I can best call the progressive side of world politics. That letter I have republished here.

In 1963 I had occasion to write to him of my concern at a second attempt to assassinate him: I implied that something was seriously wrong with a regime in which there were two attempts at assassinating the political head of state: I knew that in 1957 over a large part of Ghana Nkrumah could have walked for days without a single attendant. His reply to this letter I found most lacking in his customary political sense and as obviously I cannot publish his reply, I do not publish my original letter. But I have always paid attention to politics in Ghana; I could see there was trouble ahead and I was deeply disturbed at the way things were going. For one thing I had always found that many ordinary people in the Western world looked hopefully at Africa on account of the impact upon them of Ghana. I therefore wrote a long memorandum to Nkrumah about the continuing and growing crisis in newly-independent African states. Unfortunately I never sent it—one has to be careful in relations with political leaders, especially leaders of new states. But shortly afterwards I had occasion bitterly to regret that I had not sent him the memorandum.

The continuous crisis in Ghana had reached a climax when Nkrumah dismissed his Chief Justice for giving a judicial decision of which he disapproved. I have to emphasise that, as the book will show, this act showed the degeneration not only of the regime but of his own conception of government. As usual most commentators seemed to believe that Nkrumah, an African inexperienced in the ways of parliamentary democracy, was drunk with the wine of power, had once more proved the inability of Africans to govern except as some reactionary tribal chief in modern dress. I on the contrary realised at once that Africa had crossed a Rubicon. In order to drive home the significance of this dismissal I have gone to the length of saying to public audiences that an unscrupulous head of government might find it necessary to shoot his Chief Justice while trying to escape, arrange for him to run over by an errant motor lorry, have a bunch of doctors declare him to be medically unfit and, Kremlin-fashion, put him out of the way in an asylum, send him on a long holiday and beg the British Government to make him a life peer on resignation, even invite him to dinner and poison him. But what a head of state does not do is to dismiss his Chief Justice after he has given a major decision on a matter in which the whole country is interested. *The very structure, juridical, political and moral, of the state is at one stroke destroyed and there is automatically placed on the order of the day a violent restoration of some sort of legal connection between government and population.* By this single act, Nkrumah prepared the population of Ghana for the morals of the Mafia. Those learned societies which passed resolutions disapproving of his act should have known that Nkrumah could have said the most admirable things about the rule of law. It wasn't that he did not know. What was important was that he knew all the arguments against such a step and its inevitable consequences.

I wrote to him at once making clear the far-reaching consequences of the mistake he had made. I asked him to write to me or ask some trusted secretary to do so. I told him that if I had been able I would have come to talk to him: he needed as most of these leaders do some old associates who could talk to him without any sense of past obligation or future hopes. I suspected the pressures which had driven him to this fateful action. He never replied and after a month I wrote three articles in a West Indian newspaper using the situation in Ghana as a peg on which to hang my long-felt premonitions of the African degeneration. These articles I now republish. I have no need either to add to or subtract from them. One passage in the articles ( ) [left blank in original] foreshadows with a clarity that even I find astonishing the present dilapidation of government in Banda's Malawi, at the time still Nyasaland.

I had not come to an end of my relation with Ghana. Some months ago I was asked to write for a political journal to be published in Accra. I declined to write anything about Africa—I knew the hopelessness of the situation in which the African leaders found themselves, and knew that *all* that I had to say would not be published in any African paper. Ultimately I compromised by suggesting and agreeing to write a study of Lenin's final reflections on Soviet Russia, the first underdeveloped country to face the problem of the transition to the modern world. The last chapter in the book is a reprint of the article. It deals with Lenin's summation of what Soviet Russia had done and had not done by 1923. It could have been written with contemporary (and future) Africa in mind. As far back as 1958 I had sent a bound copy of these writings of Lenin to Nkrumah to mark his fiftieth birthday. But it seems that only after an ocean of blood, sweat and tears will African politicians be able to understand Lenin's prophetic warnings and drastic revolutionary proposals for solution.

The future of Africa will be rooted in the African experience of African life. Yet nobody, European or African, can make anything clear and consistent of the developing pattern in Africa unless upon the basis of the substantially documented and widely debated historical experiences of Western civilisation. That must first be established so that he who runs or merely looks at television may read. Recently an event has taken place in Africa which unfolds in sharp, even glaring colours, the not very distant future impending over that continent. The event was the general strike in Nigeria which compelled the government to make impressive concessions to the demands of organised labour. It is the greatest action of organised labour ever to take place in Africa and (exactly contrary to the tiresome shouts of approval of would-be Marxists, European and African) the whole experience of Europe for a hundred years marks this event as the beginning of the end of any kind of democratic progress in the largest state in Africa. A few hundred thousand Nigerian workers can challenge a government and even for a period compel acceptance of their demands. But they cannot govern Nigeria any more than Lenin's Soviets could govern Russia. This much is certain. The proletariat of Nigeria, outnumbered and lacking for example the profound experience of the British proletariat in the privileges and responsibilities of democracy, will not be able to, will not be allowed to dominate the political and social life of Nigeria. It can be predicted, it would be blinding both eyes not to see, that the attempt will be made by those who have control of the many-millioned peasantry to discipline and tame the Nigerian proletariat. Whence begins [a] new matter of which it can be said with confidence that it will not be modelled on the British two party parliamentary system. Yet even if the parliamentary democratic pattern is an illusion for Nigeria, despite the Africanness of Africa it is on the patterns developed in Europe that must begin any prognostication by which to trace and perhaps influence the developing social explosions in Africa.

Modern Europe begins in France in 1848 and Karl Marx in 'The Eighteenth Brumaire' of Louis Bonaparte pointed a fearsome finger at what he then saw at the dominating political reality of the age which was beginning.

> It is immediately obvious that in a country like France, where the executive power commands an army of officials numbering more than half a million individuals and therefore constantly maintains an immense mass of interests and livelihoods in the most absolute dependence; where the state enmeshes, controls, regulates, superintends and tutors civil society from its most comprehensive manifestations of life down to its most insignificant stirrings, from its most general modes of being to the private existence of individuals; where through the most extraordinary centralisation this parasitic body acquires a ubiquity, an omniscience, a capacity for accelerated mobility and an elasticity which finds a counterpart only in the helpless dependence, in the loose shapelessness of the actual body politic—it is obvious that in such a country the National Assembly forfeits all real influence when it loses command of the ministerial posts, if it does not at the same time simplify the administration of the state, reduce the army of officials as far as possible and, finally, let civil society and public opinion create organs of their own, independent of the government power. But it is precisely with the maintenance of that extensive state machine in its numerous ramifications that the *material interests* of the French bourgeoisie are interwoven in the closest fashion. Here it finds posts for its surplus population and makes up in the form of state salaries for what it cannot pocket in the form of profit, interest, rents and honorariums. On the other hand, its *political interests* compelled it to increase daily the repressive measures and therefore the resources and the personnel of the state power, while at the same time it had to wage an uninterrupted war against public opinion and mistrustfully mutilate, cripple, the independent organs of the social movement, where it did not succeed in amputating them entirely.

That is what I saw in Ghana in 1960 and this is what has been mounting in ever-widening circles as the outstanding social and political development in contemporary Africa. The African state enmeshes, controls, regulates, superintends and tutors civil society from its most comprehensive manifestations of life down to its most insignificant stirrings. At least it attempts to do so, and where it fails it will compromise for static acquiescence. That is so and must be so. The contemporary state has not only a finger in every pie, it initiates the gathering of material for all new pies, and finds it necessary to claim at least a token share in all the old pies. This is so more particularly in underdeveloped countries and overwhelmingly so in dynamic underdeveloped countries determined to "catch up with and in time surpass" the advanced countries. Stalin to whom we owe the phrase at least caught up with and surpassed many millions of his own subjects.

The concentration on the one-party aspect of the term one-party state is a typical myopia of people who insist on looking for two parties and are horrified to find only one. In actuality they see none. In the African one-party state the term party is a euphemism. It is the state, that expanding source of dignities, wealth and power in countries and among people which have very little of these and are accustomed to being excluded from them.

In underdeveloped countries and in African countries in particular, the struggle for the state power is a struggle for everything that matters, not only for the existing reality but for all previous promises, prospects, visions and dreams of the future. The proliferation of the state power affects the hopes and the will of the whole population. Illiterate, without a sense of history or destiny, the great African mass is utterly bewildered by this new master which seems to be the only fruit of the great hopes and sometimes bitter struggles for independence. To African intellectuals it seems that it will take ages before the masses can intervene effectively or assist in the foundation of something new and worthwhile. The drive seems to be either to join those feeding at the trough or to contract out, whether by going abroad or staying at home. A rigid study of Ghana intellectuals (if that were possible) during the last twenty years would throw a revealing light on present-day Africa. Miseducated for their tasks in British universities, they are further miseducated by the illusions and (well-meaning) falsifications of British liberals and socialists, who show a surprising tolerance, at times even enthusiasm (somewhat palled) for these gangs in possession mouthing political formulae.

A key document for all of Africa (except South Africa) is the Despatch by Governor Sir Robert Armitage, replying to the Report of the Nyasaland Commission of Enquiry, the Commission popularly known as the Devlin Commission. The chaos in Africa today and the chaos of Western professional thought on Africa can be most clearly seen in the harsh sense of a new reality which emerges from every line written by the Colonial Governor and the determined fictitiousness of the well-meaning Mr. Justice Devlin. Both the Devlin Commission and the Despatch of the Governor have this much in

The poet wants to be an architect of this unique civilisation, a commissioner of its blood, a guardian of its refusal to accept.

> But in so doing, my heart, preserve
> me from all hate
> do not turn me into a man of hate of
> whom I think only with hate
> for in order to project myself into
> this unique race
> you know the extent of my boundless
> love
> you know that it is not from hatred
> of other races
> that I seek to be cultivator of this
> unique race.

He returns once more to the pitiful spectre of West Indian life, but now with hope.

> for it is not true that the work of man
> is finished
> that man has nothing more to do in the
> world but be a parasite in the world
> that all we now need is to keep in step
> with the world
> but the work of man is only just beginning
> and it remains to man to conquer all
> the violence entrenched in the recesses
> of his passion
> and no race possesses the monopoly of beauty,
> of intelligence, of force, and there is
> a place for all at the rendezvous of
> victory.

Here is the centre of Cesaire's poem. By neglecting it, Africans and the sympathetic of other races utter loud hurrahs that drown out common sense and reason. The work of man is not finished. Therefore the future of the African is not to continue not discovering anything. The monopoly of beauty, of intelligence, of force, is possessed by no race, certainly not by those who possess Negritude. Negritude is what one race brings to the common rendezvous where all will strive for the new world of the poet's vision. The vision of the poet is not economics or politics, it is poetic, *sui generis*, true unto itself and needing no other truth. But it would be the most vulgar racism not to see here a poetic incarnation of Marx's famous sentence, "The real history of humanity will begin."

In this poem Cesaire makes a place for the spiritual realities of the African way of life in any review and reconstruction of the life of modern man. Cesaire's whole emphasis is upon the fact that the African way of life is not an Anachronism, a primitive survival of history, even prehistoric ages, which needs to be nursed by unlimited quantities of aid into the means and ways of the supersonic plane, television, the Beatles and accommodation to the nuclear peril. Cesaire means exactly the opposite. It is the way of life which the African has not lost which will restore to a new humanity what has been lost by modern life with

> its rebellious joints cracking under
> the pitiless stars
> its blue steel rigidities, cutting through the
> mysteries of the flesh

These are poetic divinations of worlds to come. They are the waves of reality in which present-day Africa must live if it is to live at all. A fierce call in French for revolution *a tout court* has had the blessing of Jean-Paul Sartre, who once again uses Africa as a rod to scourge the torpid European revolution. Meanwhile the African waits, for the call which will bridge the distance between his tribal existence and the modern existence he sees and longs for.

One final word about the form the book has taken. Beginning with Kierkegaard and Nietzsche and reaching a completion in Sartre, modern philosophy expresses its modernity by assuming the form of a personal response to extreme situations, and is no less philosophical for that. I record here a sequence of political responses to an extreme political situation, the African situation, as it has developed, during the last thirty years. The last dated section of the book is Lenin's writing on the Russia of 1923. I venture the prophecy that by 1973, fifty years after it was written, it will be the most contemporary of documents about Africa. One new African state, the state of Mali, seems to be striving to make a living reality of what hitherto exists only on paper.

Introduction. Ghana and the Worlds of C. L. R. James

1. C. L. R. James, *The Black Jacobins: Toussaint L'Ouverture and the San Domingo Revolution* (New York: Vintage, 1963), vii.
2. James, *Black Jacobins*, 417.
3. Paget Henry, "C. L. R. James, Political Philosophy, and the Creolizing of Rousseau and Marx," *CLR James Journal* 15, no. 1 (2009): 178–205, 193.
4. James, *Black Jacobins*, 418.
5. Kevin K. Gaines, *American Africans in Ghana: Black Expatriates and the Civil Rights Era* (Chapel Hill: University of North Carolina Press, 2006).
6. Yevette Richards, "African and African-American Labor Leaders in the Struggle over International Affiliation," *International Journal of African Historical Studies* 31, no. 2 (1998): 301–34. For more on Vicki Garvin, see Dayo Gore, *Radicalism at the Crossroads: African American Women Activists in the Cold War* (New York: New York University Press, 2011), 100–165; and Robeson Taj Frazier, *The East Is Black: Cold War China in the Black Radical Imagination* (Durham, NC: Duke University Press, 2015), 159–92.
7. Norman Manley to Padmore, 23 March 1957; Padmore to Eric Williams, 15 March 1957, Sc/BAA/187, Bureau of African Affairs Papers, George Padmore Library, Accra, Ghana.
8. Paul Buhle, *C. L. R. James: The Artist as Revolutionary* (London: Verso, 1988), 136.
9. C. L. R. James, *At the Rendezvous of Victory: Selected Writings* (London: Allison & Busby, 1984), 258.
10. Padmore to J.G., April 1953, box 154-41, folder 14, Nkrumah Papers, Moorland Spingarn Research Centre of Howard University, Washington, DC. The Colonial Office also tried to monitor this connecting point. See National Archives United Kingdom: KV2 1850–51.
11. Buhle, *C. L. R. James*, 137.
12. John Williams, *C. L. R. James: A Life beyond the Boundaries* (London: Constable, 2022).

13. James to Padmore, 30 September 1957, box 7, folder 196, C. L. R. James Collection, University of the West Indies-Augustine, Trinidad, and Tobago.

14. George Padmore, *The Gold Coast Revolution* (London: Dennis Dobson, 1954), 35.

15. Eric Williams, *Capitalism and Slavery* (Chapel Hill: University of North Carolina Press, 1944).

16. Kent Worcester, *C. L. R. James: A Political Biography* (Albany: State University of New York Press, 1966), 153–54.

17. Eric D. Duke, *Building a Nation: Caribbean Federation in the Black Diaspora* (Gainesville: University Press of Florida, 2016), 35.

18. Bridget Brereton, *A History of Modern Trinidad, 1783–1962* (London: Heinemann, 1981). For the Caribbean left and early federation moves, see Gerald Horne, *Cold War in a Hot Zone: The United States Confronts Labor and Independence Struggles in the British West Indies* (Philadelphia: Temple University Press, 2007). For United States involvement in the British West Indies in this period, see Jason Parker, *Brother's Keeper: The United States, Race, and Empire in the British Caribbean, 1937–1962* (Oxford: Oxford University Press, 2008).

19. Editorial, "A Few Plain Words," *Nation*, January 8, 1960, 1.

20. C. L. R. James, "The People of the Gold Coast: They Created Ghana," *Nation*, March 4, 1960, 10. See also *Nkrumah and the Ghana Revolution*, 56.

21. Quoted in Buhle, *C. L. R. James*, 146.

22. Christian Høgsbjerg, "C. L. R. James and the British New Left," *Socialist History* 51 (2017): 71–95.

23. Worcester, *C. L. R. James*, 171.

24. David Austin, "In Search of a National identity: C. L. R. James and the Promise of the Caribbean," in *You Don't Play with Revolution: The Montreal Lectures of C. L. R. James*, ed. David Austin (Oakland, CA: AK, 2009), 1–26.

25. David Austin, "All Roads Led to Montreal: Black Power, the Caribbean, and the Black Radical Tradition in Canada," *Journal of African American History* 92, no. 4 (2007): 516–39, 533–35; Paul Hebert, "A Microcosm of the General Struggle: Black Thought and Activism in Montreal, 1960–1969" (PhD diss., University of Michigan, 2015).

26. Kate Quinn, "Black Power in Caribbean Context," in *Black Power in the Caribbean*, ed. Kate Quinn (Gainesville: University Press of Florida, 2014), 42.

27. Quinn, "Black Power in Caribbean Context," 40–41. In the same volume, see also Rupert Lewis, "Jamaican Black Power in the 1960s," 53–75.

28. David Austin, *Fear of a Black Nation: Race, Sex, and Security in Sixties Montreal* (Toronto: Between the Lines, 2013).

29. Brinsley Samaroo, "The February Revolution (1970) as a Catalyst for Change in Trinidad and Tobago," in *Black Power in the Caribbean*, ed. Kate Quinn (Gainesville: University Press of Florida, 2014), 97–116, 97, 101.

30. Quinn, "Black Power in Caribbean Context," 42.

31. Fanon Che Wilkins, "A Line of Steel: The Organization of the Sixth Pan-African Congress and the Struggle for International Black Power, 1969–1974," in *The Hidden 1970s: Histories of Radicalism*, ed. Dan Berger (Piscataway, NJ: Rutgers University Press), 97–114.

32. Monique Bedasse, *Jah Kingdom: Rastafarians, Tanzania, and Pan-Africanism in the Age of Decolonization* (Chapel Hill: University of North Carolina Press, 2017), 169–81.

33. Robin Kelley, "Introduction," in *A History of Pan-African Revolt* (Oakland, CA: PM, 2012), 31.

34. Jeffrey S. Ahlman, "Road to Ghana: Nkrumah, Southern Africa and the Eclipse of a Decolonizing Africa," *Kronos* 37 (2011): 23–40; Meredith Terretta, "Cameroonian Nationalists Go Global: From Forest 'Maquis' to a Pan-African Accra," *Journal of African History* 51, no. 2 (2010): 189–212, 192; Leslie James, *George Padmore and Decolonization from Below* (Basingstoke: Palgrave Macmillan, 2015), 180–92. For the relationship between Togo and Ghana, see Kate Skinner, *The Fruits of Freedom in British Togoland: Literacy, Politics and Nationalism, 1914–2014* (Cambridge: Cambridge University Press, 2015), 2.

35. For the cultural and symbolic nationalism developed by Nkrumah-era Ghana, see Harcourt Fuller, *Building the Ghanaian Nation-State: Kwame Nkrumah's Symbolic Nationalism* (New York: Palgrave Macmillan, 2014). For CPP development projects and resettlement, see Stephan F. Miescher, "'No One Should Be Worse Off': The Akosombo Dam, Modernization, and the Experience of Resettlement in Ghana," in *Modernization as Spectacle in Africa*, ed. Peter J. Bloom, Stephan F. Miescher, and Takyiwaa Manuh (Bloomington: Indiana University Press, 2014), 184–204. For these development projects in the Cold War context, see also Stephan F. Miescher, "'Nkrumah's Baby': The Akosombo Dam and the Dream of Development in Ghana, 1952–1966," *Water History* 6, no. 4 (2014): 341–66.

36. The CPP plan to nurture disciplined, socialist, and cosmopolitan citizens involved the creation of groups like the Ghana Young Pioneers and Builders Brigades and witnessed rallies and marches, self-help projects, and competitions. These generated familial, gender, and generational tensions in Ghanaian communities. See Jeffrey S. Ahlman, *Living with Nkrumahism: Nation, State, and Pan-Africanism in Ghana* (Athens: Ohio University Press, 2017).

37. As Jean Allman has shown, Nkrumah's development-oriented projects did not transpire as straightforward proof of Nkrumah as the model modernizer and revolutionary. His recruitment of Hanna Reitsch, the famous West German pilot who was intimately tied to the Nazi war effort, complicates Nkrumah's anticolonial, antiracist project and, ultimately, offers a richer appreciation of the man and the era. Jean Allman, "Phantoms of the Archive: Kwame Nkrumah, a Nazi Pilot Named Hanna, and the Contingencies of Postcolonial History-Writing," *American Historical Review* 118, no. 1 (2013): 104–29.

38. Margaret Busby, interview with the author, 8 March 2018.

39. James, *George Padmore and Decolonization*, 172–77.

40. J. Williams, *C. L. R. James: A Life beyond the Boundaries*.

41. C. L. R. James, Grace C. Lee, and Pierre Chaulieu, *Facing Reality* (Detroit, MI: Bewick Editions, 1974), 7, 8.

42. C. L. R. James, "Rousseau and the Idea of General Will," in *You Don't Play with Revolution: The Montreal Lectures of C. L. R. James*, ed. David Austin (Oakland, CA: AK, 2009), 105.

43. Henry, "C. L. R. James, Political Philosophy, and the Creolizing of Rousseau and Marx."

44. James, *You Don't Play with Revolution*, 111–12.

45. C. L. R. James, *Notes on Dialectics: Hegel, Marx, Lenin* (Westport, CT: Lawrence Hill, 1980), 11.

46. Kate Skinner, "Who Knew the Minds of the People? Specialist Knowledge and Developmentalist Authoritarianism in Postcolonial Ghana," *Journal of Imperial and Commonwealth History* 39, no. 2 (2011): 297–323, 306.

47. Frederick Cooper, *Decolonization and African Society: The Labor Question in French and British Africa* (Cambridge: Cambridge University Press, 1996), 58–110.

48. Anthony Bogues, *Black Heretics, Black Prophets: Radical Political Intellectuals* (London: Routledge, 2016), 97–99.

49. Terence Ranger, "The Invention of Tradition in Colonial Africa," in *The Invention of Tradition*, ed. Eric Hobsbawm and Terence Ranger (Cambridge: Cambridge University Press, 2012), 211–62.

50. James's emphasis on the family as the fundamental unit in Africa would also form a key part of Walter Rodney's analysis of African politics. See Rodney, *How Europe Underdeveloped Africa* (Cape Town: Pambazuka, 2012).

51. James, Lee, and Chaulieu, *Facing Reality*, 8.

52. Bogues, *Black Heretics, Black Prophets*, 1056.

53. I have offered only cursory remarks on James's interpretation of Tanzania and African socialism. For readers interested in this issue, alongside study of James's work there is a wealth of new scholarship on Tanzanian history in this period. As a starting point, see Priya Lal, *African Socialism in Postcolonial Tanzania: Between the Village and the World* (New York: Cambridge University Press, 2015); Emma Hunter, *Political Thought and the Public Sphere in Tanzania: Freedom, Democracy and Citizenship in the Era of Decolonization* (Cambridge: Cambridge University Press, 2015); and James Brennan, *Taifa: Making Nation and Race in Urban Tanzania* (Athens: Ohio University Press, 2012).

54. Bogues, *Black Heretics, Black Prophets*, 123.

55. C. L. R. James, "Nkrumah Then and Now," unpublished manuscript, 1964–65, box 128-19, folder 417, Dabu Gizenga Collection, Moorland Spingarn Archives at Howard University, Washington, DC.

56. James, *At the Rendezvous of Victory*, 20–45.

57. I am grateful to Robert Hill for emphasizing this as motivation for James's work.

58. What does exist are essays published in the *Nation* immediately after Padmore's death in 1959. C. L. R. James, "Notes on the Life of George Padmore," *Nation*, October 2, 1959, 17.

59. In 1968, James sent enquiries to archives and police records in Paris, Copenhagen, Hamburg, and London requesting information on Padmore's early life. He corresponded with Immanuel Geiss in Hamburg, St. Clair Drake in Chicago, and the National Library in Accra about the project. Box 7, folder 194, C. L. R. James Collection, University of West Indies–St. Augustine, Trinidad and Tobago.

60. James to Victor Rabinowitz, 17 July 1968, box 7, folder 194, C. L. R. James Collection, University of West Indies–St. Augustine, Trinidad and Tobago.

61. Taped interview, Dabu Gizenga with C. L. R. James, 19 April 1973, box 128-27, Dabu Gizenga Collection, Moorland Spingarn Archives at Howard University, Washington, DC.

62. David Ljunggren, "Every G20 Nation Wants to Be Canada, Insists PM," Reuters, 25 September 2009, http://www.reuters.com/article/columns-us-g20-canada -advantages-idUSTRE58P05Z20090926.

63. Tim Fontaine, "What Did Justin Trudeau Say about Canada's History of Colonialism?," CBC, 22 April 2016, http://www.cbc.ca/news/indigenous/trudeau -colonialism-comments-1.3549405.

Introduction. 1977 Edition

1. The severity of Nkrumah in relation to Dr. [K. A.] Busia, Dr. [J. B.] Danquah and other oppositionists drew no protests nor anguish from me. They were advocates neither of democracy nor even of the Christianity they professed. They aimed at establishing an enclave of power among the Ashanti who despite their many virtues have the least claim in Africa below the Sahara to either democracy or Christianity. Not only do they make no claim to either: neither Busia, Danquah nor [Joseph] Appiah ever made any such claims for them.

2. Certainly the West Indians (British, French and Spanish), the most articulate of the formerly colonial coloured peoples, are an embodiment in the twentieth of what Dostoyevsky saw in the nineteenth century.

PART I

Chapter 1. The Myth

1. In this respect the BBC comedians who call themselves "The Goon Show" understand what is required more profoundly than all the learned men of good will who are unable to distinguish between the forces in Africa making for civilisation and those making for barbarism.

Chapter 8. The Party under Fire

1. The Case for West Indian Self-Government (reprinted in C. L. R. James, *The Future in the Present*, London, 1977).

PART II

Chapter 1. Government and Party

1. Speech delivered in Accra, July 1960.

Chapter 3. Slippery Descent

1. I always called Nkrumah Francis and not Kwame. That is why this letter is addressed as it is.

Chapter 4. Lenin and the Problem

1. Written for a political journal in Ghana in 1964.
2. C. L. R. James, *World Revolution: The Rise and Fall of the Communist International, 1917–1936* (London: Secker and Warburg, 1937).
3. V. I. Lenin, "Report on the Tax in Kind at the Tenth Party Congress," in *Selected Works*, vol. IV, 112–13.
4. Lenin, *Selected Works*, vol. VII, 351–78.
5. Lenin, *Selected Works*, vol. VIII, 165–76.
6. Lenin, *Selected Works*, vol. IX, 406.
7. "Under the conditions prevailing in Russia at present, freedom and rights for the co-operative societies mean freedom and rights for capitalism. It would be stupid and criminal to close our eyes to this obvious truth."

Appendix 1. Correspondence, 1957

1. I am grateful to John Williams for much of the background to these interactions. See John Williams, *C. L. R. James: A Life beyond the Boundaries* (London: Constable, 2022).

Appendix 2. "Africa: The Threatening Catastrophe— A Necessary Introduction," 1964

1. Christian Høgsbjerg, "C. L. R. James and the British New Left," *Socialist History*, no. 51 (2017): 81.

2. Dunduzu Kaluli Chisiza, *Africa, What Lies Ahead* (New York: African-American Institute, 1962).

3. The severity of Nkrumah in relation to Dr. [K. A.] Busia, Dr. [J. B.] Danquah and other oppositionists drew no protests nor anguish from me. They were advocates neither of democracy nor even of the Christianity they professed. They aimed at establishing an enclave of power among the Ashanti who despite their many virtues have the least claim in Africa below the Sahara to either democracy or Christianity. Not only do they make no claim to either. Neither Busia, Danquah nor [Joseph] Appiah ever made any such claims for them.

4. Mr. Chisiza I believe to be the finest political mind produced in modern Africa. I also show that he knew what would take place not only in Nyasaland but in all Africa and if he did not commit suicide, his violent end remains unsatisfactorily explained to this day. I have ventured to give an estimate of the process by which he met his death. At the time of writing I had not fully absorbed the urgency of the fears of Sir Robert Armitage and the similar but greater fears of Dr. [Hastings] Banda.

5. Certainly the West Indian (British, French and Spanish), the most articulate of the formerly colonial coloured peoples, are an embodiment in the 20th of what Dostoevsky saw in the 19th century.

6. C. L. R. James, *The Black Jacobins* (New York: Vantage Press 1963).

7. Aimé Césaire, *Cahier d'un retour au pays natal.*

Index

self-government: African, 16, 209, 217; Ghana revolution and, 33–34, 39–43, 49, 68–74, 114, 117–20; the myth and, 24–28; Nkrumah and, 79, 84, 89, 94–98; positive action and, 104, 107–12; revolution and, 78; revolutionary theory and, xiii–xiv, xxii, xxiv. *See also* government and governance

self-organization, xxi–xvii

Sir George Williams affair, xvii

slavery, xiii, xxi, 11, 25, 29, 54–61, 140, 189, 213–16

"Slippery Descent" (James), xxiv–xxvi, 152–57

Small, Richard, xvi

socialism: Africa and, 11, 182–87, 208, 212–14, 217, 224n53; Ghana and, 154; governance and, 131, 136–37, 142–48; the myth and, 32; Nkrumah and, 193–95, 223n36; revolution and, 13, 16, 69, 72; revolutionary theory and, x, xiii–xiv, xviii, xx–xxi, xxv–xxviii, 51–52, 55–56; Russia and, 160–61, 165, 168–70, 174–77

South Africa, xxix, 24, 30, 40, 138–39

sovereignty, ix, xxviii, 136–37

Soviet Communist Party, 11

Soviet Union. *See* Russia

speeches, 96–99, 126–28

Spheres of Existence (James), xx

sports, 44, 47, 97–98

Stalin and Stalinism, 10–14, 31, 51–52, 160, 171–73, 195, 202, 208, 211–15

state, the. *See* Ghana

strikes, xxii–xxiii, 27, 36, 40, 58–59, 72, 94, 106–17

student movements, xxix

Tanganyika, 24, 30, 156–57. *See also* Tanzania

Tanzania, x, xvii–xxx, 19, 179–82, 185–86, 224n53

Tories, 29

totalitarianism, xxiv, 28, 57, 81, 131, 154, 172

Trades Union Congress, xxiv, 42, 111

trade unions. *See* unions

tradition, xxvi–xxvii

tribes and tribalism: Africa and, xxvi–xxvii, 15–16, 154, 156, 201, 217, 220; Ghana and, 42–45, 68, 82, 193, 209–10; the myth and, 31; Nkrumah and, 51

Trinidad, x–xix, xxiii–xxx, 27, 100, 200

Trinidad Evening News, 152

Trotsky and Trotskyism, 52, 56–60, 86–87, 109, 116, 160–65, 171–72

Trudeau, Justin, xxxi

Tse-Tung, Mao, 158

Tshombé, Moïse, 199

Tunis, 126, 158

two-party systems, 11, 157, 212

Uganda, 24, 27, 30, 156–57

unions: Nkrumah and, 99; positive action and, 111; revolution and, 43–44, 73–74, 144, 194–95; revolutionary theory and, xvi, xxii–xxiv, 51–52, 59, 62; Russia and, 162–64; trade, 39, 42, 70, 170. *See also* ex-servicemen and the Ex-Servicemen's Union

United Gold Coast Convention (UGCC), 105

United Gold Coast Convention, 34–35, 39, 68–74, 83–84, 106

United Nations, 12, 24, 125, 213

United States: the myth and, 29; revolution and, xx, 11, 43, 47, 70, 96, 130–31, 140–42, 146, 158–60, 189–90; revolutionary theory and, x–xv, xxxi, 51–54, 57, 61–63; unions and, 44

unity, 42–47, 72, 78, 86, 122, 136, 163

University of Woodford Square, xxv, 100–101

urbanization, 44, 103

Uriah Butler, Tubal, 27

violence: Ghana revolution and, 47–48, 66, 107–9, 125–27; Nkrumah and, 82, 95–96; police, xvii; revolution and, 8–14, 17, 27, 38–40, 173, 205, 210–16; revolutionary theory and, xvii, 57–61. *See also* non-violence

Weber, Max, 50

Weekes, George, xvi

Western civilization: Africa and, 157, 179, 206, 215–16; the myth and, 25, 30–31; Nkrumah and, 83, 99; revolution and, 9–11, 14–18, 131; revolutionary theory and, xxii–xxiii, xxx, 50–51, 158–59

West Indian Federal Labour Party, 6, 135, 203

West Indies: Africa and, 91, 219; James and, 5–8, 27, 139, 142, 199, 202–5; the myth and, 29; Nkrumah and, 149–51; revolution and, 16–17, 145–47; revolutionary theory and, x, xv–xvi, xxviii–xxx, 51–53, 62–63, 225n2. *See also* British West Indies Federation

Williams, Eric, xi–xv, xix, xxiv–xxvi, 100–101, 139

women, xix, xxvi, 39–40, 45–46, 89, 96, 108–9, 171–72, 180, 185

workers: Africa and, 180–81, 184–85, 206; governance and, 143–44, 147; James on, 155, 200; the myth and, 27; Nkrumah and, 99–103; positive action and, 108, 111; pre-revolution, 41–46; revolutionary theory and, xxi, xxiv–xxvii, 57, 62–63, 197; Russia and, 161–64, 169–78. *See also* proletariats

Workers and Farmers Party, xvi

Workers and Peasants Party, 200

World Revolution (James), 189